An admirable statement of the aims of the Library of Philosophy was provided by the first editor, the late Professor J. H. Muirhead, in his description of the original programme printed in Erdmann's *History of Philosophy* under the date 1890. This was slightly modified in subsequent volumes to take the form of the following statement:

'The Muirhead Library of Philosophy was designed as a contribution to the History of Modern Philosophy under the heads: first of Different Schools of Thought—Sensationalist, Realist, Idealist, Intuitivist; secondly of different Subjects—Psychology, Ethics, Aesthetics, Political Philosophy, Theology. While much had been done in England in tracing the course of evolution in nature, history, economics, morals and religion, little had been done in tracing the development of thought on these subjects. Yet "the evolution of opinion is part of the whole evolution".

'By the co-operation of different writers in carrying out this plan it was hoped that a thoroughness and completeness of treatment, otherwise unattainable, might be secured. It was believed also that from writers mainly British and American fuller consideration of English Philosophy than it had hitherto received might be looked for. In the earlier series of books containing, among others, Bosanquet's *History of Aesthetic*, Pfleiderer's *Rational Theology since Kant*, Albee's *History of English Utilitarianism*, Bonar's *Philosophy and Political Economy*, Brett's *History of Psychology*, Ritchie's *Natural Rights*, these objects were to a large extent effected.

'In the meantime original work of a high order was being produced both in England and America by such writers as Bradley, Stout, Bertrand Russell, Baldwin, Urban, Montague, and others, and a new interest in foreign works, German, French and Italian, which had either become classical or were attracting public attention, had developed. The scope of the Library thus became extended into something more international, and it is entering on the fifth decade of its existence in the hope that it may contribute to that mutual understanding between countries which is so pressing a need of the present time.'

The need which Professor Muirhead stressed is no less pressing today, and few will deny that philosophy has much to do with enabling us to meet it, although no one, least of all Muirhead himself, would regard that as the sole, or even the main, object of philosophy. As Professor Muirhead continues to lend the distinction of his name to the Library of Philosophy it seemed not inappropriate to allow him to recall us to these aims in his own words. The emphasis on the history of thought also seemed to me very timely: and the number of important works promised for the Library in the very near future augur well for the continued fulfilment, in this and other ways, of the expectations of the original editor.

H. D. LEWIS

MUIRHEAD LIBRARY OF PHILOSOPHY

General Editor: H. D. Lewis

Professor of History and Philosophy of Religion in the University of London

Action by SIR MALCOLM KNOX
The Analysis of Mind by BERTRAND RUSSELL
Belief by H. H. PRICE
Brett's History of Psychology edited by R. S. PETERS
Clarity is Not Enough by H. D. LEWIS
Coleridge as Philosopher by J. H. MUIRHEAD
The Commonplace Book of G. E. Moore edited by C. LEWY
Contemporary American Philosophy edited by G. P. ADAMS and W. P.
    MONTAGUE
Contemporary British Philosophy first and second Series edited by
    J. H. MUIRHEAD
Contemporary British Philosophy third Series edited by H. D. LEWIS
Contemporary Indian Philosophy edited by RADHAKRISHNAN and J. H.
    MUIRHEAD 2nd edition
The Discipline of the Cave by J. N. FINDLAY
Doctrine and Argument in Indian Philosophy by NINIAN SMART
The Elusive Mind by H. D. LEWIS
Essays in Analysis by ALICE AMBROSE
Ethics by NICOLAI HARTMANN translated by STANTON COIT 3 vols
The Foundation of Metaphysics in Science by ERROL E. HARRIS
Freedom and History by H. D. LEWIS
The Good Will: A Study in the Coherence Theory of Goodness by H. J.
    PATON
Hegel: A Re-examination by J. N. FINDLAY
Hegel's Science of Logic translated by W. H. JOHNSTON and L. G.
    STRUTHERS 2 vols
History of Aesthetic by B. BOSANQUET 2nd edition
History of English Utilitarianism by E. ALBEE
History of Psychology by G. S. BRETT edited by R. S. PETERS abridged
    one volume edition 2nd edition
Human Knowledge by BERTRAND RUSSELL
A Hundred Years of British Philosophy by RUDOLF METZ translated by
    J. H. HARVEY, T. E. JESSOP, HENRY STURT
Ideas: A General Introduction to Pure Phenomenology by EDMUND
    HUSSERL translated by W. R. BOYCE GIBSON
Identity and Reality by EMILE MEYERSON
Imagination by E. J. FURLONG
Contemporary Philosophy in Australia edited by ROBERT BROWN, and
    C. D. ROLLINS

Muirhead Library of Philosophy

EDITED BY H. D. LEWIS

THE SUBJECT OF
CONSCIOUSNESS

THE SUBJECT OF CONSCIOUSNESS

BY

C. O. EVANS

LONDON: GEORGE ALLEN & UNWIN LTD
NEW YORK: HUMANITIES PRESS INC

FIRST PUBLISHED IN 1970

© *George Allen & Unwin Ltd, 1970*

BRITISH SBN 04 126002 3

U.S.A. SBN 391 00037 3

PRINTED IN GREAT BRITAIN
in 11 on 12pt Imprint
BY W & J MACKAY & CO LTD,
CHATHAM, KENT

TO MERLYN

PREFACE

In this book I develop a philosophical theory of the self the purpose of which is to explain how it is that our experience of being selves is an experience of being continuous subjects of experience. That is to say, the theory is offered as an explanation of self-awareness.

On many current theories of the self put forward by philosophers working in the empiricist tradition self-awareness is reduced to awareness of the states which at the time the self is in. This is not what I understand self-awareness to be. I believe that self-awareness is the awareness of the self as the conscious subject of the states of the self. This book is both an attempt to show how this is possible and an attempt to show what awareness of the conscious subject consists in. Essentially, in my dispute with the reductive view I attempt to show what self-awareness is not, by showing what it is.

It would be fitting to describe the work as an exercise in *constructive* philosophy. It develops a conceptual apparatus specifically for the purpose of presenting a philosophical theory. On this account the book needs to be read consecutively to be understood. The concepts fashioned in the early chapters are applied systematically as the theory is unfolded in the later chapters. Because the theory has some of the characteristics of a system it has ramifications that go beyond the problems of the self and reach into the foundations of the Philosophy of Mind.

Although the book is not written from a phenomenological point of view, many of its conclusions are relevant to phenomenology. If some have already been anticipated by phenomenologists this would add to my confidence in them, and I would add that phenomenologists might nevertheless derive some interest from seeing how someone working, broadly speaking, within the analytic tradition had reached them.

To think of those who have had a hand in the coming into being of this book is to think of some of the happiest associations of my life.

I would not have had the opportunity to write the book had it not been for the help of Professor W. H. Walsh and Mr Philip Grove. I am most grateful to both of them.

I wish to record my thanks to the University of Edinburgh for awarding me a research fellowship which freed me from teaching and gave me the time for the research out of which this book has grown.

The greatest philosophical influence on its content has come from three friends: my teacher, Dr Frederick Broadie; a former colleague, Professor D. C. S. Oosthuizen; and a former student of mine, Mr John Schumacher. I am deeply indebted to each of them for the unstinting way they have given me the benefit of their impressive philosophical resources.

I would like to make particular mention of Daantjie Oosthuizen whose sudden death at the age of 43 made the completion of this book a sad task. He more than anyone was looking forward to its appearance, and only he would have been able to appreciate how much it has gained from his suggestions and criticisms. His death is a loss to me, a loss to philosophy, and a loss to his country.

I am privileged to be able to thank Professor H. H. Price for his encouragement and for his constructive comments on a draft of the manuscript. I am sure he will not mind my saying that he was particularly pleased to see the views of the French psychologist TH. Ribot getting detailed consideration, since he believes that the neglect of Ribot has been our loss.

It is a similar privilege and pleasure to thank Professor H. D. Lewis for his close reading of the manuscript and for his valuable suggestions.

I wish to record my thanks to Rensselaer Polytechnic Institute for the typing of the manuscript.

Finally, I owe everything to my wife for all the deprivations she has put up with on account of this book.

CONTENTS

CHAPTER ONE

INTRODUCTION

[1] Two distinctively different philosophical issues have usually been discussed under the heading of *personal identity*. One concerns itself with our knowledge of the identity of persons other than ourselves, and the other concerns itself with self-awareness. Although the expressions 'personal identity' and 'self-identity' have commonly been used interchangeably by philosophers, I would like to suggest that there is point in reserving the first expression to describe the problem of the identity of persons, and the second to describe the problem of self-awareness.

Many philosophers would not agree that there are two different problems involved. In this introduction I try to make out a case that there are. If there were a difference between the problem of personal identity and that of self-identity, it would follow that the two questions, (*a*) What is a person? and (*b*) What is the self? are different questions and not merely different formulations of the same question.

It might be thought that what makes the two questions different is not the use of the word 'person' in (*a*) and the word 'self' in (*b*), but the use of the indefinite article in (*a*) and the definite article in (*b*). Were this the case it would be possible to make the two questions identical by the simple expedient of using the indefinite article in both. With this I would concur. But the significant point is that we *cannot* use the *definite* article in both cases. The sentence 'What is *the* person' is ungrammatical.

It will emerge in due course that there are more powerful reasons for refraining from posing the problem of self-awareness in terms of the concept of a person. At this point, however, all that needs to be pointed out is that the nature of self-awareness has been a preoccupation of philosophers and their curiosity about self-awareness is not satisfied either by knowledge of the identity of other persons or by knowledge of the criteria on which such knowledge is based. It is less misleading, therefore, to phrase the problem 'Of what are we aware in self-awareness?' in terms of the question, 'What is the self?', than it is to phrase it in terms of a question about persons. Furthermore the question 'What is a person?' leaves it open whether or not the reader himself is included within the class of persons. This is not left open with the question 'What is the self?' For that question is one which the reader must address to himself if he is to understand it. The question pragmatically implies token-reflexivity – it becomes for each reader the question, 'In what does my identity as a self consist?'

Many of the best philosophers writing today on personal identity would strongly resist an attempt such as this to insert a wedge between the concepts 'person' and 'self'. Indeed they would prefer to avoid the word 'self' altogether, and discuss the problem exclusively in terms of the word 'person'. Their approach is based on the contention that there is no distinction between identity in one's own case and identity in the case of others, and hence that an understanding of the identity of persons in general is *eo ipso* an understanding of one's own identity.

It needs to be pointed out, however, that this contention could not even be stated unless each of us knew that he was a member of the class of persons. This would give rise to the question of what entitles us to make this knowledge claim. It would be tempting to say that it is analytically true that persons and persons only are able to raise questions about their own identities. The trouble with this move is that it makes it impossible to equate persons with human beings, because it must be left at least a logical possibility for a being other than a human being to raise the question of self-identity. But I shall let that pass.

The approach just alluded to – let me call it the *persons-approach* – is part of a programme of deliberate reversal of the traditional approach to epistemology. The tradition emanating from Descartes was to begin an epistemological enquiry with one's own case, and, from that starting point, arrive by inference at knowledge claims about things apart from oneself. However, philosophers have since come to believe that many of the insoluble problems of knowledge can be traced back to the premiss that one must start with one's own case. From their point of view, therefore, the suggestion that the problem of one's own identity is distinct from the problem of the identity of other persons appears to be a regression to the unfortunate method of starting with one's own case.

It is fear of such regression, I believe, that has made philosophers wary of references to the self, and has caused them to see the problem of personal identity as primarily a problem of the identity of other persons, and only derivatively a problem of self-identity. According to the *persons-approach* we learn all there is to know about self-identity by understanding in what the identity of other persons consists.

The *persons-approach* has been very successful, and the philosophy of personal identity is one area in which definite progress has been made. Philosophers would therefore have good cause to be suspicious of the apparent re-introduction of a distinction which threatens this hard-won progress. I hope to show that the distinction I have in mind poses no such threat, and that the recognition of a separate problem of self-identity leaves intact the progress made in our understanding of personal identity. I shall in fact be arguing for an even stronger claim than this: namely, that the two problems are complementary and that only when both problems have been solved will we have an adequate understanding of our own identities.

If I am right about this, then a solution to the one problem must not contradict the solution to the other problem. That is to say, an answer to the question 'What is the self?' must not contradict the answer to the question 'What is a person?' Furthermore, an answer to the first question must not be thought to supply the answer to the second question and vice versa. I wish to stress this because it rules out any attempt to arrive at a theory of personal identity by reverting to the traditional method of starting with one's own case. Once it is realized that the distinction between person and self has no such implication, nothing is lost in at least allowing the distinction to go forward for the sake of argument.

The problems of personal identity and self-identity can only be logically separate from each other if the identity sought is different in the two cases. I shall argue that this is indeed the case.

The concept of identity is a difficult one to understand at the best of times, and this difficulty is added to in discussions of personal identity because identity is apt to be confused with identification. In answer to the question 'Which is it?' we provide what I shall call *referential identification*. In answer to the question 'What is it?' we provide what I shall call *sortal identification*. (I shall not be concerned at the moment with a third type of identification in which we answer the question 'Whose is it?' by providing what may be called *possessive identification*.) It is clearly the case that successful referential identification will give us some broad knowledge of the sort of object identified. It can reveal whether the object in question is a physical object, an animal, or something less solid like thunder and lightning. The relevance of this point is brought out by Shoemaker who notes:

'To say what sort of criteria we use in making judgments about the identity of objects of a certain kind is to say something, often a great deal, about the nature (essence, concept) of that sort of object. Thus it is that the problem of personal identity is a problem about the nature of persons.'[1]

It must nevertheless be insisted that referential identification has a different logical function from sortal identification.

[2] The *persons-approach* connects personal identity with questions of identification. Its method is to reach sortal identification through a discovery of the conditions necessary for successful referential identification. Its point of view is exhibited in the question, 'What must we *take* a person to be if we are to achieve successful referential identification of persons (as we are)?' It would follow on this approach that if referential identification of persons depended on identification of their bodies, then we must take a person to be at least a bodily *x*. This would lead to a consideration of such questions as, 'Is it sufficient to *take* a person to be a certain body, or is such a sortal identification incomplete?'

I have said enough for it to be evident that the *persons-approach* is primarily concerned with the identity of *other* persons and only derivatively concerned with the identity of one oneself. This is inevitable once referential identification is made the key to personal identity. For in normal circumstances none of us makes either a referential or a sortal identification of himself to himself. It is only to others that we referentially identify ourselves. Thus even when we do refer to ourselves it is only because we are obligated to consider ourselves in relation to other people; it is for their benefit that we make identifying references to ourselves. To say that I can identify myself to myself is as absurd as it is to say that I can introduce myself to myself. (The sense in which one discovers who he is following amnesia is not in question here.)

To the objection that we do seem to make identifying references to ourselves in soliloquy (when there is no question of identifying the speaker to hearers) the correct reply is that we continue to use

[1] S. Shoemaker, *Self-Identity and Self-Knowledge* (New York, 1963), p. 5.

public language in soliloquy (for want of a better), but that in soliloquy the referring expression 'I' is not used for the purpose of identification. I leave it open here whether the personal pronoun has any function at all in soliloquy, or is simply redundant as Geach maintains.[1] Moreover from a logical point of view soliloquy is conceptually more complex than dialogue, so the former should be explicated in terms of the latter.

The *persons-approach* attempts to tell us what we must *take* ourselves to be. It aspires to be theoretical knowledge of what we are, and its attempt to find out what we are is an attempt to fit us into the scheme of things; to explain in what respects we are like and in what respects unlike other things such as material objects, organic entities, fanciful robots, and spiritual beings (granted there are such). It is an attempt, in short, to locate us among the furniture of the world.

Another aspect of the *persons-approach* needs to be stressed, because its implications do not seem to have been fully appreciated by those who adopt it. It should lead to an account of what we have reason to *take* persons to be, and should not lead to an account of what we *know* persons to be. We do not know that persons are what we take them to be apart from supporting philosophical argument. I cannot, in other words, have immediate knowledge – knowledge not based on argument or evidence – that I am one of the following: a mere body, a pure ego, a bundle of perceptions, a non-spiritual substance, or a unique type of basic particular. It would be odd for a philosopher to say that he knows that he is nothing but a body, but at least intelligible for him to say that he takes himself to be nothing but a body. It is conceivable that I know *that* I am a person without knowing what a person is, but I may *take* a person to be any of these things. Thus I understand the problem of personal identity to be the problem of what to *take* ourselves to be, provided the qualification is added that the conception we form of persons permits persons to make referential identifications of one another.

Enough has now been said about the problem of personal identity for a meaningful contrast to be made with what I have suggested should be regarded as the separate problem of self-identity. As persons we are aware of each other, but we are also aware of ourselves. We possess self-awareness. The problem of self-identity, then, is the problem of the identity of the self of

[1] P. Geach, *Mental Acts* (London, 1957), p. 120.

which we have this awareness. For those philosophers for whom the *persons-approach* exhausts the problem, self-awareness of necessity reduces to the possession of the *concept* of oneself, or to the having of an *idea* of oneself.[1] And this concept of necessity reduces to that of a person. Apart from the dubiousness of the latter equation, however, it cannot be denied that it is *prima facie* implausible to interpret awareness of something as an *idea* of something. Normally an awareness is taken to be experiential in a way that an idea or concept is not. Thus 'I am aware of myself' contrasts with 'I have a concept or idea of myself'. The dilemma facing philosophers who adopt the *persons-approach* is that given their refusal to consider one's own case, the only analysis of self-awareness open to them is the reductive analysis in terms of which being aware of oneself is having an idea of oneself.

What needs to be recognized is that in addition to having an idea of what we must take ourselves to be (personal identity), each of us also has the experience of being a self. It is with this experience that we are concerned when we deal with self-awareness. On this basis I have reserved the description 'the problem of self-identity' for the problem of ascertaining in what the identity of the self consists of which we claim awareness. And I have given the name 'the self-approach' to the method that I take to be the right method to employ if we are to reach a solution to the problem.

Of course it is possible on the *persons-approach* to deny that we are aware of ourselves in any sense not covered by their analysis. *Persons-approach* philosophers may claim that the so-called self-awareness is nothing more than the self's recognition that his experiences are *his* experiences; that the awareness of being a self just consists in having experiences of this, that and the other kind. However, on this view it is not ruled out in principle that an experience of the sort I have been discussing could feasibly be had. Rather it presents a challenge, i.e. to produce an experience of the appropriate sort. It may be read as corresponding to Hume's method of challenge.[2] Such a move may preserve the consistency of the theory, but, I claim, experience just does not bear it out. If no other explanation of self-awareness was forthcoming, then one might have little option but to accept this interpretation. However, there is I believe an alternative, and my aim is to put forward a

[1] P. F. Strawson, *Individuals* (London, 1959), p. 89 f.
[2] See D. G. C. MacNabb, *David Hume: His Theory of Knowledge and Morality* (London, 1951), p. 18.

theory of self-identity that is based on the experience each of us has of being a self.

What the *persons-approach* seems to ignore is the awareness we have of ourselves and with it our knowledge that we have this awareness, which I shall call our *native knowledge of the self*.[1] Knowledge of what we take the self to be is not such knowledge. Whereas the latter sort of knowledge is theoretical and hence propositional in nature, native knowledge of self is non-theoretical and non-propositional; it is the knowledge we have of a self because selves are what we ourselves are. In short, it is experiential knowledge of the self.

I shall try to give a preliminary indication of the nature of this native knowledge we possess. Such knowledge can be reached by a consideration of the relation between a self and his experiences. For grammatical reasons I shall refer to the self as the subject. I do so because we cannot speak grammatically of 'the self of experiences', or 'the person of experiences', whereas we can comfortably speak of 'the *subject* of experiences'. Now most philosophers, when they refer to the relation between a subject and his experiences, have a special vocabulary for the purpose. Among the variety of expressions used to describe the relation in question are the following: 'belonging to', 'owning', 'having'. Alternatively the experiences are said to be 'experiences *of* a subject', 'states of a subject', 'predicates characterizing a subject', or 'experiences ascribed to a subject'. I list these expressions because I would like to make the point that these expressions are most naturally understood from a third person point of view. They are not the most apt expressions we can find to disclose what is true in our own cases. When we come to the relation between ourselves as subjects and our own experiences, the experiences appear as experiences *to* the subject. The subject 'undergoes' an experience, 'enjoys' an experience, 'suffers' an experience, is 'aware of' an experience, and so on. In sum, from the subject's point of view, experiences happen *to* him.

This distinction between on the one hand an experience being an experience *of* a person and on the other hand an experience being an experience *to* a subject is central to an appreciation of the distinction between the *persons-approach* and the *self-approach*.

---

[1] It may be called knowledge with as much or as little justification as our knowledge of our own pains may be called knowledge. It expresses our ability to report our awareness of the self.

For in the case of others, all we can say is that an experience is an experience *of* a person; it is only in our own case that we can say that an experience is an experience *to* a subject. The point is most significant. Once we cut ourselves off from the fact that experiences are experiences *to* a subject, and confine our analysis to the experiences *of* a person, we can make of the subject any unknown somewhat without it making the slightest difference. Very conveniently this frees the personal identity theorist from the embarrassment of having to explain (which in his own terms he is unable to do) in what sense a subject must be conscious if an experience is to be an experience *to* him. The consciousness of the subject can be reduced to the attributing of conscious experiences to him. The subject's being conscious apart from his having one particular experience is then understood in terms of his having other contemporaneous experiences beside the one in question. We are then left with no alternative to the following conclusion: the consciousness of the subject = the experiences of the subject.

Such an account fails to do justice to our experience of experiences. An experience, no matter how internal, is always presented to the subject as an experience *to* him; as something over against himself; as something put forth from himself. To use a metaphor, the subject lives in his own logical space which is separate from the logical space of any particular experience. If this metaphor could not be cashed there would be no point in using it. But it will take the rest of the book to cash it. I introduce it at this point simply to draw attention to a problematic aspect of the relation between a subject and his experiences which can only be avoided by refusing to give any account at all of the subject for consciousness. The problem of self-identity then as I see it is the problem of accounting for the identity of the conscious subject *qua* conscious subject. It is of such conscious subjects that those adopting the *persons-approach* go on to ask 'What are they?' The *persons-approach* seeks to offer a theoretical account of what we must take those selves to be which it is the aim of the *self-approach* to identify experientially.

The puzzle about self-identity, I believe, is the puzzle about the nature of the subject *qua* conscious subject, and the problem is one of understanding what to make of our being conscious subjects to which our experiences appear to us to be related. What seems to be needed is an account of how we have this experience of being a subject, which is distinct from an account of the relation of the subject to the experiences he has. For anyone interested in this problem theories of personal identity will not supply the answers. If I am right this is quite properly so, because the *persons-approach* is not concerned with this particular set of problems. Thus anyone wishing to have an answer to the problem of self-identity must feel that the *persons-approach* does not give him what he wants, and in spite of accepting, perhaps, a particular theory developed on the *persons-approach*, he will still feel that the theory has not removed his perplexity.

Contemporary philosophers could not be expected to be sympathetic to such an undertaking, because they are only too well aware of the pitfalls that lie in its way. Most would see it floundering between the Scylla of Serial Theories of the self, and the Charybdis of the Pure Ego Theory of the self. The challenge presented by this book is its claim to show that it is possible to navigate successfully between the two. Because I have come to think it possible to navigate such a course, I have come to believe that philosophers have been over-hasty in thinking that it could not be done. It is possible for philosophers to become too familiar with philosophical arguments, and because of their familiarity to take for granted their soundness, when a closer inspection would have revealed their weakness. Thus it has become automatic to contrast the Pure Ego Theory with the Serial Theory (or Bundle Theory as it is sometimes called), as though there were no *tertium quid*. A case in point is the following comment made by Aune:

'For one thing, since no phenomenal self is introspectively apparent, as Hume and others have insisted, the only other alternative seems to be a conception of the self as a bundle of experiences.'[1]

The decisive refutation of this antithesis between the Pure Ego Theory and the Serial Theory is the production of a plausible third alternative. The present study in its entirety may be viewed as such an attempt, for it is an attempt to construct a theory of the self on entirely experiential lines which yet succumbs to neither its Scylla nor its Charybdis.

[3] The distinction between the *persons-approach* and the *self-approach* which I wish to draw is necessitated also by a reading of

[1] B. Aune, *Knowledge, Mind, and Nature* (New York, 1967), p. 69.

traditional theories of the self. This I shall now try to show, and I shall prepare the way with a further point about our native knowledge of the self.

I have asserted that native knowledge of the self is non-propositional, and that due to this it is difficult to put into words. This fact can be exhibited by appreciating a certain affinity between the question 'What is the self?' and the question raised by St Augustine: 'What is time?' St Augustine's well-known retort to the question 'What is time?' seems even more applicable as a retort to the question 'What is the self?': namely, 'If no one asks me, I know; if I wish to explain it to one that asketh, I know not.' In spite of this difficulty there have been attempts to describe the self from within, and I shall instance one such attempt for the purpose of assessing the implications involved in making such attempts. MacNabb, in his defence of a Berkeleyan view of the self against the Humean view says the following:

'I suggest that there is much plausibility in Berkeley's view, that we have an experience which we call the self, or soul, an experience different in kind from our other experiences, more internal than the most personal emotion we feel, and not needing or able to be represented in thought by an image, since in all thinking it is actually present.'[1]

On this account our selves are, so to speak, 'with us' all the time and this accounts for our feeling of complete familiarity with the self, of which MacNabb's passage gives such a distinct impression. This is, to be sure, the way we feel about ourselves when we are not asked what the self is. But no sooner have we found words to describe this experience, than the self-defeating character of the description becomes evident. MacNabb, we notice, refers to an *experience* 'which we call the self'. This means that the self *is* an experience. And the question at once arises: 'Who experiences *this* experience?' It cannot be the self, since the self has been identified with the experience experienced. We are left with the feeling that the experiencer who experiences the self has been left out of the picture after all, and the suspicion remains that the experiencer in question is the self we have been trying to identify all along. As the fruit-laden branches receded out of reach whenever Tantalus attempted to grasp them, so does the self seem to elude us when we

[1] MacNabb, *David Hume: His Theory of Knowledge and Morality*, p. 147.

attempt to grasp it. Equally, when we do not attempt to grasp it in introspection, it seems as close to us as was the fruit to Tantalus when he made no attempt to reach for it.

The seeming fruitlessness of the attempt to reach the self experientially has led some philosophers to the conclusion that the self must lie outside experience, and must be unknowable in itself. On this view our knowledge of the self is essentially inferential. We know of its existence only through its manifestations. We know what the self experiences and what it accomplishes, but what it is in itself remains forever a mystery. We call it the self, the mind, the ego, or the subject, but apart from dignifying it with a name, we cannot say what it is. Such, in essence, is the Pure Ego Theory of the self.

Other philosophers have refused to entertain the idea of a self that lies outside any possible experience, and yet have agreed with the Pure Ego Theorists that inner experience does not present the self *per se*. The solution they have proposed is that the self is constituted by its experiences. Theories of this nature are variants of what is called the Serial Theory of the self.

Despite the fact that these two types of theory stand at opposite extremes to each other, they have a common presupposition. The presupposition is that the type of account that can be given of material objects can also be given of the self: in other words, these theories of the self in effect transpose to the self a theory formulated in the first instance as an account of the relation between a material object and its properties. By implication, therefore, they treat the self as an object. Thus in the case of the Pure Ego Theory the reasoning which led to the conclusion that the self is pure subject is identical with the reasoning that whatever property we ascribe to a substance is an attribute of the substance, and what we know of a substance is always one of its attributes and never the substance itself. The substance becomes an unknowable something in which attributes 'inhere', and its sole *raison d'être* is to be a 'support' for a collection of attributes. In short, the Pure Ego Theory is simply the application to the self of the general doctrine of substance and attribute.

If a dialectical movement is to be found anywhere in philosophy it is surely in the movement from theories of substance to phenomenalistic theories. Once a substance is declared to be nothing more than an unknowable support for attributes, it is inevitable that some way of accounting for the compresence of a group of attributes should be sought that is free of the intellectual embarrassment of an unknowable support. The simplest alternative is to attribute the unity of a group of attributes to no other fact than the fact that they constitute a group. It is because they cohere together, it is argued, and not because they inhere in a substance, that a group of attributes is deemed to form a unity. In phenomenalist terms, what is called a substance is nothing but a collection of attributes.

As is well known Hume gave such a phenomenalist analysis of the one substance that had until then escaped – namely, the self. Where others had argued that the self could be known only through its manifestations Hume tough-mindedly asserted that the self was identical with its manifestations; the self being nothing but a bundle of perceptions. Here too, therefore, we have an instance of a theory that was designed to account for our knowledge of material objects simply being taken over and applied to the self.

The fault I find with both the Pure Ego Theory and the Serial Theory – thesis and antithesis, as it were – is that for all the difference it makes they might as well not be about ourselves at all. The theories take no cognizance of our native knowledge of ourselves. They show no awareness that it might beg the question simply to assume that selves can be given the same type of analysis as objects. In effect they do not see it as giving us a unique advantage as compared with our knowledge of objects that *we* are selves; that we have native knowledge of ourselves, and of ourselves alone; and that it is this that puts the ground of our knowledge of the self on altogether a different footing from the ground of our knowledge of objects.

That the two traditional theories do not make use of the fact that we are in the best possible position to give an account of the self should lead us to suspect that they are wrongly viewed as contributions to the problem of self-identity, and that they should instead be viewed as contributions to the problem of personal-identity. After all not only is no appeal made to our native knowledge of ourselves, but also our native knowledge of self does not lend support to one or other of the traditional rival theories. The Pure Ego Theory preserves the unity and the endurance of the self, but it does so at the cost of making the self non-experiential, and that is at odds with our native knowledge of ourselves. Contrariwise, the Serial Theory makes it difficult to understand the self *qua* subject: It gives no intuitively acceptable account of the unity and the endurance of the self, although it gives full recognition to the experiential nature of the self.

The use to which I have just put our native knowledge of the self reveals by implication what I mean by calling it non-propositional knowledge. I have claimed that in terms of it we can say that experience does not bear out the accounts of the self with which the traditional theories present us. The situation is, I think, rather like this: in virtue of my native knowledge of the self I can tell when a theory of the self does not receive the endorsement of my experience of being a self. To the theorist I can say that I know that the self is not as he describes, but if he asks me what description of the self does fit my experience, I do not know. To put it differently, I can test a theory of the self in terms of my own experience, but I do not judge the suggested theory by comparing it with the theory of the self I know to be true. My judgement is not based on any *theory* at all: it is based on experience of being a self – quite another matter. It is this that makes it true to say, borrowing from St Augustine: 'when no one asks me, I know what I am, but when I am asked I do not know'.

If then neither the Pure Ego Theory nor the Serial Theory receives the corroboration of our native knowledge of the self does this not mean that they are theories concerning what we must *take* ourselves to be? For it will be recalled that I argued that a theory of what the self must be taken to be is not disclosed by our native knowledge of the self, and does not receive the endorsement of this experiential knowledge. Unfortunately there are considerations weighing against such an interpretation of the theories we have been dealing with. The aim of theories of personal-identity is to arrive at a sortal identification of persons. So far so good: the theories in question seem to have that aim. On the other hand, the additional condition was laid down that persons had to be subject to referential identification. This condition, I shall try to show, cannot be met by the theories in question.

I do not wish to argue for this proposition on the ground that we run into difficulties as soon as we try to provide criteria for the identification either of Pure Egos, or of selves *qua* series of experiences. Those difficulties have been impressively exposed by Strawson and Shoemaker. Rather I wish to adopt a different approach. Referential identification of persons is a necessary presupposition of our ability to make statements about persons – both statements ascribing characteristics to ourselves and statements ascribing characteristics to others. That is to say, both self-ascriptive statements (avowals) and other-ascriptive statements are statements about persons. It follows that any sentence in which the grammatical subject is a personal pronoun is a sentence in which the personal pronoun is an expression referring to a person. In turn it follows that self-ascriptive statements and other-ascriptive statements entail corresponding statements about persons. Thus the statement 'I am angry' entails the statement 'A person is angry'. Similarly the statement 'He is overweight' entails the statement 'A person is overweight'. From this it is obvious that we can form propositional functions ('— is angry', '— is overweight') and consider the question: 'What type of expression can meaningfully fill the blank to complete the sentence?' Such a procedure, I now want to suggest, can be used to determine whether a theory of the identity of a subject is a theory of personal-identity or a theory of self-identity.

It would work in the following manner. If a theorist wishes to argue that the self as described by him is the intended referent in sentences about persons, then he must consent that a sentence is meaningful when the blank in a propositional function such as the above is replaced by a description of the intended referent. A theorist who is prepared to defend such a proposition as meaningful is a *persons-approach* theorist dealing with the problem of personal identity. If not, the theorist must be classified as a *self-approach* theorist dealing with the problem of self-identity.

Thus a theory according to which we are nothing but bodies would answer to the *persons-approach* because it is possible to fill the sentence-blank with the expression 'a body'. This would give us sentences such as, 'A body is angry', and 'A body is overweight'. Now I would be the first to concede that this is an odd thing to say, but that is not the point. The point is that such a proposition would have to be defended by a philosopher who held the view that we are nothing but bodies. It hardly needs to be said that such theorist must be prepared to go to the limit with his analysis and affirm the meaningfulness of such sentences as 'A body is thinking'. In other words, the blank-filling must be applicable to sentences involving mental predicates as well as to those involving physical predicates.

When a theorist is not prepared to allow that an expression characterizing the self according to his theory can fill all such sentence-blanks and the sentence still be defended as meaningful, we can be sure that we are not dealing with a theory of personal identity, but a theory of self-identity.

Thus a Pure Ego Theorist would not wish to make the truth of his theory depend upon the meaningfulness of such sentences as,

'A Pure Ego is angry (or overweight)'. Neither could a Serial
Theorist allow the truth of his theory to depend on the meaningfulness of such sentences as, 'A bundle of perceptions is hungry (or
overweight)'.

This principle would therefore disqualify the two traditional
theories from being theories of personal identity. I have already
argued that they are not theories of self-identity, because they
neither appeal to native knowledge of the self, nor receive the
corroboration of such knowledge. Of what then *are* they theories?

Only one conclusion seems to remain and that is that they aspire
to be theories of *both* personal identity and self-identity. I have
however argued that this is impossible. This would explain why the
two theories fall between two stools. They are neither the one thing
nor the other because they try to be both. They are intended to
explain both what the subject is experienced as being, and what the
subject must be *taken* to be. If I am right, however, these are
separate questions requiring separate answers, and the unsuccess-
fulness of the two theories can be attributed to the failure of their
advocates to keep the two questions distinct.

One of the merits of the *persons-approach*, therefore, is that it has
forced on us the realization that we have two sorts of questions we
can ask about the identity of selves, and this enables us to see where
the traditional theories fall down. The lesson to be learned is that a
theory of self-identity is *not* to be evaluated in terms of whether the
self can be the subject of ascriptive sentences. On the contrary a
theory of self-identity attempts to offer an account of a self even
when such a self is not yet thought of as a language-user – a self-
ascriber. Just as the having of experiences is not dependent on one's
ability to report their occurrence, so being a self is not dependent
on one's ability to use first-person and third-person sentences.
Thus the difference between the *persons-approach* and the *self-
approach* comes to this: the former asks what we must *take* ourselves to be, given the condition that we *are language-users*; the
latter asks what it is to be a subject to which experiences occur,
quite independently of this condition. The two approaches operate
on entirely different logical levels, and both approaches are, I
believe, equally legitimate.

The above discussion gives us a possible insight into why the
persons-approach is nowadays just about the only one in the field.
The traditional theories such as the Pure Ego Theory and its antithesis the Serial Theory were thought to be theories intended to

reveal the identity of the self *qua* subject of experience. Thus interpreted they represented attempts to find out what could be discovered about the self from one's own case. Since these theories have mostly been thought to be unsuccessful, their failure has impugned the respectability of the very idea of giving an account of the experiential self. This meant that the only respectable problem left was that of explaining what we must take to be the subjects referred to in our ascriptive sentences.

But this seems to me to be the wrong conclusion to reach in the light of the failure of the two traditional theories. They failed, not because they attempted an impossible task, but precisely because they were not genuine theories of *self-identity* resting on an examination of one's own case. They failed because they ignored our native knowledge of the self, and tried to apply to the self theories constructed for the purpose of explaining our knowledge of material objects.

On this assumption I have tried to make good the omission by proposing a theory of self-identity that does rest on our native knowledge of the self. Should the reader still be in doubt whether I have set myself a genuine task, I can only ask him to judge in the light of the theory I am proposing. Thus I am in a sense suggesting that the validity of the problem should be assessed in terms of the meaningfulness of the theory developed in the chapters that follow.

It will be discovered that I frequently turn to the views of nineteenth- and early twentieth-century philosophers many of whom are now no more than names to most philosophers. I have done this in order to re-establish a connection with the stage philosophy had reached when the problem of self-identity as I have defined it was still a live issue, and before the *persons-approach* came to dominate the philosophical scene.

My introduction of the *self-approach* may have given rise to a scepticism in the mind of the reader concerning the sorts of argument and evidence I will appeal to in developing my solution to the problem of self-identity. It is easy to anticipate a philosopher's reaction to the statement that an account is to be given of the self which hinges on the experience the subject has in his own case. He will suspect that he is about to be introduced to some very mysterious type of experiencing, which he has no hope of matching with any corresponding experience of his own, and that the case will therefore rest on some ultimately untestable experiential claim. Alternatively, he will suspect that the subject as uncovered in any

such investigation will prove to be so private and elusive that only
the writer will know what he is referring to and no reader will
succeed in identifying it. That is to say, he will be sceptical whether
any attempt to communicate this experience of the self, or to
identify the self allegedly experienced, can succeed.

To allay such suspicions it will be as well for me to reveal the
empirical bias of my own philosophical point of view. C. D. Broad,
writing in this instance of moral theory, laid down two principles
which, when applied to the theory of the self, I would claim to be
exemplified in my own approach. The first principle is:

'Other things being equal, a theory is to be preferred if it does not
have to postulate anything of a kind which is not already admitted
as a fact and found to be readily intelligible.'[1]

This principle is in operation throughout this work, and no appeal
will be found anywhere in it to strange forms of experience, or to
the postulation of strange entities. The second principle is:

'Other things being equal, a theory is to be preferred if it does not
have to suppose that all men are *fundamentally mistaken* on certain
matters with which the whole race is and has always been constantly
concerned.'[2]

This principle supports my attempt to account for self-awareness
as a phenomenon readily admitted by all except those philosophers
whose theories forbid them to concede its existence.

Broad pointed out that as far as moral enquiry is concerned these
two principles pulled in opposite directions, but this is not true of
their application to the theory of the self I shall advance. The two
principles not only work in harmony throughout this enterprise,
but go so far as to provide a neat formulation of the methodological
aims of the entire work. It would offend against Broad's two
principles to imagine that the experiential self can only be found
after a deep search for some ultra recondite fact of experience. We
have the experience of being selves throughout our waking moments,
and an account of the self which depended on some recondite fact,
which it would take the discipline of a Platonic philosopher to discover, would not be believable. No account of the self can be

[1] *The Philosophy of C. D. Broad*, ed. A. Schillp (New York, 1959), p. 814.
[2] *Ibid.*

successful if it fails to explain the accessibility of a subject's self to himself. Any account which was by its nature recondite would immediately be rejected as contrary to our native knowledge of ourselves. The self must be shown to be knowable by means of experience; and by means of experiences none would dispute. A theory which fails to make the self knowable in this way automatically becomes a theory of what the self must be taken to be, and not a theory of what it is experienced as being: that is to say, it might pass as an answer to the problem of personal identity, but could not pass as an answer to the problem of self-identity.

CHAPTER TWO

CONSCIOUSNESS

I. PROBLEMS OF EXISTENCE AND MEANING

[1] The task of the *self-approach* is to give an account of self-identity and this, on my interpretation, is an account of the self *qua* subject of consciousness. Such an account must begin with consciousness, for apart from consciousness no question about the subject of consciousness can arise. I cannot know what it is to be a self if I am not conscious. Equally I cannot be a self if I cannot at least be conscious. Such native knowledge as I have of myself cannot therefore be divorced from the fact that I am conscious, and from the fact that in being conscious I am a self. Consciousness will therefore have to be subjected to an analysis if we are to give a philosophical account of the self. To comply with the *self-approach* the consciousness to be analysed must be first-person consciousness. Certain nineteenth-century British philosophers adopted what is essentially the *self-approach*. To support their views on the relation between a subject and his experiences they appealed to what they called 'the deliverances of consciousness'. Among these philosophers were J. F. Ferrier, Sir William Hamilton, and Shadworth Hodgson. It would be doing them no injustice to call them 'philosophers of consciousness', because to them it was a truth above argument that a sound philosophy began with an analysis of consciousness.

Standing in the way of any attempt to re-establish links with their tradition in philosophy are those philosophers and psychologists who more recently have denied the very existence of consciousness. The philosophers of consciousness would no doubt have greeted the proposition 'Consciousness does not exist' with the disbelief with which G. E. Moore greeted such propositions as 'Time is unreal' and 'There is no external world'. I shall therefore begin this enquiry into the nature of consciousness by considering what philosophers might have in mind when they ostensibly deny the existence of consciousness. My aim is not merely to clear a route back to a bygone tradition, but, more importantly, to explain how I myself understand the notion of consciousness and how I shall use it in the present study.

To deny the existence of consciousness seems a paradox, because it seems to imply that we are all unconscious, or that we should look upon ourselves as Cartesian automatons: it seems to imply that we are incapable of feeling and have no sense experience. Now it would plainly be ridiculous to believe any such thing, and we cannot seriously believe that this is what the philosopher denying the existence of consciousness has in mind. When a philosopher's position seems to be outrageously false, it is wise to consider the possibility that he is denying a particular philosophical account of the facts, and not the incontrovertible facts themselves.

Let us therefore find out what at least one philosopher has in mind when he denies the existence of consciousness. I refer to William James' famous paper 'Does "Consciousness" exist?'[1] which is the classical statement of the position. The first point that should strike us, is that William James puts the word 'consciousness' in inverted commas. This should warn us that he is not referring to consciousness as ordinarily understood, but to a specific philosophical doctrine of 'Consciousness'. The word 'consciousness' had been taken up into the technical terminology of a number of philosophical systems, and it was to its employment in these systems that he took exception. This the following passage makes clear.

'To deny plumply that "consciousness" exists seems so absurd on the face of it – for undeniably "thoughts" do exist – that I fear some readers will follow me no farther. Let me then immediately explain that I mean only to deny that the word stands for an entity, but to insist most emphatically that it does stand for a function. There is, I mean, no aboriginal stuff or quality of being, contrasted with that of which material objects are made, out of which our thoughts of them are made; but there is a function in experience which thoughts perform, and for the performance of which this quality of being is invoked. That function is *knowing*.'[2]

This passage leaves us in no doubt that what James is denying is not in fact the existence of consciousness, but the correctness of certain types of description of consciousness: viz. those that entail its

[1] William James, *Essays in Radical Empiricism* (London, 1912), ch. 1.
[2] *Ibid.*, p. 3.

being an 'entity' or 'aboriginal stuff'. That is to say, James is disputing the truth of the descriptions certain philosophers give of consciousness. This is a far less radical challenge than is implied in the unqualified statement that consciousness does not exist. Other philosophers have not been as meticulous as James in putting the word 'consciousness' in inverted commas, before denying its existence, thus making their position seem needlessly provocative and paradoxical.

I proceed now to the substance of James' objection: his claim that consciousness is not an 'entity' or 'aboriginal stuff'. Although not mentioned by James, a statement made by Hamilton gives a good idea of the sort of view he was objecting to:

'Consciousness may be compared to an internal light, by means of which, and which alone, what passes in the mind is rendered visible. Consciousness is simple, – is not composed of parts, either similar or dissimilar. It always resembles itself, differing only in the degrees of its intensity; thus, there are not various kinds of consciousness, although there are various kinds of mental modes, or states, of which we are conscious.'[1]

When in *The Concept of Mind* Ryle remarks that the myth of consciousness is a piece of para-optics,[2] he too no doubt had passages such as this in mind. But there is no need to go back as far as Hamilton to find examples of the view James and Ryle are attacking. G. E. Moore's 'Refutation of Idealism' in which he offers his analysis of sensation provides the most notable instance of the doctrine of 'consciousness' to which they took exception.

Extracts from Moore's article are actually quoted by James as representing the view he was objecting to. Moore maintains:

'We have then in every sensation two distinct elements, one which I call consciousness, and another which I call the object of consciousness. This must be so if the sensation of blue and the sensation of green, though different in one respect, are alike in another: blue is one object of sensation and green is another, and consciousness, which both sensations have in common, is different from either.'[3]

[1] Bowen, *The Metaphysics of Sir William Hamilton*, p. 120.
[2] G. Ryle, *The Concept of Mind* (London, 1951), p. 159.
[3] G. E. Moore, *Philosophical Studies* (London, 1960), p. 17.

If it is doubted that this passage commits Moore to the proposition
that consciousness is a sort of 'aboriginal stuff', the next passage in
which he elaborates his meaning, settles the issue.

'For the element "consciousness" being common to all sensations
may be and certainly is regarded as in some sense their "substance"
and by the "content" of each is only meant that in respect of which
one differs from another.'[1]

Although Moore claims that this is only one of two possible ways of
describing the position, he does not give any indication that he is
opposed to this formulation.

Now it is quite clear that when philosophers such as James and
Ryle deny the existence of 'consciousness', they are not denying
that we are conscious in the ordinary sense of the word. They are
denying rather views such as those held by Hamilton and Moore as
exemplified in their contention that all our experiences contain an
element in common which they, rather confusedly, also name 'consciousness'. The fact that Moore, for instance, means by 'consciousness' something entirely different from what is ordinarily
meant by consciousness is proved beyond a shadow of a doubt in
the following passage:

'. . . The moment we try to fix our attention upon consciousness
and to see *what*, distinctly, it is, it seems to vanish: it seems as if
we had before us a mere emptiness. When we try to introspect the
sensation of blue, all we can see is the blue: the other element is as
if it were diaphanous.'[2]

In the ordinary sense of 'consciousness' the presence or absence of
consciousness is not something that we can only detect after taking
great pains. On the contrary the impact of the presence of consciousness is powerful and immediate – if I may be permitted for
the moment to speak in these terms. Moreover, as ordinarily understood 'consciousness' is not to be conceived of as something over
and above the occurrence of thoughts and feelings. We are, therefore, free to determine the meaning of consciousness as ordinarily
understood, without fear that we might be referring to something
which in no sense exists, and without falling foul of James and Ryle.

[1] *Ibid.*, p. 23.
[2] *Ibid.*, p. 25.

[2] Any attempt to discover the meaning of consciousness as it is ordinarily used would meet with the immediate objection of Ryle, who argues, quite rightly, that the word is ordinarily used in a number of different contexts for a variety of purposes.[1] Ryle himself has done us the service of distinguishing five different uses to which the word 'conscious' and its cognate 'self-conscious' are put in real life. I do not wish to dispute the fact that the word is used in these five senses, and indeed I believe I can add a sixth. I would not deny, either, that a great deal of confusion has been caused by the fact that philosophers who have given the concept of consciousness a prominent place in their philosophical systems have failed to keep the various senses distinct. One frequently finds a philosopher like Hamilton sliding from one sense of the word to another seemingly without being aware of doing so. Where I do wish to take issue with Ryle is in connection with his unspoken assumption that these several uses are all on a par with one another – none being more basic than any of the others. As against Ryle I shall argue that there is a basic meaning of 'consciousness' which we may understand philosophers to have in mind when they use the word. I shall further argue that a philosopher may make use of this basic meaning without this carrying the implication that he is using the word in a special philosophical sense which is different from any of its ordinary uses (as we discovered to be true of Moore).

The criterion I shall use in respect of which a particular sense to the word 'consciousness' is basic can at once be defined. A sense of 'consciousness' is basic if a person's being conscious in that sense does not entail his being conscious in any other sense, whereas his being conscious in any other sense does entail his being conscious in that sense. I propose now to give excerpts of Ryle's analysis of the different ways in which the words 'conscious' and 'consciousness' are used, so that we can consider whether there is not among them a sense of consciousness which is basic in the sense I have defined.

'(a) People often speak in this way; they say, "I was conscious that the furniture had been rearranged", or, "I was conscious that he was less friendly than usual". In such contexts the word "conscious" is used instead of words like "found out", "realized" and "discovered" to indicate a certain noteworthy nebulousness and consequent inarticulateness of the apprehension . . .

[1] *The Concept of Mind*, pp. 156–7.

'(b) People often use "conscious" and "self-conscious" in describing the embarrassment exhibited by persons, especially youthful persons, who are anxious about the opinions held by others of their qualities of character or intellect.

'(c) "Self-conscious" is sometimes used in a more general sense to indicate that someone has reached the stage of paying heed to his own qualities of character or intellect, irrespective of whether or not he is embarrassed about other people's estimations of them . . .

'(d) Quite different from the foregoing uses of "conscious", "self-conscious" and "unconscious", is the use in which a numbed or anaesthetised person is said to have lost consciousness from his feet up to his knees. In this use "conscious" means sensitive or sentient and "unconscious" means anaesthetised or insensitive. We say that a person has lost consciousness when he has ceased to be sensitive to any slaps, noises, pricks or smells.

'(e) Different from, though closely connected with this last use, there is the sense in which a person can be said to be unconscious of a sensation, when he pays no heed to it. A walker engaged in a heated dispute may be unconscious, in this sense, of the sensations in his blistered heel, and the reader of these words was, when he began this sentence, probably unconscious of the muscular and skin sensations in the back of his neck, or in his left knee. A person may also be unconscious or unaware that he is frowning, beating time to the music, or muttering.

"Conscious" in this sense means "heeding"' . . .[1]

To this list I would like to add:

(f) "Conscious" is sometimes used synonymously with "distracted by". "I couldn't concentrate on Mark Antony's speech, because I was conscious of the actor's accent all the time."

Of these six senses of consciousness sense (d) is the only one which could be considered basic: namely the sense in which 'conscious' means 'sentient'. However as it stands, Ryle's description of this sense of consciousness is not sufficiently clearly drawn. A person is 'sensitive' or 'sentient' while he is fast asleep, and yet no one can be conscious in any of the other senses while in a dreamless sleep. Before we have a sense of 'conscious' which is truly the basic sense, we have to rule out this possibility.

This has been done very clearly by John Wisdom. The interest

[1] *Op. cit.*, pp. 156–7.

of his analysis lies in the fact that he is concerned to determine the fundamental sense of consciousness.

'I cannot analyse what I mean by "conscious", but I want to make known to you what I attribute to a thing when I call it "conscious". When using the word in this special sense I will write it *conscious*. And I will now set down the clues to what I mean by conscious.

'(i) *Conscious* implies *either feels* or *is aware*.

'(ii) Consider the change which comes over a man as he comes round from chloroform or from *dreamless* sleep. You know quite well the change I mean. That kind of change I call "becoming *conscious*". Of course as you come round from chloroform all sorts of *bodily* changes are taking place – the nerves are recovering from the chemical poison; and as you come round from sleep more blood flows to the brain. So that, strictly, there is nothing that can be called "*the* change" which takes place when one comes round from chloroform and sleep. Nevertheless, these bodily changes are not ones you thought of when I spoke of *the* change; you never thought of blood and brain. That kind of change which you immediately thought of when I spoke of the change from sleep or chloroform is the one I express by "becoming *conscious*".

'(iii) *Conscious* does not mean *alive*. A tree is alive but not conscious. An amoeba is certainly alive yet quite likely not conscious.

'(iv) *Conscious* does not mean *living and sensitive*. A man in a dreamless sleep is a living and sensitive being; but he is not at that time conscious in my sense, i.e., *conscious*. Of course such a man is conscious compared with a tree or a dead man; more accurately there is *a* sense of "conscious" in which it is correct to say that he is a conscious being. He is conscious in the derived and hypothetical sense that, if he were shaken, he would become *conscious* (fundamental sense).

'This hypothetical sense of "conscious" is less fundamental than that in terms of which mental facts are to be defined, that is *conscious*. For "conscious" (in this hypothetical sense) has a meaning derived from, i.e. defined in terms of, *conscious*. In other words, if we split up the meaning of the hypothetical sense, we find that one of its elements is *conscious* . . .

'(v) S is *conscious* implies neither (1) that S is conscious of his environment nor (2) that S is conscious of himself. As to (1), a man is *conscious* when he is dreaming . . . and therefore when unconscious of his environment. I do not deny, on the contrary I assert, that there is *a* usual and therefore perfectly respectable sense in which "conscious" is used, which *does* imply "conscious of his environment". Thus, when we say "Is he conscious?" meaning "Has he regained consciousness?" (after an accident), we *do* mean "Is he now again conscious *of his environment*". But it will be seen that this third way of using "conscious" is yet another sense derived from our first, that is, the sense we write *conscious*. For "conscious" (sense 3) means "*conscious* of environment".

'As to (2), a man may be conscious and yet be unconscious of himself . . . It is important to add clause (2) because some psychologists use "conscious" in a sense which implies consciousness of self. Thus they would deny that animals are conscious, because, although they would admit that dogs smell bones and are therefore *conscious*, they would deny that a dog ever thinks to himself, "I shall do so and so", e.g. "take a bone". In other words, they deny that an animal is ever *conscious* of itself and they express their view very misleadingly by saying that animals are not conscious. This fourth sense of "conscious" is obviously also derived from *conscious*. So we may write:

'(vi) *Conscious* is the fundamental sense of "conscious" – that is the sense in terms of which all other senses are defined.'[1]

Wisdom's analysis brings into the open all the ambiguities latent in Ryle's description of sense (d). There are two major points of disagreement between Ryle and Wisdom, and over both points I am, with some qualification, in agreement with Wisdom. Firstly, he believes that a fundamental sense of 'conscious' may be distinguished. As we have seen Ryle fails to determine the relations of dependency which hold between the various senses of consciousness he distinguishes, and he denies by omission that there is a basic sense of consciousness. Secondly, Wisdom asserts that the other senses of consciousness can be defined in terms of the fundamental sense. I, on the other hand, asserted that the other senses entailed the basic sense, but were not in turn entailed by it. We both therefore assert a dependence of other senses of consciousness on the fundamental sense, although we see this dependence differently. My relation of dependence is weaker than Wisdom's, and it would still stand even if his claim that other senses of conscious can be defined in terms of '*conscious*' proved to be false.

[1] J. Wisdom, *Problems of Mind and Matter* (Cambridge, 1963), pp. 12–15. This work was first published in 1934.

It should be noted that Ryle's list of different senses of 'conscious' is a different type of list from Wisdom's. Ryle's list is a list of possible usages of the word 'conscious' in ordinary language, whereas Wisdom's list reveals a number of possible philosophical distinctions that may be made by taking 'conscious' in various senses. Thus while it is true that Wisdom's basic sense of 'conscious' *is* a defining sense for his list, it is doubtful whether it *could* be a defining sense for Ryle's list. Since my entailment relation between the basic sense of 'conscious' and its other senses applies to Ryle's list as well as to Wisdom's, it is more flexible than Wisdom's defining relation.

[3] Although Wisdom claims that the derived senses of 'conscious' can be defined in terms of the fundamental sense of 'conscious', it is clear from what he says that he does not believe that the fundamental sense – *conscious* – can be defined. For this reason he gives us 'clues' instead. Wisdom's belief about the indefinability of consciousness is shared by many philosophers, including Hamilton who says:

'Nothing has contributed more to spread obscurity over a very transparent matter, than the attempts of philosophers to define consciousness. Consciousness cannot be defined; we may be ourselves fully aware what consciousness is, but we cannot, without confusion, convey to others a definition of what we ourselves clearly apprehend.'[1]

Let us consider then what seems to be the difficulty about defining consciousness. Hamilton seems to be suggesting that a definition of consciousness would not be a definition of the use of the word 'consciousness', but a description of the phenomenon itself which the word designates. He seems to have in mind a definition which is 'real' as opposed to 'nominal' or verbal. He presumably thinks of such a definition as a description of the phenomenon that specifies its essential characteristics. Such a description would be definitional in the sense that it could be said that nothing failing to fit the description could possibly constitute consciousness, and further that nothing fitting the description could possibly fail to constitute consciousness. That this is what he means seems to be confirmed by his referring to a definition, not of a *term*, but of 'what we ourselves

[1] Bowen, *The Metaphysics of Sir William Hamilton*, p. 125.

clearly apprehend'. From this point of view a mere verbal definition of consciousness must fail.

We can appreciate this by treating Wisdom's first clue to consciousness, not as a clue, but as a definition: (i) would then become *'Conscious'* means *feels*, or *is aware*.[1] It is plain that such a definition does no more than supply possible synonyms for the word 'conscious'; possible alternative designations of the phenomenon but not possible descriptions defining it. Such a verbal definition would not be to the point because exactly the same request to have the concept defined arises again in respect of the definiens – in the present case 'feels' or 'is aware'. This is because a person puzzled about the nature of consciousness is hardly likely to be less puzzled about the nature of feeling or awareness. It is presumably for this reason that Wisdom hesitates to propose (i) as a definition rather than as a clue. He recognizes that as a definition it hardly adds anything to our understanding.

Let us for the moment concede the rejection of the appropriateness of verbal definitions of consciousness, and, returning to defining descriptions as such, raise the question: Under what conditions might that type of definition have point? It would have point, I suggest, for a person who had not encountered the phenomenon the definition was about. In lieu of a direct encounter, a description gives some impression of the phenomenon. The description will then have the added function of enabling a person to recognize the phenomenon in the event of his encountering it.

Now it is true that in some cases we may fail to find a description that seems to portray a phenomenon adequately. When that happens we may then be forced to say that words fail us, and that there is nothing for it but for a person to encounter the phenomenon for himself. In that situation we may feel inclined to say that the phenomenon cannot be defined – cannot be given a defining description.

If I am right, a defining description has point for someone who has not encountered the relevant phenomenon, and it follows that it is only when a defining description would have point that there is room for the admission that the phenomenon is indefinable. But neither of these conditions applies to consciousness. It is logically impossible for a person not to have encountered consciousness: nothing can be a person and not have encountered consciousness. Again, it is logically impossible to give a defining description of

[1] See above, p. 43.

consciousness to a person who had not encountered consciousness. For a precondition of the possibility of communicating the definition is the consciousness of the person receiving the communication. Thus a defining description of consciousness necessarily lacks point. But in that case the assertion that consciousness *is* indefinable in the above sense must also lack point. I conclude that the idea of giving a 'real' definition of consciousness is absurd. If this is what Hamilton had in mind when he said that consciousness was indefinable then we can agree with him. But we can object to his manner of making his point. For the claim that consciousness is indefinable inevitably suggests that it is either too transparent to describe or too elusive to pin down, and neither of these is the right reason for concluding that consciousness is indefinable.

It is important to stress the absurdity of the request for a definition of consciousness in the sense in question. If we say no more than that consciousness is indefinable we leave the impression that the request for a definition was in order but simply could not be met. Such an impression is false and injurious. The doctrine of the indefinability of consciousness has, I believe, been detrimental to the whole notion of consciousness.

Philosophers quite rightly stay clear of indefinable terms wherever possible, and when they are told that consciousness is indefinable their instinct is to try to manage without it.

But if I am right a request for a definition of consciousness cannot be the self-contradictory sort of request I have been considering. It can more plausibly be seen as a request by someone to whom the meaning of the word 'consciousness' is unknown, to be informed of its meaning. We must be able to give the meaning – or meanings – of the word 'consciousness' just as we must be able to give the meaning of any word belonging to language.

We need not be as cautious as was Wisdom, when he would commit himself to no more than the giving of 'clues'. I shall, therefore, contradict Hamilton and maintain that consciousness *is* definable. It should however be clear that what I have in mind is a verbal definition as opposed to a 'real' definition (defining description).

To put it in a nutshell definitions of consciousness presuppose experience of what it is to be conscious on the part of both hearer and speaker. Consequently it is pointless to propose a definition as a substitute for encountering consciousness, and it is equally pointless to point out that no definition can substitute for an actual encounter. We are forced to conclude that the only meaningful form of definition that can be given of consciousness is a verbal one. This I shall now try to give.

If a definition is to be successful, the definiens must consist of terms which are understood by the hearer. If we could appeal to no words which were known to the hearer, we would be precluded from giving a definition. Thus these 'verbal' definitions can only be given to practised language-users. This means that if a person asks the question 'What is consciousness?' we are entitled to take it for granted that he understands other words – words no language-user could properly speaking be said to lack – which we can make use of in our definition and which we are not going to be asked to define in turn. Given this condition we can define 'conscious' in the basic sense as follows: to be conscious is, *inter alia*, to perceive, to feel emotions and sensations, to have images and recollections, and to have desires, intentions, and thoughts.

I shall make some observations about this definition. In the first place I have omitted reference to a subject. There are two reasons for this: (*a*) I do not want to limit consciousness to persons such that only persons can be conscious, and (*b*) Since I am staying within the *self-approach* no question arises of having to correlate consciousness with behaviour. Thus from the point of view within which the definition is proffered the hearer is the reader himself, and he must understand it in terms of his own encounter with perceiving, and so forth. Secondly, the list is not meant to be exhaustive, and nothing is implied concerning how many of these 'mental events' need occur together for one to be conscious. Lastly, the mental concepts in terms of which I have defined consciousness must be understood in a non-dispositional, or episodic, sense.

Consciousness as so defined is similarly understood by James Mill who writes:

'It is easy to see what is the nature of the terms Conscious and Consciousness, and what is the marking function which they are destined to perform. It was of great importance for the purpose of naming, that we should not only have names to distinguish the different classes of our feelings, but also a name applicable equally to all those classes. This purpose is answered by the concrete term Conscious; and the abstract of it, Consciousness. Thus, if we are in any way sentient; that is, have any of the feelings whatsoever of a living creature; the word Conscious is applicable to the feeler, and

Consciousness to the feeling: that is to say, the words are Generical marks, under which all the names of the subordinate classes of the feelings of a sentient creature are included. When I smell a rose, I am conscious, when I have the idea of a fire, I am conscious; when I remember, I am conscious, when I reason, and when I believe, I am conscious; but believing, and being conscious of belief, are not two things, they are just the same thing: though this same thing I can name at one time without the aid of the generical mark, while at another time it suits me to employ the generical mark.'[1]

If we take Mill's definition of consciousness, and qualify it along the lines Wisdom's account suggests to us, we have the account of consciousness I have been trying to reach. We ought not to be dissuaded from accepting Mill's account because of the faulty example at the end of the passage. Had Mill made the distinction between dispositional and episodic senses of mental concepts he would not have needed to have made the dubious claim that believing and being conscious of belief are the same thing.

2. THE NATURE OF THE CONCEPT

[4] We may usefully compare the function of the word 'conscious' with the function of the word 'colour'. Often we are simply interested in the fact that something is coloured, or has colour, without being interested in which determinate colour it has. And yet we do not on that account imagine that an object can be coloured without being of a determinate colour, or of a number of determinate colours. What is true of the word 'colour' is also true of the word 'conscious' as I have defined it. A person cannot be conscious without its being true that he is either perceiving, or having thoughts, emotions, etc. In this sense 'conscious' and 'consciousness' are, as Mill says, generic terms.

I wish now to offer an explanation of the advantage of this generic term, which to my knowledge has not been fully appreciated. In the passage of James Mill's which I have just quoted he said in this regard, 'It was of great importance, for the purpose of naming, that we should not only have names to distinguish the different classes of our feelings, but also a name applicable equally to all

---

[1] James Mill, *Analysis of the Phenomena of the Human Mind*, ed. by J. S. Mill (London, 1869), I, pp. 225–6.

those classes.' He does not, however, tell us what its importance is. Perhaps he took its importance to be obvious; perhaps it is. There is, however, one respect in which the importance of having the generic term 'conscious' is not obvious, and this respect is of philosophical importance. It can best be brought out by returning to the comparison of the generic term 'conscious' with the generic term 'colour'.

An expanse of colour may be comprised of one particular hue or several. If the former, then the particular hue exhausts the colour of the expanse. If the latter, then the sum of the particular hues exhausts its colour. The existence of colour is nothing over and above the existence of particular hues of colour. We may think of a multi-coloured expanse as built up of a mosaic of individual hues. Now there is a temptation to think of consciousness in this way too, and to assume that if it is a condition of being conscious that a person must have one or more determinate experiences, then his consciousness is identical with the sum of such determinate experiences; consciousness being conceived of as a mosaic of particular experiences, as it were. On this conception when a subject specifies the particular experiences he is undergoing at a particular time, he exhausts the description he gives of himself as conscious at that time. In other words, to say that a subject is conscious is just an abbreviation for saying that he is either seeing such-and-such, or hearing such-and-such, or thinking such-and-such and so on through all the 'particular classes of our feelings' as Mill describes them. Obviously this list should not be understood disjunctively: a number of these determinate 'feelings' can occur simultaneously. It is usual, for instance, to see, hear, and think contemporaneously. An implication of viewing consciousness in this way would be that it would entitle us to draw the inference that if we took a sufficiently short time span we should be able to specify all the individual 'feelings' that together make up a particular consciousness during that time.

In other words if 'consciousness' is the name of a class of mental 'events', then it must be possible to define the class extensionally by denoting all the members belonging to it. If such were the case, there would be complete logical parity between 'conscious' and 'colour' considered as generic terms. This view of consciousness may fitly be described as the mosaic view of consciousness. This is the model of consciousness that underlies the classical atomistic theory of consciousness.

I shall argue that this mosaic view of consciousness is false, and that the assumption of parity between 'conscious' and 'colour' breaks down. My rejection of this view constitutes my most important divergence from the traditional empiricist view of consciousness.

Let us imagine setting out to draw up a list of all the feelings of which a person's consciousness is made up during a time-span of a few seconds – cashing the consciousness for the real coin of thoughts, feelings, perceptions, and desires. The job would be completed when we had entered the very last 'feeling' on our list. This can be most effectively illustrated in the case of visual perception. At the moment specific objects are in my visual field: I see various things, each of which must be entered in my list as a particular perception. I at once notice a disconcerting development. The more I look, the more I see. When the separable objects seem to have been exhausted, I can pass on to noticing irregularities in the surfaces of the objects, marks, shadows, and other details. I soon realize that my description of what I see can go on indefinitely. I cannot exhaust all there is to see in my visual field. It is the source of as many different perceptions as I care to have. At least in the case of visual consciousness, therefore, it is not the case that consciousness is equivalent to a determinate set of constituents.

Now it may be argued that under normal circumstances we are not busy probing our visual fields to discover how many different things and aspects and properties of things we can spot. Normally there are just a few things which hold our attention, and these are what we see, and *these* are determinate. This I concede, but it does not save the position. I will see a few objects in the centre of my visual field discretely and separately, and no doubt they will be the first to go down in my list. But what of the remainder of my visual field? Can I be sure that it is also furnished with equally distinct and separate objects? Is it not more probable that towards the borders of my visual field there is a penumbra within which it is impossible to distinguish separate objects? Could I not find out by having a look? It is logically impossible to do so for two reasons: (*a*) because if I focus my eyes on the borders of my visual field, I of necessity alter my visual field, thus destroying one of the conditions of the experiment, and (*b*) because the question is to discover whether what we see and to which we are not paying attention, breaks up into discrete objects in the same way as does the visual area to which we are paying attention. Here too it is logically impossible to verify the claim that the objects to which we are not attending are as clear and distinct as those to which we are, because in order to do so we have to attend to the parts of the visual field which were previously unattended to. But then they become objects which are attended to, and they cease to be the objects we wanted to find out about: i.e. objects which were not being attended to.

I have gone far enough, I feel sure, to demonstrate the completely unrealistic nature of the assumption that visual consciousness is made up of a distinct and separable set of constituent experiences. When an item is picked out of the visual field and described in some such statement as 'I see a tree' we must realize that under normal conditions we at the same time see vastly more than we describe.

Of course in this connection visual consciousness is a rather special case,[1] and it is not as clear in the case of other forms of perceptual consciousness that we cannot exhaustively describe what enters the sense field in question. When the content of the sense field is rich (as in the auditory field would be the case if one were listening to an orchestra) the situation is analogous to the visual field, but often the sense field is impoverished (as in the auditory field would be the case if one heard but a single sound) and then the analogy breaks down. Nevertheless this counterinstance is not serious for a variety of reasons. Firstly, although my examples are confined to single senses, our list cannot be so confined if it is to exhaust the 'feelings' that go to make up consciousness. The position would only be serious if it were possible for *all* the sense fields to be impoverished at the same time. This is not likely to happen outside a psychological laboratory, and even then it would not be decisive. For, secondly, if we classify the somatic field as falling under perceptual consciousness – and for the present purpose we may – then at least the somatic field is always rich. (I would not know what it would be for the somatic field to be impoverished short of general anaesthesia and then we would no longer be dealing with consciousness.) In short although unusual circumstances may be conceived in which it might be possible to give an exhaustive description of the constituents of an impoverished consciousness, it would definitely be false to claim that under normal conditions such a description can be given of consciousness.

I have confined these remarks to perceptual consciousness because it is not as obviously true of non-perceptual consciousness

[1] See below, pp. 192–3.

– thinking, reverie, imagining – that its constituents cannot be exhaustively described. I shall not deal with this complication because I shall later dispose of the point by arguing that non-perceptual consciousness is dependent on perceptual consciousness. It will not matter, therefore, should it not be the case that the constituents of non-perceptual consciousness are similarly une-numerable. I shall have much more to say on this subject in succeeding chapters however; for the present purpose I hope I have established that there is a logical disparity between the generic terms 'conscious' and 'colour', and that it is the peculiar merit of the terms 'conscious' and 'consciousness' that they convey the true impression that our lives are at every moment packed with a dense amorphous conglomeration of experiences, or 'feelings' as Mill called them. No matter how full we make our description of what we are conscious of at any one time, this will always be the merest sample of the mass of feelings, which go to make up consciousness at that time. Anyone wishing to focus attention on this particular aspect of the mental will find himself seriously handicapped if he tries to dispense with the term 'consciousness'.

[5] I have argued that Mill's definition of consciousness in terms of the experiences of seeing, hearing, feeling, thinking, imagining, etc., is the right one. The relation I have been arguing for between consciousness and the variety of conscious phenomena can be explicated in terms of a technical term that Ryle has given us for the purpose. In his terms consciousness is a polymorphous concept.[1] That is to say it would not be true to say that a person was conscious in the basic sense unless it was also true to say of him that he was enjoying at least one experience in at least one of its modes. But in the past few philosophers have taken the course I am advocating of drawing the line here by insisting that con-sciousness is nothing over and above a congeries of experiences or feelings. Many of them have gone on to argue that if the one word 'consciousness' can be used to cover such a variety of mental manifestations, it must be in virtue of the fact that all these mani-festations have some property in common, and that until we have identified that property, we have not reached the heart of the matter. Hamilton, who by and large successfully resists the temptation of taking consciousness to be a special faculty, reveals

---

[1] See, A. R. White, *Attention* (Oxford, 1964) on polymorphous-concepts.

nevertheless, in the following passage, to what extent he is in the grip of the idea of a common property:

'But before proceeding to show in detail what the act of consciousness comprises, it may be proper, in the first place, to recall in general what kind of act the word is employed to denote. *I know, I feel, I desire*, etc. What is it that is necessarily involved in all these? It requires only to be stated to be admitted, that when I know, I must *know that I know*, – when I feel, I must *know that I feel*, – when I desire, I must *know that I desire*. The knowledge, the feeling, the desire, are possible only under the condition of being known, and being known by me. For if I did not know that I knew, I would not know, – if I did not know that I felt, I would not feel, – if I did not know that I desired, I would not desire. Now, this knowledge, which I, the subject, have of these modifications of my being, and through which knowledge alone these modifications are possible, is what we call *consciousness*.'[1]

Leaving aside the soundness or otherwise of what Hamilton says, we see underlying it the assumption of the existence of a property common to all the 'manifestations' of consciousness, in virtue of which the word 'consciousness' can be applied to them. The same assumption was operative in Moore's analysis of sensation, where consciousness was held to be the element which several sensations had in common. Now we have every reason to be suspicious of this assumption as it applies to consciousness. For we are entitled to ask for the evidence on which is based the claim that consciousness is a common property. The answer, I suspect – for none is explicitly forthcoming – is that it must stand for a common property, for otherwise so heterogeneous a collection of instances (manifestations) could not be subsumed under the one concept. That is to say, the evidence for the existence of a common property is none other than the fact that the one word 'consciousness' is used to cover these diverse instances. Thus the existence of a common property is arrived at by deduction from the existence of the concept for which it is assumed to stand. If my suspicion is well-founded, it would enable us to understand why philosophers have insisted that there is such a common property in spite of the difficulty they have experienced in producing evidence of its

[1] Bowen, *The Metaphysics of Sir William Hamilton*, p. 126.

existence. It would also throw light on Moore's famous observation that consciousness 'is as it were *diaphanous*'. We can take this observation to be a sign of how tenuous is the evidence for the common property. Alternatively we could treat it as evidence of the fact that the putative common property is a myth. On either interpretation we have seen enough of the difficulties faced by the common property view for the basic assumption to be challenged. Moreover it scarcely needs to be said at the present time that the assumption that every general term stands for a common property is not compelling.

We would be well advised, therefore, to try an approach that is not based on the assumption that consciousness stands for a common property. For this reason I follow James Mill in treating consciousness as a concept which covers reference to actual thoughts, perceptions, images, dreams and so forth. Used in this way, it enables us to refer to any of these occurrences, and is an abbreviation for them. By adopting this view we are spared the difficulties that are created by thinking of consciousness as something over and above such occurrences as I have listed. Whether such a 'reductionist' theory of consciousness is successful may be judged by its performance in the argument of this book, for the word 'consciousness' will be understood in this sense throughout. It should not be forgotten, however, that when I use the term 'consciousness' I do so on the understanding that I reject the view that consciousness can be exhaustively specified in terms of any determinate set of referents of which it is the abbreviation. This is the novel twist I give to the meaning of the term, and it is absolutely crucial to my argument.

[6] Now that the basic notion of consciousness has been explicated, it is necessary to say something about the circumstances in which consciousness can be an object of analysis. Here the distinction between the *self-approach* and the *persons-approach* becomes relevant. The object of the *self-approach* is to posit consciousness for the sake of analysis without making any theoretical assumptions about it. From this point of view all we need to know is the truth of the proposition 'There is consciousness'. Now from the point of view of the *persons-approach* this statement would only be meaningful as an unhappy way of stating the proposition 'Something is conscious'. But this is because the *persons-approach* is concerned with the question 'Who or what is conscious?' and this theoretical

sort of question is deliberately excluded by the *self-approach*. Thus the proposition 'There is consciousness' represents the closest we can come to a theory-neutral description of the datum to be analysed.

Let it be granted that the proposition 'There is consciousness' is as close as we can come to a presuppositionless description of a datum. It still does not follow that we *have* a datum fitting the description. The proposition might after all be false. What evidence do we possess of the truth of the proposition 'There is consciousness?' It is not a necessary truth: there probably was a time when the proposition was false, and there may come a time when it is no longer true.

Fortunately we do not have to worry ourselves about the truth conditions of the proposition. It is enough to know that whenever the proposition has a reader it will be true. It will be true because the reader himself will instantiate the proposition. Thus no reader can doubt the truth of the proposition; and the existence of a datum for analysis is assured in virtue of the fact that the reader supplies his own datum. But this does not mean that the reason for the reader's assurance of the truth of the proposition 'There is consciousness' is his ability to utter the self-ascriptive proposition 'I am conscious'. It is his *reading* the proposition 'There is consciousness' that makes it veridical, not his ability to use a self-ascriptive utterance at the time. To put the main point picturesquely, when this book does not have a reader the proposition 'There is consciousness' may be false, but it cannot be false at such times as it has a reader. It cannot therefore be meaningfully denied that at least one consciousness exists.

It is worth pointing out that the no-ownership theory of the self[1] must make an even more radical use of the proposition 'There is consciousness' than I am doing. For on that theory a self-ascriptive statement is logically dependent upon the relationship between a consciousness and a certain human body. And this means that the utterance 'I am conscious' is logically dependent on the utterance 'There is consciousness' and not the other way around. I nowhere make the claim made by the no-ownership theorist that the utterance 'I am conscious' can be derived from the utterance 'There is consciousness'. I have maintained that that would be to confound the *self-approach* with the *persons-approach*.

[1] See M. Schlick, 'Meaning and Verification', reprinted in *Readings in Philosophical Analysis*, ed. Feigl and Sellars.

3. SIR WILLIAM HAMILTON AND HIS CRITICS

[7] Now that the question of the definability of consciousness has been cleared up, and an explanation has been given of the sense in which consciousness may be said to be a real phenomenon, we are in a position to consider the view of a leading philosopher of consciousness, Sir William Hamilton. After giving a brief survey of his position, I shall state the views of his critics, J. S. Mill, Shadworth Hodgson, and William James, who take exactly the opposite position to Hamilton. My purpose in doing this is not to endorse the view of one party or the other, but rather to show the impasse that was reached in the analysis of consciousness at a time when this was considered a central philosophical enterprise. Only if this impasse can be broken can the *self-approach* once again come into its own alongside the *persons-approach*. We have already seen that Hamilton regards all consciousness as self-consciousness.[1] The following passage sets out his view more definitively.

I.   'I shall commence wit that great fact to which I have already alluded, – that *we are immediately conscious in perception of an Ego and a Non-ego, known together, and known in contrast to each other*. This is the fact of the Duality of Consciousness. It is clear and manifest. When I concentrate my attention in the simplest act of perception, I return from my observation with the most irresistible conviction of two facts, or rather two branches of the same fact; – that I am, – and that something different from me exists. In this act, I am conscious of myself as the perceiving subject, and of an external reality as the object perceived; and I am conscious of both existences in the same indivisible moment of intuition. The knowledge of the subject does not precede, nor follow, the knowledge of the object; – neither determines, neither is determined by, the other.'[2]

Lest it be thought that it is only in perception that the ego presents itself in this way, let me hasten to add that this duality is present, in Hamilton's view, in every act of consciousness. This is made clear in another place, where he tells us:

II.   'We may lay it down as the most general characteristic of
consciousness, that it *is the recognition by the thinking subject* of
its own acts or affections.'[1]

These passages seem to commit Hamilton to the view that no
distinction can be drawn between consciousness and self-consciousness. Unfortunately none of his statements of his position
makes it quite clear which of three possible interpretations of his
words is the right one. (*a*) He could mean that in all consciousness
we know *that* it is a self which is conscious, but we do not have any
acquaintance with the self which is conscious. To put it slightly
differently, in every conscious act there is the recognition of the
fact that a self is conscious, but apart from knowledge of this bare
fact, nothing about the self is known. (*b*) He could mean that in all
consciousness it is not only a fact that a self is conscious, but that
there is a genuine acquaintance with the self which is presented
along with the act of consciousness: (*b*) would differ from (*a*) in
affirming that we both know *that* a self is conscious, and have a
direct intuition of the self. (*c*) He could mean that in all consciousness the self knows not only the content or object of consciousness,
but its mode of presentation. Thus I know, not only that I am conscious of a visual object, but at the same time that this visual object is
one I am *perceiving*, and not *imagining*. The position is made more
complicated for us, because Hamilton would not describe any of
these three possibilities as self-consciousness, which term he reserves
for an altogether different distinction. It will be useful to explain
what this latter distinction is, but before doing so we need to make up
our minds on the question of which of the three positions listed as (*a*),
(*b*) and (*c*) represents Hamilton's position. Passage I seems to support
(*a*), while passage II points to (*c*). On the other hand, a third passage
seems to favour interpretation (*b*):

III.   'The various modifications of which the thinking subject, Ego,
is conscious, are accompanied with the feeling, or intuition,
or belief, – or by whatever name the conviction may be called,
– that I, the thinking subject, exist. This feeling has been
called by philosophers the apperception, or consciousness, of
our own existence; but, as it is a simple and ultimate fact of
consciousness, though it be clearly given, it cannot be defined
or described.'[2]

[1] *Ibid.*, p. 131.   [2] *Ibid.*, p. 254.

This passage undoubtedly lends support to (b), but it might just as well be taken to be an unhappy way of stating (a).

Perhaps the following passage will be allowed to have settled the issue in favour of (a).

IV. 'In so far as mind is the common name for the states of knowing, willing, feeling, desiring, etc., of which I am conscious, it is only the name for a certain series of connected phenomena or qualities, and consequently expresses only what is known. But in so far as it denotes that subject or substance in which the phenomena of knowing, willing etc., inhere – something behind or under these phenomena – it expresses what, in itself, or in its absolute existence, is unknown.'[1]

In passage IV we recognize the Pure Ego Theory in all its starkness. According to it we have some special indefinable sort of knowledge of the sheer fact of the existence of the self, but what this self is we still do not know. It lies outside experience. Hamilton's description of the Duality of Consciousness thus reduces itself to the assertion that every act of consciousness is presented as the consciousness of a subject, or self. Self and consciousness exemplify the logical behaviour of correlatives.

In view of the unapproachability of the self in Hamilton's Philosophy, we may well wonder what for him passes as self-consciousness. His solution is rather neat.

V. 'Perception is the power by which we are made aware of the phenomena of the External world; Self-consciousness, the power by which we apprehend the phenomena of the Internal.'[2]

I think we may take this conception of self-consciousness to be negatively defined: viz. an internal phenomenon is any phenomenon which does not belong to the External world. It would then be possible to maintain that self-consciousness is one of the sub-species of consciousness; to be contrasted with perception, and memory, which are two other forms of the 'Presentative Faculty' of consciousness. Such a proposal may be criticized on the ground

---

[1] W. Hamilton, *Lectures on Metaphysics*, Vol. I, p. 138.
[2] *Op. cit.*, p. 396.

that self-consciousness is made a rag-bag for all instances of presentative consciousness which cannot be classed either as perceptions or as memories. It lacks the character of a coherent category in its own right. Furthermore it is open to serious objection. Not all memories are memories of events in the external world, and those which are not should be eligible for classification under the heading of self-consciousness. This would cut across Hamilton's distinctions. As a passing shot I might add that it would be odd to say that in being aware of an after-image or a hallucination one was being self-conscious.

A more promising interpretation can be put on proposition V than the one we have just seen to be unsatisfactory. When Hamilton refers to the 'phenomena of the Internal' he could be interpreted to mean those cases of consciousness in which we ourselves are the objects of our states of consciousness. On this interpretation the facts I know about myself through consciousness, as distinct from the facts I know about objects through consciousness, are what I know through self-consciousness. This interpretation would fit in more happily with the meaning the term 'self-consciousness' is often taken to have in ordinary usage. It approximates to Ryle's sense (c) of 'self-conscious'.[1] The most favourable example in support of this interpretation is provided by such statements as 'I am in pain', 'I am feeling angry', 'I feel thirsty'. These statements may be understood as descriptions of states of consciousness in which I myself am the object of consciousness. I do not believe we can decide between these alternative interpretations of self-consciousness without a detailed analysis of consciousness of the sort I propose to undertake, and for this reason I do no more than note these two interpretations of Hamilton's conception of self-consciousness. Both alternatives agree in this, that in self-consciousness there is no direct awareness of the self as such, and self-consciousness is not thought of as a sort of second-order awareness; an awareness of awareness.

[8] J. S. Mill attacked Hamilton for maintaining that the distinction between subject and object was an ultimate deliverance of consciousness which could not be doubted.[2] He conceded that to

---

[1] See above, p. 42.

[2] J. S. Mill, *An Examination of Sir William Hamilton's Philosophy* (London, 1865), ch. 9, 11 and 12. Mill's views are not found in one place but have to be pieced together from scattered statements.

the adult intelligence introspection certainly reveals the Duality of Consciousness which Hamilton had identified, and he also admitted that to such a mind any other possibility was inconceivable. But the essence of his criticism of Hamilton is that he mistakes acquired characteristics of consciousness for original ones.[1] Mill argues that it comes to seem inconceivable to us that the distinction between ego and non-ego might not be a necessary condition of consciousness, because the habit of so regarding it has been ingrained from our earliest years. He sums up the position as follows:

'These philosophers, therefore, and among them Sir W. Hamilton, mistake altogether the true conditions of psychological investigation, when, instead of proving a belief to be an original fact of consciousness by showing that it could not have been acquired, they conclude that it was not acquired, for the reason, often false, and never sufficiently substantiated, that our consciousness cannot get rid of it now.'[2]

Hodgson sides with Mill in denying that consciousness in its original form was polarized into subject and object. He distinguishes three distinct stages of consciousness, which he calls *primary* consciousness, *reflective* consciousness, and *direct* consciousness, in that chronological order. Primary consciousness is a preconceptual stage of consciousness, which corresponds with what Mill calls 'original consciousness', and both of them ascribe this form of consciousness to the consciousness of infants prior to the commencement of conceptualization. Primary consciousness is characterized by the absence of any reference to the self, on the one hand, and the absence of any reference to 'things' on the other hand. It is when the stage of *direct* consciousness is reached that consciousness exhibits the typical duality identified by Hamilton. For Hodgson direct consciousness gives us our common sense view of the world.[3] James likewise rejects Hamilton's position:

'Experience . . . has no such inner duplicity; and the separation of it into consciousness and content comes, not by way of subtraction, but by way of addition.'[4]

[1] *Ibid.*, pp. 149-50.
[2] *Ibid.*, pp. 150-1.
[3] Shadworth H. Hodgson, *The Philosophy of Reflection* (London, 1878), I.
[4] James, *Essays in Radical Empiricism*, p. 9.

James is in agreement with Mill and Hodgson in their denial that consciousness in its pristine state has any inner articulation into a self and that which is presented to the self. Those who, like Mill, Hodgson, and James, deny the existence of any sort of independent entity which we can identify as the self, have the responsibility of explaining how we come to have a conception of self, and precisely what this conception amounts to. Sheer denial is not enough. This fact is acknowledged by the three philosophers I have just mentioned.

In the passage just quoted James said of any dichotomy within consciousness that it comes 'not by way of subtraction, but by way of addition'. How then, in James's opinion, is this 'addition' effected? He explains:

'A given undivided portion of experience, taken in one context of associates, play(s) the part of a knower, of a state of mind, of "consciousness"; while in a different context the same undivided bit of experience plays the part of a thing known, of an objective "content". In a word, in one group it figures as a thought, in another group as a thing. And, since it can figure in both groups simultaneously we have every right to speak of it as subjective and objective both at once.'[1]

Alongside this passage let me place one from Hodgson making essentially the same point:

'These thoughts and feelings are not only thoughts and feelings, but bundles of constantly connected thoughts and feelings, that is, "things". The connection between them belongs to them. Therefore they are *things*, as well as, and without ceasing to be, states of *consciousness*. They have a double aspect; that which was undistinguished has, I now see, a distinction into consciousness and object of consciousness.'[2]

The point, I think it is true to say, is the one Wittgenstein had in mind when he said, 'I am my world.'[3]

---

[1] *Ibid.*, pp. 9–10.
[2] Hodgson, *Philosophy of Reflection*, I, 111.
[3] L. Wittgenstein, *Tractatus Logico-Philosophicus*, ed. C. K. Ogden (London, 1922), 5.631.

[9] This brief survey has shown that the philosophers who adopted the *self-approach* reached diametrically opposite conclusions on the relation between the self and consciousness. Each took the testimony of consciousness to endorse his own position. Moreover, all the philosophers have given the impression that their own views were so evidently true that they could not be backed up by evidence more compelling than the bare statement of each position itself would be. Some philosophers regard the Duality of Consciousness as one of those ultimate facts which it would be meaningless to wish to ground in some facts still more ultimate. Others again state with equal conviction the view that the facts give no support to the claim that the self is anything apart from a particular aspect of consciousness itself. The positions are *stated* rather than argued for. It is not surprising, therefore, that later philosophers should have become suspicious of a form of enquiry, which, because of the alleged indefinability of the concepts concerned, seemed to reduce itself to the making of pronouncements – especially as the pronouncements contradicted one another. This eventuality, one suspects, had much to do with the increasing unpopularity among philosophers of appeals to the testimony of consciousness.

If the *self-approach* is to get us anywhere it is clearly necessary for an analysis of consciousness to be given which appeals to considerations which no one would be willing to deny. By this I mean that the analysis should rest on distinctions that cannot be denied except by a philosopher who is prepared to reject much of our 'language of mind'. In other words it is my intention to make my analysis rest upon distinctions that I shall argue are necessary to an understanding of our mental concepts as they are employed outside of philosophical contexts. In this way a particular analysis of consciousness can be supported by argument instead of by appeals to self-evidence. Such a development of the *self-approach* will put us in a position, I believe, to determine whether Hamilton is right to affirm the Duality of Consciousness, whether Mill, Hodgson, and James, are right to deny it, or whether both parties to the dispute are partly right and partly wrong. The analysis is being undertaken in the hope that it will lead to the discovery of the identity of the subject of consciousness.

I shall end this historical review of the progress to date of the *self-approach* with a brief look at the view of one philosopher who has made a beginning in taking the subject in the direction I am advocating.

[10] Samuel Alexander gives an analysis of consciousness that is very much in the spirit of the present undertaking.[1] He comes closer than any of the philosophers so far mentioned to giving a satisfactory account of the experiential basis of our native knowledge of ourselves. Not only does his account give us some insight into this native knowledge of the self, but it also is praiseworthy for its attempt to analyse consciousness in terms other than the distinction between subject and object. If, after all, what we are trying to comprehend is the manner in which consciousness posits subject over against object, it is unhelpful to be just informed that it evidently does so. For this reason an analysis of consciousness that describes its inner articulation in some other terms seems to be the more philosophical alternative.

Alexander analysed an experience into two elements which he called 'an act of *mind*' and 'the appearance of a *thing*'. The two elements are further characterized as follows: 'The act of mind is an enjoyment, the object is contemplated.' He also asks us to view an experience as an experienc*ing* and an experienc*ed*. The relation between these two elements is said to be one of 'togetherness' or 'compresence'. One of Alexander's central ideas is that minds themselves are never contemplated, they are never their own objects of knowledge. In his own words, 'my own mind is never an object to myself in the sense in which the tree or table is'. However, minds and objects 'are distinct and relatively independent existences compresent with each other'. To complete the picture it only needs to be added that Alexander identifies minds with selves. 'I am my mind,' he states, 'and am conscious *of* the object.' On this view the self is a component of experience – it is the enjoying – and it is experiential through and through despite the fact that it is never itself an object of experience. Alexander could thus have said in reply to Hume that the self cannot be its own object of experience, but nevertheless it is experienced in every experience of objects (as the enjoying of the experience). On Alexander's theory the experience of being a self would consist in our enjoying of our experiences. Looked at in this way MacNabb's description of the self as an experience of a peculiarly internal sort could be construed as a misleading description of the experiential self. It would in effect be to confuse the enjoying of an experience with an experience of enjoyment. Alexander's theory has the great merit of bringing us the insight that to claim that the self is experiential is

[1] S. Alexander, *Space, Time, and Deity* (London, 1920), p. 11 ff.

not incompatible with the claim that there is no special experience of the self, alongside of other experiences, but different from them. His view helps us to appreciate that having an experience of being a self is not some experience the self has in addition to its other experiences. Having an experience of being a self accompanies every experience, just as the enjoying of an experience, for Alexander accompanies every experience. To put the matter in Rylean terms it cannot be asked of the experience of being a self, as it can of experiences in general, 'When did you have that experience?' 'How often have you had it?' 'In what circumstances do you obtain it?' Unlike experiences of which such questions may meaningfully be raised, the experience of being a self is pervasive in the sense that it is actual all the while one is having such datable experiences.

Since I shall not build on Alexander's idea I shall not offer a critique of it. I mention it as an interesting proposal in the right direction. It does, however, still suffer from the weakness we found in the earlier accounts of the deliverances of consciousness: namely, that no evidence can be offered in favour of the claim that each experience has the two aspects described by Alexander. Thus even if he is right he is powerless to answer an opponent who denies his distinction. Furthermore there is a troublesome ambiguity in Alexander's use of the term 'experience'. If experience is broken down into an experienc*ing* and an experienc*ed*, the experienc*ed* is susceptible of interpretation as either (*a*) the content of the experience, or (*b*) the object independent of the experience. If we take Alexander to mean (*a*), then his theory is open to the objection that it is by no means clear that enjoying an experience is anything over and above the having of the content of the experience. If we take him to mean (*b*), then the experience can only be the enjoying of it. On both interpretations, therefore, there is a danger of the two aspects of experience collapsing into each other. Should that happen, Alexander could not claim to have arrived at a position any different from the orthodox Serial Theorist.

[11] I shall sum up this chapter by extracting those points that will henceforth be presupposed in the development of my argument. (1) The word 'conscious' has a basic sense such that for a person to be conscious in any of the dependent senses he must be conscious in the basic sense. (2) 'Conscious' in the basic sense can be defined. It is a generic concept that may be defined in terms of its several instances. Most important of all, its retention enables us to refer

to its instantiations without its following that its instances are fully determinable. This feature of the concept is not shared by the concept of experience which many philosophers have preferred to use in its place. As will emerge in the course of the argument this alone is sufficient reason for the retention of the concept as a philosophical term. (3) The concept has application for the reader because it applies in his own case. In this sense we can affirm 'There is consciousness' without prejudging the question whether there is any subject of consciousness to be revealed through its analysis.

CHAPTER THREE

ATTENTION

I. CONSCIOUSNESS AND CHANGE

[1] The object of this chapter is to show that consciousness is given a structure by attention. After certain preliminaries of a terminological nature, and a section on consciousness and change, I argue in support of Ward's doctrine that attention is a universal feature of consciousness. I give reasons for believing that what we take to be the presence of attention in consciousness is the polarization of consciousness into elements occupying its foreground relative to others which form its background. The hypothesis that all normal forms of consciousness have this structure is examined in the case of two of its forms which give least promise of supporting it. It is shown that even in such conditions of seeming nonattention the hypothesis is confirmed. Finally, distinctions between different forms of consciousness, proposed by Hamilton and Ribot, are examined and rejected in favour of distinctions between 'interrogative', 'executive', and 'unordered', attention.

In the preceding chapter I argued that although 'consciousness' was a collective name for our several experiences, it could not be eliminated in favour of direct reference to individual experiences, because no meaning could be attached to the assertion that at any one time an individual had a determinate number of experiences which could be exhaustively specified. Nevertheless it will be necessary to refer in a topic-neutral way to the experiences of which consciousness is comprised. I shall use the expression 'element(s) of consciousness' – 'element(s)' for short – for this purpose. Unfortunately no designation which could be chosen entirely avoids misrepresentation of the position. Even the term 'element of consciousness' suggests a certain atomistic independence of one element from the next, and this could give rise to the idea that consciousness is an aggregate of such elements. This is an idea I want to resist, and so when I refer to the elements of consciousness, it should be borne in mind that I do so with the reservation that I endorse the view expressed by William James:

'The traditional psychology talks like one should say a river consists of nothing but pailsful, spoonsful, barrelsful, and other moulded forms of water. Even were the pails and the pots all actually standing in the stream, still between them the free water would continue to flow. It is just this free water of consciousness that psychologists resolutely overlook. Every definite image in the mind is steeped and dyed in the free water that flows round it. With it goes the sense of its relations, near and remote, the dying echo of whence it came to us, the dawning sense of whither it is to lead. The significance, the value, of the image is all in this halo or penumbra that surrounds and escorts it . . .'[1]

Besides needing to refer to the elements of consciousness, it is also necessary to be able to refer to their temporal relations to one another. James's metaphor of a stream has graphic value in this connection. He describes consciousness as a 'stream of thought'. This creates the image of elements of consciousness floating along in the current of time. For the breadth of the stream we can conceive of all those elements that are compresent at a particular moment, and for the length of the stream we can conceive of a series made up of a succession of such compresent elements. Philosophers have referred to this twofold organization of consciousness in different ways. Broad has described the counterpart of the breadth of the stream as the 'transverse unity of a cross-section of the history of a mind', and the counterpart of the length of the stream as the 'longitudinal unity' of a mind.[2] Grice has referred to the contemporaneous elements as a 'total temporary state' of consciousness. A continuous succession of elements (Broad's 'longitudinal unity' of the mind) Grice refers to as a series of total temporary states.[3] I shall adopt Grice's terminology because it is more convenient than Broad's. For the present we shall sufficiently understand what is meant by a total temporary state from the following explanation offered by Grice:

'A total temporary state is composed of all the experiences any one person is having at any given time. Thus if I am now thinking of Hitler and feeling a pain, and having no other experiences, there will be occurring now a total temporary state containing as ele-

[1] William James, *The Principles of Psychology* (London, 1891), Vol. I, p. 255.
[2] C. D. Broad, *The Mind and Its Place in Nature* (London, 1951), p. 560.
[3] H. P. Grice, 'Personal Identity', *Mind*, L. (1941).

ments a thought of Hitler and a feeling of pain. Now since total temporary states may be said to occur at various times, they may be said to form temporal series.'[1]

It is evident from the above account of a total temporary state that it is a theoretical possibility for a total temporary state to contain but a single element. It would represent the logical limit to consciousness in one direction. A total temporary state which lacked even one element would not be a state of consciousness at all. Now when in the course of my enquiry I have spoken of *normal* forms of consciousness, the qualification was intended to exclude precisely this possibility of a consciousness a total temporary state of which contained no more than one element. Special significance is attached to this possibility but the matter is left to succeeding chapters. The normal state of affairs, I maintain, is one in which total temporary states have a plurality of elements.

The proposition that a total temporary state normally contains a plurality of elements is indisputable. We do not cease to have visual impressions when we hear a sound; we do not necessarily cease to hear things when we have thoughts; we do not cease to be aware of any of these things when we have tactile sensations, and so on. Of course our absorption in any of these experiences might diminish our awareness of the others, but this I am not denying. When all our senses are working we receive impressions from them simultaneously, provided of course that the necessary stimuli are present. But even if it be granted that a total temporary state normally consists of more than one element, it is theoretically possible for there to be a series of identical total temporary states. This would constitute a perfectly static consciousness in which no existing element perished and no new element appeared. Accordingly, it also needs to be shown that this is not normally, if ever, the case. I shall argue, on the contrary, that a series of total temporary states will be a series of changing elements, in which although some elements will persist from one state to the next, others will be new. It may be thought that the truth of this proposition goes without saying. Strawson, in his book on the *Critique of Pure Reason*, reveals his concurrence with Kant's acceptance of it. Speaking of Kant's thesis 'that experience essentially exhibits temporal succession', he says,

[1] *Ibid.*, pp. 341–2.

'The thesis is treated by Kant throughout as an unquestionable datum to which we cannot comprehend the possibility of any alternative, and as such we may be content to regard it.'[1]

Nevertheless, I shall attempt to account for this feature of experience as an introduction to one of the themes that will figure prominently in the later development of my position.

[2] The thesis that consciousness is dependent on change is neatly expressed in the proposition: '*Semper idem sentire idem est ac non sentire.*'[2] It has been convincingly argued for by a noted French psychologist, TH. Ribot, who was a contemporary of William James'. I shall try to develop the position he sets out in the following passage:

'All our organs of perception are at the same time sensorial and motor. To perceive with our eyes, ears, hands, feet, tongue, nostrils, movements are needed. The more mobile the parts of our body, the more exquisite is their sensibility, the less perfect their mobile power, the more obtuse their sensibility. Nor is this all; without motor elements, perception is impossible. We will call to mind a previous statement that if the eye be kept fixed upon a given object without moving, perception after a while grows dim, and then disappears. Rest the tips of the fingers upon a table without pressing, and the contact at the end of a few minutes will no longer be felt. But a motion of the eye, or of the finger, be it ever so light, will re-arouse perception. Consciousness is only possible through change; change is not possible save through movement. It would be easy to expatiate at great length upon this subject, for although the facts are very manifest and of common experience, psychology has nevertheless so neglected the role sustained by movements, that it actually forgot at last that they are the fundamental condition of cognition in that they are the instrument of the fundamental law of consciousness, which is relativity, change. Enough has now been said to warrant the unconditional statement, that where there is no movement there is no perception.'[3]

---

[1] P. F. Strawson, *The Bounds of Sense* (London, 1966), p. 25.
[2] Pointed out to me by Professor H. H. Price. I do not know if this dictum originated with Hobbes, but it certainly expressed his thought: viz. '. . . it being almost all one for a man to be always sensible of one and the same thing, and not to be sensible at all of any thing.' *The Metaphysical System of Hobbes*, ed. M. W. Calkins (Illinois, 1948), p. 119.
[3] TH. Ribot, *The Psychology of Attention* (London, 1890), p. 52.

As a psychologist Ribot is concerned to identify the physical conditions that support consciousness, and his theory is that the consciousness of a percipient (man or animal) is dependent on the bodily movements it makes when it actuates its sense-organs. His account presupposes therefore that consciousness is a property of a physical being. However, from the standpoint I am adopting I cannot consistently make that assumption, for to do so would mean my taking a stand of a theoretical order on the relation between consciousness and bodily existence, and this is not the concern of the *self-approach* which I am adopting. I shall therefore try to show that a conceptual point lies behind Ribot's theory, and that this conceptual point is not dependent on his scientific assumptions.

First of all, the movement claimed by Ribot to be necessary to consciousness cannot be understood as simple physical movement. It must be looked upon as an aspect of action – of what we *do*. Our movements, in this sense, necessarily enter into descriptions of what we are doing. Secondly, our sense-organs should not be thought of as mere physical mechanisms which may be identified apart from their function. Conceptionally considered, a sense-organ should be understood as that *with* which certain sorts of activity can be performed. Thus having a particular sense-organ necessarily enters into a full description of a certain sort of doing. On this view it is analytically true that we see with our eyes, whereas it is a synthetic truth that we see with the orbs located in our head. The significance of this point is that it enables us to mention our sense-organs without committing ourselves about their physical nature. If we bring these two points together we get the result that consciousness is dependent on certain activities that involve sense-organs and their movement. Examples of such activities are 'looking for something', 'feeling for something', and, at a more complex logical level, 'reading'. I shall give the name 'sense-organ activities' to those activities that cannot be engaged in by a percipient lacking the requisite sense-organ. A point not brought out by Ribot, but one which will be shown to be of considerable importance later on,[1] is that these sense-organ activities will bring about changes in consciousness because of the kinaesthetic sensations to which they give rise. One of our ways of knowing that we have succeeded in engaging in a particular sense-organ activity is through the relevant qualitative changes that we experience as kinaesthetic sensation. Such activities

1 See below, pp. 125–6.

therefore ensure that when they are engaged in, consciousness will exhibit the characteristic of temporal succession.

Ribot's thesis takes it for granted that we are dealing with the world we all know, a world which itself manifests variety and change, and he is only concerned with the conditions that make consciousness possible in this world. He is not concerned with the conditions that would have to be satisfied in every possible world. Given our world of variety and change it is true that our sense-organ activity will usually result in a temporal succession of elements of consciousness. As I look about me, for instance, I am bound to have a variety of visual experiences, and since it takes time for me to look about me, the visual experiences are bound to be successive. It is also true of this world that since noticeable changes occur within it which are not instantaneous, and since such changes can be broken down into stages, our experience of such change can be described as successive in that we can be said to have experienced first one stage of the change and then the next, and then the next, and so on. It may strike the reader that changes taking place in the world may be perceived without the appropriate sense-organ having to move, in which case consciousness would seem to be supported by change in the world and not by movement connected with the relevant sense-organ. This Ribot would not deny, but he would reply that such a state of affairs could not long be sustained by a normal consciousness. But this side of his theory will receive detailed examination in a later section of the book.[1]

The experiences that come about as a result of sense-organ activity may be put under the heading of *perceptual consciousness*. This allows me to point out that not all consciousness is perceptual consciousness. And the question arises: Is our non-perceptual consciousness also dependent upon the movement that enters our doings? Prima facie it would seem that I could continue to have images and recollections, not to mention thoughts, even if all my sense-organs were out of action; i.e. I had no perceptual consciousness. This raises many complex questions, but as we shall see Ribot's theory rests on a denial of this possibility. However, even if we allow such a possibility we would be talking of a consciousness completely foreign to us. It would not therefore refute the claim that *our* variety of consciousness is dependent on our sense-organ activities. In any case I shall be arguing that non-perceptual consciousness is dependent on perceptual consciousness, and if

[1] See below, pp. 123–5.

that is true it follows that the whole of consciousness is dependent on the movement connected with sense-organ activity. To be explicit the inference is this: if movement is a necessary condition of perceptual consciousness, and perceptual consciousness is a necessary condition of non-perceptual consciousness, then movement is a necessary condition of both perceptual and non-perceptual consciousness; i.e. the whole of consciousness.

Thus by relating consciousness to what we do – to our sense-organ activities – we can offer an explanation of the Kantian point that consciousness exhibits temporal succession. Our doings take time and involve a sequence of changes themselves and in being aware of what we are doing we are aware of some of these temporal changes. In this way consciousness reflects temporal change.

In the foregoing I sought to show that a total temporary state contained a number of elements, and that successive total temporary states in a series would differ from one another in that in normal circumstances each would contain some elements not shared by the others. On this basis I proceed to an examination of the precise relationship between consciousness and attention.

[3] I shall begin by considering the view of the philosophically-minded psychologist James Ward. Essentially what he maintains is that attention and consciousness are identical.[1] That is to say we cannot be aware of anything without giving it some attention, and this for the simple reason that to be aware of it is to attend to it. This means that as far as Ward is concerned it would be meaningless for one to say that he was aware of something but hadn't given it *any* attention. The most he could say is that he was aware of it although he hadn't given it *much* attention. Seeming absence of attention is explained in Ward's theory as a low degree of attention.

To better acquaint ourselves with the issues involved, it will be helpful to find out whether there is any difference between a state of inattention and a state of nonattention. *Webster's Dictionary* treats the words 'inattention' and 'nonattention' as synonymous, but their use does seem to have different 'pragmatic implications'. We use the word 'inattention' to describe a state of mind of one who is not paying attention to what he is supposed to be doing. An inattentive person is one whose attention is diverted from that to which he is supposed to be giving his attention to something to which he is not supposed to be giving it. When, however, there is

[1] James Ward, *Psychological Principles* (Cambridge, 1918), ch. III, sec. 1 and 2.

nothing to which a person *is* supposed to be paying attention, it would be misleading to say that he was *in*attentive, but correct to say that he was *non*attentive.

This suggests that Ward's theory would be true of inattention but not of nonattention. He could retort, however, that the fact that there was nothing to which a person was supposed to be paying attention would not preclude its being the case that he *was* nonetheless paying attention to something. Thus Ward could not so easily be made to abandon the theory according to which every element of consciousness is an object of attention of at least some degree. Let us therefore see how his theory stands up to a paradigmatic counterexample – a state we would call sheer nonattention. Such a state is described by William James, who puts forward a theory of attention which contradicts Ward's by maintaining that there is a condition of consciousness which is free of any trace of attention whatsoever:

'Everyone knows what attention is. It is the taking possession by the mind, in clear and vivid form, of one out of what seem several simultaneously possible objects or trains of thought. Focalization, concentration, of consciousness are of its essence. It implies withdrawal from some things in order to deal effectively with others, and is a condition which has a real opposite in the confused, dazed, scatter-brained state which in French is called *distraction*, and *Zerstreutheit* in German.

'We all know this latter state, even in its extreme degree. Most people probably fall several times a day into a fit of something like this: The eyes are fixed on vacancy, the sounds of the world melt into confused unity, the attention is dispersed so that the whole body is felt, as it were, at once, and the foreground of consciousness is filled, if by anything, by a sort of solemn sense of surrender to the empty passing of time. In the dim background of our mind we know meanwhile what we ought to be doing: getting up, dressing ourselves, answering the person who has spoken to us, trying to make the next step in our reasoning. But somehow we cannot *start*; the *pensee de derriere la tete* fails to pierce the shell of lethargy that wraps our state about. Every moment we expect the spell to break, for we know no reason why it should continue. But it does continue, pulse after pulse, and we float with it, until – also without reason that we can discover – an energy is given, something – we know not what – enables us to gather ourselves together, we wink our eyes, we shake our heads, the background-ideas become effective, and the wheels of life go round again.'[1]

Now certainly on his own description of attention, James is quite right when he avers that anyone in this condition is not paying attention. Nevertheless, it seems to me that he lays himself open to attack from Ward's quarter by equating attention with the highest degree of attention. When James describes attention as the mind's taking possession of an object 'in clear and vivid form', we are given a description that best suits optimal attention. If therefore in conformity with Ward's position we look for traces of minimal attention in the state of distraction so vividly described in the above passage, we should not be altogether surprised to find what we are looking for. The clue is given in James's reference to the 'foreground' and 'background' of consciousness. In the state of ennui described, consciousness is still differentiated, according to James, into a foreground and a background. Ward would no doubt argue, and I see no reason to disagree with him, that the division of consciousness into a *foreground* and a *background* is the hallmark of attention. Indeed these are the very words frequently used for the precise purpose of describing the effect of attention on consciousness. What is more, the picture of a foreground against a background is also implicit in James's own characterization of attention when he says of it: 'Focalization, concentration, of consciousness are of its essence.'

James's passage is introspective writing at its best, but I question his belief that attention is entirely lacking even in as 'distracted' a condition of consciousness as the one described. After all the presence of attention is implied by his own words when he says 'Every moment we expect the spell to break'. For surely expectation is a state of attention.[2]

There is a possible ambiguity in his thought on the question of attention-free states of consciousness. As we have seen, in his description of attention he refers to the mind taking possession of an object in a clear and vivid form, but this is open to two interpretations.

On the one hand, attention may take a clear and vivid form because the object of attention is itself clear and vivid: clarity and vividness in this sense being intrinsic to the object itself. On the

[1] James, *The Principles of Psychology*, Vol. I, pp. 403–4.
[2] My attention was drawn to this point by John Schumacher.

other hand, the object may itself be vague and amorphous, and the more clearly and vividly attention is given the object, the more vague and amorphous it is seen to be. Thus in the first case, even if a less than optimal degree of attention were given to the object, the object would still be clear and vivid. While in the second case, even if optimal attention were given to the object, it would remain vague and amorphous. These constitute two distinct senses in which the mind can take possession 'in a clear and vivid form', and it is apparent that James's description is ambiguous as between them.

If we now bear in mind these two possibilities, and return to the passage we are examining, we notice that James describes the foreground of consciousness as filled 'by a sort of solemn sense of surrender to the empty passing of time'. Now if anyone senses anything of the sort, he certainly would not want to describe what he sensed as 'clear and vivid'. But this does not preclude the person from trying to give his whole attention to such an experience. It may be that the more he attends to the experience the more convinced he becomes of its essential vagueness and indeterminateness. The same may be said for the experience James allies with it, in which 'the whole body is felt'. He has no right to conclude, therefore, that if the foreground of consciousness consists of elements which are not clear and vivid, attention has not been brought to bear. I conclude that although James's view of attention is inconsistent with Ward's, the example he has given of a condition of consciousness lacking all attention, fails of its purpose. Nevertheless the failure is a lesson in itself. If such a state of distraction as the one described exhibits an important characteristic of attention, this is itself strong evidence for the conclusion that no consciousness will be found without the presence of at least a dim flicker of attention. For if that is not an example of a consciousness devoid of attention, one may well ask what is.

The condition of consciousness in question would be better described as one characterized by the *diffusion of attention*, rather than by its total absence. However, the notion of a diffused attention runs directly counter to the description James gives of attention when he says of it that 'Focalization, concentration, of consciousness are of its essence'. This assertion seems to express the orthodox opinion on the subject. Hamilton, too, says of attention, 'It is consciousness concentrated'.[1] In view of the importance of this

[1] Bowen, *The Metaphysics of Sir William Hamilton*, p. 160.

contention, it must be given closer scrutiny to determine whether it really is at odds with Ward's claim that some degree of attention is present under all conditions of consciousness.

[4] William James resorts to visual metaphor when he speaks of the 'focalization' of attention, and we shall see in a moment that Hamilton uses an elaborate visual analogy to describe attention. It is in fact difficult to avoid talking about attention in visual terms, nor do I think we should refrain from so portraying it. Visual descriptions, and visual distinctions, are far richer and have a greater degree of subtlety than their alternatives, and it would be foolish for us to handicap ourselves by avoiding their use. But we must be watchful not to be deceived by the analogy into thinking that what is true of the analogue is true generally; for it might be that we are unwittingly dealing with a non-analogous feature of the analogue.

When James talks of 'focalizing' attention, and the 'foreground' and 'background' of consciousness, he is using ideas which find their natural home in visual perception. Hamilton quite un-abashedly takes the analogy with vision to the limit when he says,

'Consciousness may be compared to a telescope, attention to the pulling out or in of the tubes in accommodating the focus to the object.'[1]

Now the idea of focusing, and the idea of concentrating, carry with them the idea of something being focused, and the concentration taking place around a centre. Both ideas point to a 'centre of attention'. Furthermore, once we have the picture of a centre, we think of the centre as standing out from its surroundings, and we can describe the centre as in the foreground as contrasted with what is outside the centre, which is relegated to the background.[2] The usefulness of the visual model is enhanced because it so easily accommodates the idea of degrees of attention.

The structural relationship between foreground and background will be determined by the nature of the centre. On the one hand there could be a large centre with ill-defined edges which

[1] *Ibid.*, p. 160.
[2] Gestalt Psychology furnishes plenty of evidence of the fact that anything seen as a centre automatically seems to stand out from a background.

imperceptibly merge into the background; on the other hand, there could be a highly concentrated centre which stands out in sharp contrast against the background. We may think of the operation of a spot-light to give us a picture of one sort of centre passing into the other. If a spot-light is completely out of focus for a certain distance, it will throw a wide, diffuse, beam giving a low degree of illumination. As we correct the focus, the circumference of the beam contracts, and the intensity of illumination correspondingly increases, until the point is reached at which the spot-light is fully in focus, and we have a brightly lit area with a sharply defined circumference. It is important to realize that both the badly focused beam, and the sharply focused one cast light on an area that may be described as consisting of a centre occupying the foreground and a complementing background.[1]

By analogy, the centre of attention could have a low degree of concentration (produced by a badly focused beam), or a high degree of concentration (produced by a sharply focused beam). Moreover any distinction at all between a foreground and a background would entail the existence of some degree of attention, no matter how little (corresponding to a beam of some degree of concentration). Hence, when James distinguishes between a foreground to consciousness and a background in the case of a 'distracted' consciousness, he *ipso facto* describes a consciousness differentiated by attention.

That which is at the centre of attention is frequently described as the object of attention. This description, too, we owe to a visual analogy, since objects are among the things we are said to *see*. In view of the fact that there is no standard description of that on which attention may be said to be centred, I shall employ the term 'object of attention' specifically for that purpose. An *object of attention* is thus, by definition, anything on which attention is focused. It must be understood that the visual connotations of the

---

[1] It is no accident that we describe an object in focus as being situated in the *centre* of the field of vision. It is based on a fact in physiology. 'In the centre of the retina, in the *fovea centralis* (the pit in the middle of the so-called yellow spot) there are only cones, and no rods at all. From there toward the periphery of the retina the number of cones decreases and the rods become more and more numerous. The *fovea centralis* is of paramount importance in our vision. This tiny spot is the only place where you see a sharp image. If you see something in the lateral field of your retina and want to investigate it more thoroughly, you turn your eye so as to cause the image of that object to be projected exactly onto your *fovea centralis*.' W. von Buddenbrock, *The Senses* (The Univ. of Michigan Press, 1958), p. 80.

word 'object' have no relevance to the defined term 'object of attention'. A thought, a sensation, or an imaginary object are as properly called 'objects of attention' as are visual objects.

The discussion of James's point of view has served two purposes. Firstly, it has suggested the idea that consciousness may be organized into a foreground and a background. Secondly, it has introduced the idea of an attention-free consciousness. Both of these ideas are important for the hypothesis I now wish to advance. The hypothesis is that the differentiation of consciousness into a foreground and background is a feature of all normal forms of consciousness. I have already shown the appropriateness of describing the operation of attention in visual terms. And I have discussed the applicability to attention of the model of a foreground marked off from a background through the presence of a 'centre' on which attention is focused. From that discussion it becomes obvious that we would experience no difficulty in showing that those forms of consciousness that exhibit a high degree of attention could be appropriately described in terms of a foreground and a background. The object of attention would function as the 'centre' marking off foreground from background. The crucial test of the hypothesis would be to see whether a *seemingly* attention-free consciousness also displayed this distinction between foreground and background. I have pointed out that the hypothesis seems true in the case of the 'distracted' consciousness described by James.

I now wish to offer more detailed support for the hypothesis by showing that it is borne out in the case of two forms of consciousness. These are, firstly, a pure sensuous consciousness, and, secondly, a state of reverie. If the hypothesis were false, these two forms of consciousness would show it. If, however, the hypothesis is confirmed for such prima facie unpromising forms of consciousness, we can take it to have been established. Anyone wishing to dispute the correctness of the hypothesis would have to show that these two forms of consciousness together with the normal forms, which it must be conceded *are* attentive forms, do not exhaust the known forms of consciousness. It should be noted that the first form of consciousness can be satisfied by a single total temporary state, and it, therefore, tests the hypothesis in the one dimension of consciousness. The second form of consciousness is only satisfied by a series of total temporary states, and it, therefore, tests the hypothesis in the other dimension of consciousness.

2. REJECTION OF THE NOTION OF AN ATTENTION-FREE CONSCIOUSNESS

[5] I begin with the case of a pure sensuous consciousness. I should point out that as far as human beings are concerned a pure sensuous consciousness might be just an abstract possibility (i.e. not realized). That is to say, it might represent an ideal limit to consciousness in one direction which is only approached but never actually reached. My argument is that even as an abstract possibility it does not constitute a counter-instance. What I am calling a pure sensuous consciousness can best be explained through an example. We have all had the experience of being asked out of the blue what we are thinking about. On occasion we say that we have not been thinking about anything in particular, not because we wish to be secretive about our thoughts, but because it seems the truthful answer to give. It might be the case that the question was put at a time when we were not having thoughts about anything, but were simply enjoying our present sensations. Lying on a beach sunbathing could be a circumstance in which this would be true. I might be conscious of the sun burning into me, the lapping of the waves, the light coming through my eyelids, the indistinct sound of voices, and so on. Naturally if asked what I was thinking about I would not take the question to be aimed at discovering what I was conscious of. I would take it to be directed at anything I was thinking about which I took to be relevant or interesting to the questioner, and, from that point of view, it is often honest to say: 'Nothing.' Often in a state of euphoria one says, 'My mind is in a complete blank.' It is just such a state in which we give ourselves up to our sensations and allow our minds to go blank that I describe as a state of pure sensuous consciousness.

I wish to argue that a total temporary state of a pure sensuous consciousness does not contain a number of elements which are all equally submerged in the background, but, on the contrary, that at each moment some one element has the ascendency over the rest. If we try to check this by introspection, we run into several difficulties. In the first place it is not easy to make one's mind go blank. And secondly it is not easy to find out what takes place when one is in a state of pure sensuous consciousness without thereby destroying the state. For these reasons we are forced to rely on memory of such states, and base our findings on what we seem to remember. We may not, even in retrospect, be able to tell just which element was more to the fore than the rest at a particular time. The reason for this is that we are dealing with a fluid situation, in which one element is continually being ousted by another from the centre of consciousness. Furthermore, when in a state of nonattention we are not bothered by the question of which element is at a particular time holding the central position. Naturally, too, any element which is in the foreground will possess a poorly differentiated character. The foreground, as in the case of a badly focused spot-light, will be large and obscure, and this means that the element occupying this position will be similarly ill-formed and ill-defined. For instance, in a sunbather's consciousness a general sensation of heat may occupy the central position for a brief period, and then be replaced by an undifferentiated auditory sensation, which itself might be followed by the visual sensation caused by the light of the sun passing through closed eye-lids.

I am not suggesting that these elements are not present all at once – they are. What I am suggesting is that at any one time one element is insinuating its presence more insistently than the others. In other words, I am maintaining that James was right to divide consciousness into a foreground and a background, even in a situation which approximates as closely as experience seems to allow to one of absolute nonattention.

I have offered purely introspective evidence to back up the claim that consciousness, even in a state that can be described as one of complete nonattention, seems to be structured into a foreground and background. But even if it is agreed that introspection bears me out, it is not necessary to rest the case on the evidence of introspection alone. An explanation can, I believe, be offered for the phenomenon, which may well be convincing to those who remain unmoved by the introspective evidence.

It is Ribot's thesis that attention is grounded in the emotional nature of the organism, and in support of this view he uses the following argument:

'Any animal so organized that the impressions of the external world were all of equal significance to it, in whose consciousness all impressions stood upon the same level, without any single one predominating or inducing any appropriate motory adaptation – were exceedingly ill-equipped for its own preservation. I shall overlook the extreme case, in which predominance and adaptation would favour detrimental impressions; for an animal thus constituted must perish, being an illogical organism – a kind of in-corporate contradiction. The usual case remains, viz: the pre-dominance of useful sensations, that is, of those connected with nutrition, self-defence, and the propagation of the species. The impressions of prey to be caught, of an enemy to be avoided, and from time to time, of a female to be fecundated, become settled in the consciousness of the animal with their adapted movements. Attention, thus, is at the service of and dependent upon necessities; always connected with the sense most perfectly developed, the sense of touch, of sight, of hearing, of smelling, according to the species. Here attention is seen in all its simplicity, and here it affords the most instruction. It was necessary to descend to those rudimentary forms, in order to grasp the reason of its power: – attention is a condition of life . . .'[1]

We may agree with Ribot that if, *per impossibile*, a percipient could be absolutely indifferent to its environment, there would be no reason for it to pay attention to changes which took place in the environment of which it was aware.

We might in fact go one step further than Ribot, and question whether a percipient could continue to be conscious if its aware-ness of its environment ceased to matter to it. In any event it is possible that Ribot has pressed his point too far. We find him say-ing, for instance, that, 'man, like animals, lends his attention spontaneously only to what concerns and interests him'.[2] This view lends itself to the overstatement that man, as well as animal, can only have his attention attracted by something which has an emotional significance for him. Indeed Ribot himself says, 'Spontaneous attention without an anterior emotional state would be an effect without a cause'.[3] The danger of this position is that it becomes true by definition that if a percipient spontaneously attends that which holds the attention must be of concern or interest to it.

We may therefore agree with Ribot that spontaneous attention is grounded in emotional states, without following him to the point of saying that every instance of spontaneous attention is caused by an emotional state. But would this, as Ribot thinks, be an 'event' without a cause? Surely not, for what the emotional state does is

---

[1] Ribot, *The Psychology of Attention*, p. 33.
[2] *Ibid.*, pp. 12–13.
[3] *Ibid.*, p. 13.

give the percipient a propensity to have its attention elicited by changes in the intensity of stimuli. The position as I see it is this: no percipient is indifferent to its environment (so far I am in agreement with Ribot), but because the environment is of interest and concern, every perceptible change in it taken by the percipient to be novel must alert it. The percipient is alerted when, quite involuntarily, its sense-organs are arrested by the novel stimuli. This can best be understood in terms of one or two examples. We are all familiar with the experience in which a sudden movement, or a flash of light, catches the eye. As soon as the movement, or the light, is seen, the eye is held by the novel stimulus. The eye comes to rest on the moving or flashing object before the object is recognized, or before there is time for its relevance to be evaluated. As we say, the object has caught our attention. A similar experience occurs when an unexpected sound strikes the ear. The sound itself excites our attention, in advance of any interpretation of its significance for us. In other words, the response of the sense-organ to a novel stimulus is very much like an unconditioned reflex.

The objection that many quite startling stimuli do not arrest the sense-organ concerned can be quite easily disposed of. To an infant all environmental stimuli are novel and startling. As it accommodates itself to its environment, however, it finds progressively fewer stimuli novel: stimuli which startle because of their novelty cease to do so when a number of repetitions are found to be without repercussion. Thus, the infant may be startled by a clap of thunder which an adult ignores. As the infant develops it learns to inhibit the reflex-like response of the sense-organs to certain types of stimuli. But what is inhibited cannot be the initial arrest of the sense-organ – the stimulus is still 'picked up': the adult hears the thunderclap that startles the infant. What the adult has inhibited is any further reaction – such as the assumption of a posture of attention.

I have suggested this alternative to Ribot's theory, because it seems to me to offer an intelligible account of facts which on his theory remain a mystery. Ribot tells us that only a percipient with an emotional involvement in its environment can exhibit attention, but he does not explain how the environment is to have a reper-cussion on the percipient in the first place. This my alternative attempts to clarify.

My departure from Ribot's position has certain interesting implications. It is one of his basic contentions that the normal state of a percipient is one of nonattention, and it follows that attention is for him an exceptional phenomenon. As he explains:

'Attention . . . is an exceptional, abnormal state, which cannot last a long time, for the reason that it is in contradiction to the basic condition of psychic life; namely, change. Attention is a state that is fixed. If it is prolonged beyond a reasonable time, particularly under unfavourable conditions, everybody knows from individual experience, that there results a constantly increasing cloudiness of the mind, finally a kind of intellectual vacuity, frequently accompanied by vertigo. These light, transient perturbations denote the radical antagonism of attention and the normal psychical life. The progress toward unity of consciousness, which is the very basis of attention, manifests itself still better in clearly morbid cases, which we shall study later under their chronic form, namely, the "fixed idea", and in their acute form, which is ecstasy.'[1]

According to the way I see the matter, Ribot has been led to overemphasize the abnormality of attention. This I shall try to show. It is true that we are reluctant to attribute consciousness to an entity that cannot do things of its own accord. When a creature is not active we begin to doubt whether it is conscious. For this reason we are reluctant to admit it as a logical possibility that an object such as a tree could be conscious.[2] A tree does not *do* anything. It is a natural state of a conscious being that it should be active; that it should be doing things.

In the case of an animal, most of its waking life is devoted to activity. It is grazing or drinking; it is on the alert for danger, looking about, listening, scenting the air, and so forth. These are natural activities in the sense that the animal does not have to be taught to do them. (It has to be taught to do them recognitionally, but that is another matter.) Even an infant does not have to be taught to do such basic things as move its arms and legs, look about, and focus its eyes on objects. These 'doings' occur spontaneously at certain stages of normal growth.

If we confine the discussion of 'doings' to those involving the senses, then it would seem quite arbitrary to say that those sense-organ activities that involve movement of the sense-organs are normal, and those that involve suspension of movement are

---

[1] Ribot, *The Psychology of Attention*, pp. 8–9.
[2] See, N. Malcolm, *Knowledge and Certainty* (New Jersey, 1963), pp. 133–6.

abnormal. If looking *about* is normal, and listening *for* is normal, so surely is looking *at* and listening *to*; and yet frequently the latter activities can only be engaged in when movement is suspended. Of course if such a static activity went on too long it would become mesmerization, and that would be abnormal. But it would be no more abnormal than would the continuance of any activity long after it had lost point. It is surely obvious, too, that the exploratory use of sense-organs has value for a creature only if the sense-organs can also be used to fixate an object of interest. I shall use the expression 'sense-organ attention' to describe the involuntary fixation of a sense-organ on an object. Contrary to what Ribot says, sense-organ attention is as normal an activity as is the activity in which the sense-organs are used for the purpose of 'scanning' the surroundings. It would be obviously false to describe sense-organ attention as being 'in contradiction to the basic condition of psychic life'.

The difference between Ribot's position and mine is not as great as would appear, and with a little qualification the two can be brought into harmony. What we need to realize is that in the above passage Ribot is clearly referring to maximal attention. Now I would certainly be prepared to follow him in his claim that maximal attention is an abnormal state, which cannot be sustained for very long periods, but this is a far cry from the claim that even minimal attention is abnormal. I think it is true to say that Ribot was misled, in just the way that James was misled, by thinking exclusively of maximal attention, and assuming that what is true of maximal attention is true of all attention. He in fact points out at the very beginning of his study that he intends to confine himself to cases of attention that are 'marked and typical'.

'It is a matter of much greater difficulty to know at what point attention begins, and where it ends; for it embraces all degrees from the transient instant accorded to the buzzing of a fly, to the state of complete absorption. It will be conformable to the rule of sound method only to study cases that are marked and typical; that is to say, those which present at least one of the following two character-istics: intensity and duration.'[1]

It is evident that whereas my discussion of a pure sensuous consciousness concentrates on the end of the scale at which

[1] Ribot, *The Psychology of Attention*, p. 7.

attention is minimal, Ribot is concerned with the end of the scale at which attention is maximal. Moreover, Ribot, who distinguishes two forms of attention, 'spontaneous' attention and 'voluntary' attention,[1] makes it equally true of both forms of attention that they are 'antagonistic' to the 'normal psychical life'. In due course I shall try to show that in terms of his own theory Ribot is in error when he makes this claim in respect of spontaneous attention. We are now in a position to understand why it is that in a state described as one of nonattention, consciousness is nevertheless structured into a part which is in the foreground, and a remainder which fills the background. My example of a person lying on the beach sunbathing probably comes as close as is possible in normal conditions to a person having a pure sensuous consciousness (assuming as my example made clear that the sunbather would later claim that his mind was a blank). I maintained, on introspective grounds, that there would always be some sense experience which would constitute the foreground of the sunbather's consciousness. Why this should be so can now be explained in terms of what I have called sense-organ attention. As I explained, our sense-organs are always arrested by the most novel stimulus in the environment. Thus if the increasing intensity of the heat of the sun on his back is the most novel feature of the environment for the sunbather, that sensation will spontaneously occupy the foreground of his consciousness.[2] This it will continue to do until another stimulus occurs which is more novel than the sensation of heat. It might be the sudden break of a wave, or the shrill call of a sea-gull. Attention will then spontaneously transfer to the sound, and the sound will take the place of the previous sensation, and itself occupy the foremost position in consciousness. Since a sound is usually a transitory stimulus, after it has ceased the next relatively most novel stimulus will arrest the sense-organs and so place yet another element in the foreground. It may be that a cloud hides the sun and then immediately, even with eyes closed, the sudden darkening sensation to the sunbather's eyes leaps to the foreground of consciousness.

The fact therefore that consciousness seems always to be differentiated into a foreground and a background, even in this

---

[1] I have deliberately avoided discussing the question of the different forms of attention until this became unavoidable. My intention is to avoid obscuring the argument by introducing too many considerations at once. The subject is discussed in sections 8 and 9.

[2] In the present context the body as a whole may be thought of as a sense-organ.

condition of nonattention, must be attributed to the way our sense-organs function in relation to changes in stimuli. If what Ward means, when he contends that attention is exhibited in all consciousness, is that consciousness is always differentiated into a foreground and a background, then we have found every reason to agree with him. The examination of a pure sensuous consciousness has shown it to be a form of consciousness exhibiting a structure. This structure has a twofold character which comes about because some of its elements constitute a foreground relative to which others constitute a background. The notion of sense-organ attention was introduced in an attempt to offer an explanation of this structure.

[6] This brings me to the second form of consciousness with which I wish to test the hypothesis that all consciousness is thus structured – the state of reverie. When in such a state the mind wanders from one thought to another in a course dictated largely by the accidental association of ideas. Thoughts are interrupted by perceptions, and perceptions are in turn interrupted by thoughts. The mind seems to be free-wheeling.

Such writers as James and Ribot clearly regard this condition of consciousness as a paradigm case of the absence of attention. Ribot, for instance, referring to scatter-brained people, gives a description of their condition that applies equally to reverie in general:

'We call "distracted" people whose intelligence is unable to fix itself with any degree of persistence, and who pass incessantly from one idea to another, at the mercy of their most transient whims, or of any trifling events in their surroundings. It is a perpetual state of mobility and dispersion, which is the very reverse of attention.'[1]

We may note, before continuing, that Ribot cannot mean that these 'distracted' people are unable to attend spontaneously in the way in which he says animals attend to their sense experiences in the struggle for survival. They must at least be capable of what he has called 'spontaneous attention', and yet in this passage we are led to believe that 'distracted people' are incapable of any attention whatever. He must mean that they are incapable of what he has called 'voluntary attention'. Once again we see Ribot making generalizations about attention in all its forms from features that are applicable to only some of its forms. This is the penalty he pays for

<hr>

[1] Ribot, *The Psychology of Attention*, p. 78.

generalizing unqualifiedly from instances of attention which are 'marked and typical'. Nevertheless, apart from a theoretical description of the matter, Ribot is undoubtedly staying close to ordinary usage when he describes 'distracted' people as people incapable of attention. And it is certainly the case that a person in a state of reverie would ordinarily be described as a person in a state of nonattention. Ribot's own words fit such a state perfectly: 'It is a perpetual state of mobility and dispersion, which is the very reverse of attention.'

Now inasmuch as some of the elements of consciousness found in a state of reverie may correspond with those belonging to a pure sensuous consciousness, they have already been shown to fall into the pattern of foreground and background. This leaves the other elements comprising a state of reverie: viz. recollections, mental images, and thoughts. Probably no one would dispute the testimony of introspection, which supports the claim that consciousness exhibits the typical structure of foreground and background in the state of reverie. In reverie there is always some element in the centre of consciousness. Nevertheless there is no need to rely on introspection alone. The very expressions we use to describe reverie tell the same story. We speak of a succession of ideas crossing the mind, and I do not think it would be going too far to say that we imagine them crossing in single file. We also use the expression 'a train of thought' and in reverie the train would be describable as aimless. Whether we speak of ideas 'crossing' the mind, or a 'train' of ideas, in each case the metaphor suggests that at any one time some idea must be in the middle of its passage, and that idea is then said to be 'before' the mind. Now it will be recalled that I have argued that a total temporary state of normal consciousness will reveal the presence of a plurality of elements. Since reverie is normal consciousness in this sense it must follow that if one element in a total temporary state has the position we describe as being 'before' the mind, there will be other elements in the state of which this is not true. We may conclude from these premises that when in reverie some idea is before the mind, it is not the only element existing in consciousness at the time. This state of affairs can be described without misrepresentation as one in which the element in question occupies the foreground to a consciousness which must also have other elements in the background.

It is possible for a person to interrupt a state of reverie, and to try to recall the ideas that have been passing through his mind.

The task is not easy. At the best of times it is difficult to recall events that received but scant attention, and we are dealing with reverie about which our concern is whether it is not perhaps a state of absolute nonattention. Nevertheless, because of the propinquity of the ideas to be recalled, we can hope for some success. Now it is not necessary to my argument that we be able to recall with any great fidelity what transpired in a state of reverie we have just come out of. It is sufficient for the argument if some of its elements can be recalled. A description of what is recalled will take the form of mentioning one idea, which gives rise to another, suggests a third, recalls a fourth, and so on. In other words the description will suggest a linear pattern in which we advance from one idea to the next. No matter how fragmentary each individual thought is, it will for a fleeting second occupy the focal position in consciousness, and it is for this reason that it should seem entirely fitting for a description of what happens to mention one idea after another. In other words, we do not protest that language cannot capture the true nature of reverie owing to the fact that in language we are forced to describe ideas one at a time, whereas in reverie there is no such linear pattern. Quite the contrary. The sequential nature of description of ideas in language accurately captures the impression of their order in the mind. The position is very different from the one we meet when we describe a visual scene for instance. For there we see a number of things at once, but have to describe them one after the other.

This point can best be substantiated by quoting a piece of writing describing a state of reverie. In James Joyce's *Ulysses* we find Bloom in a carriage on the way to a funeral, lost in reverie:

BRONZE BY GOLD HEARD THE HOOFIRONS, STEELY.

rining
Imperthnthn thnthnthn.
Chips, picking chips off rocky thumbnail, chips.
Horrid! And gold flushed more.
A husky fifenote blew.
Blew. Blue bloom is on the
Gold pinnacled hair.
A jumping rose on satiny breasts of satin, rose of Castille.
Trilling, trilling: Idolores.
Peep! Who's in the . . . peepofgold?
Tink cried to bronze in pity.

And a call, pure, long and throbbing. Longindying call.
Decoy. Soft word. But look! The bright stars fade. O rose!
Notes chirruping answer. Castille. The morn is breaking.
Jingle jingle jaunted jingling.
Coin rang. Clock clacked.
Avowal. *Sonnez.* I could. Rebound of garter, Not leave thee.
Smack. *La cloche!* Thigh smack. Avowal. Warm.
Sweetheart, goodbye.
Jingle. Bloo.
Boomed crashing chords. When love absorbs. War! War!
The tympanum.
A sail! A veil awave upon the waves.
Lost. Throstle fluted. All is lost now.
Horn. Hawhorn.
When first he saw. Alas!
Full tup. Full throb.
Warbling. Ah, lure! Alluring
Martha! Come!
Clapclop. Clipclap. Clappyclap.
Goodgod heneverheard inall.
Deaf bald Pat brought pad knife took up.
A moonlight nightcall: far: far.
I feel so sad. P.S. So lonely blooming.
Listen!
The spiked and winding cold seahorn. Have you the? Each
and for other plash and silent roar.
Pearls: when she. Liszt's rhapsodies. Hisss.[1]

Bloom's musings consist of a jumble of ideas which mostly
originate in experiences he had earlier in the day, held together in
a mental dance of the mind's own making. What is of particular
interest is the literary form Joyce gives to Bloom's stream of
thoughts; short, abbreviated, consecutive. Each one seems to stand
in isolation. By laying out the words one below another Joyce
conveys the idea of the thoughts coming one after another.

For the fleeting moment each thought lives, it is in the forefront
of consciousness. The mind is drawn towards it; it has our attention.
The pattern of consciousness here, in reverie, is no different from
its pattern in pure sensuous consciousness: it is articulated as foreground against background.

[7] In arguing that consciousness is structured even in conditions
of nonattention, I have deliberately described the form this

---

[1] James Joyce, *Ulysses* (Hamburg, 1935), Vol. I, p. 264.

structuring takes, in the vaguest possible way, in terms of foreground and background. The minimum possible claim was all my argument needed. Nevertheless it might be helpful if I were to give some more definite idea of the manner in which I conceive a thought or an element of consciousness to occupy the foreground of consciousness. This can only be done by analogy. When speaking about an object in the vicinity it is usually possible to point to it. The visual field, the auditory field, or whatever sense-field it is, then organizes itself about the object. It becomes the centre of attention. Very much of a parallel situation is found, I suggest, in consciousness generally. When I have a thought, for instance, the thought becomes the cognitive referent around which consciousness organizes itself. It is as though, when I had a thought, I had already pointed out to myself which thought I was having. Now of course I do no such thing. But it is as if the reason I do not need to point it out to myself is that it already occupies precisely the position it would have, had I pointed it out. In this way it presents itself.

I have found reason to agree with Ward that some degree of attention is to be found in even the most distracted conditions of consciousness, whether it be pure sensuous consciousness or a state of reverie. In both forms of consciousness the need was found to differentiate consciousness into a foreground and background. Provided this feature of consciousness is recognized, it matters little whether it is identified as a rudimentary type of attention, or whether the word 'attention' is reserved for application to a less distracted condition of consciousness; for what James and Hamilton call 'consciousness concentrated'. If a feature of attention, which seems intrinsic to its 'marked and typical' forms, is also found to be present in nonattentive consciousness, this is worth pointing out. It might after all provide the link between non-attentive consciousness and fully attentive consciousness, and this in turn might explain how a state of nonattention could pass into a state of full attention.

It is a quite proper theoretical procedure to extend the scope of a concept to a phenomenon not previously falling under it in order to uncover a resemblance between such a phenomenon and the phenomena to which the concept was previously restricted. This, it seems to me, is what Ward has done when he alleges that some degree of attention is to be found even in conditions of consciousness normally believed to be antipathetic to its existence. If we have succeeded in tracing attention back to its earliest beginnings in consciousness, it would be churlish to object to our describing what we have found as 'rudimentary attention'. It is opportune at this point for me to make clear where I stand in relation to Ward's theory on the general question of the relation between consciousness and attention. At the moment I can give no more than a bare statement of my agreements and disagreements with him, because it is not until the next chapter that the reasons for my own position become fully evident. His view that there are degrees of attention I take to be important and true. I also agree with him that there is no consciousness without some minimal degree of attention. My fundamental disagreement with him is over his claim that to be aware is to attend, and by inference that every element of consciousness receives attention. Ward in effect makes it an analytic truth that to be aware is to attend. I do not. For me the concepts 'awareness' and 'attention' are logically different from each other. Thus I shall be arguing, in a way that Ward's position would preclude him from arguing, that although in each total temporary state of consciousness some element will be receiving attention, normally there will be many unattended elements belonging to it as well.

3. THE VARIETIES OF ATTENTION

[8] If we consent to follow Ward in talking of degrees of attention, there is no reason why we should not take a leaf out of Mill's book, and claim that attention may differ in quality as well as in quantity. I shall now take up this idea, and consider the question of whether there are different *types* of attention. Of course, in a sense, an affirmative answer has already been conceded as soon as it is agreed that 'rudimentary attention' is found in states of distraction. Ribot too, as we have noticed in passing, makes a clear-cut distinction between two different types of attention, one of which he calls 'spontaneous' attention and the other 'voluntary' attention. In terms of this classification the discussion to this point has been confined to 'spontaneous' attention. We are now ready to investigate 'voluntary' attention. I shall try to show that the traditional explanation of the distinction between different types of attention runs into difficulties, and I shall offer in its place a different explanation of what lies at the heart of the differentiation of attention into 'spontaneous' attention on the one hand and 'voluntary' attention on the other.

Ribot sets out the contrast between spontaneous attention and voluntary attention, as he sees it, as follows:

'There are two well-defined forms of attention the one spontaneous, natural; the other voluntary, artificial. The former – neglected by most psychologists – is the true, primitive, and fundamental form of attention. The second – the only one investigated by most psychologists – is but an imitation, a result of education, of training, and of impulsion. Precarious and vacillating in nature, it derives its whole being from spontaneous attention, and finds only in the latter a point of support. It is merely an apparatus formed by cultivation, and a product of civilization.'[1]

I have already drawn attention to Ribot's view that attention is an abnormal phenomenon which cannot be prolonged too long. This point of view is strongly evident in what he here says about voluntary attention. A further distinction between the two types, which he takes to be quite definitive, is that spontaneous attention is entirely effortless, while on the other hand voluntary attention is always an effort.[2]

William James shares Ribot's views, as is evident from the following passage:

'*Voluntary attention is always derived*; we never make an *effort* to attend to an object except for the sake of some *remote* interest which the effort will serve.'[3]

Ribot would endorse that statement without qualification. And the next statement of James's is also one which would fit in with Ribot's position:

There is no such thing as voluntary attention sustained for more than a few seconds at a time.[4]

James's contention is that if we *seem* to be voluntarily attending for more than a few seconds this is only because there is in fact 'a

---

[1] Ribot, *The Psychology of Attention*, p. 8.
[2] This must not be understood to be a denial that in effortless attention energy is expended. Effort in that sense is not intended.
[3] James, *The Principles of Psychology*, Vol. I, p. 416.
[4] *Ibid.*, Vol. I, p. 416.

repetition of successive efforts which bring back the topic to the mind'.

There is no doubt a distinction to be made between what Ribot calls spontaneous attention and voluntary attention, but it cannot be said that he has clarified it. In the first place, if we suppose that only *learned* attention is voluntary – and this seems to be Ribot's criterion for voluntary attention – there is no reason to believe that learned attention will always be accompanied by a feeling of effort (in the sense of overcoming a disinclination to do it). Ribot himself states that in people who have been successfully taught, attention of the sort in question ultimately becomes a habit. Now surely it must be conceded that when we do something out of habit, we do it without feeling any effort in what we are doing? We can go a step further and affirm that when something has become a habit, we are frequently unaware of having acted on the habit until the act has been completed. If so, we could not have been aware of a feeling of effort.

Bearing this in mind, I can only suggest that Ribot has convinced himself of the ubiquity of the feeling of effort in voluntary attention, because he has confined himself to the learning-situation. If a child is being taught to pay attention, he is being taught to do something he cannot yet do, and this would ordinarily give rise to a feeling of effort. But once the task is learned, it can be performed without any conscious feeling of effort. From this point of view the feeling of effort can be seen as incidental to the learning process, and not as intrinsic to the nature of voluntary attention. Alternatively, we frequently meet with the experience in which an initial attempt to attend to an activity costs a great deal of effort but that after a while, the activity begins to engross us, we become absorbed, and all feeling of effort disappears. In the light of these two circumstances Ribot would seem constrained to say that what began as voluntary attention became transformed into spontaneous attention. This would account for the disappearance of the feeling of effort.

Unfortunately this move is not open to Ribot, for on his own theory spontaneous attention is by definition *unlearned* attention,[1] and neither voluntary attention which has become habit, nor voluntary attention which has become absorption, can be described

[1] See, Ribot, *The Psychology of Attention*, ch. 2, p. 35. Thus: 'Voluntary or artificial attention is a product of art, of education, of direction, and of training. It is grafted, as it were, upon spontaneous or natural attention, and finds in the latter its conditions of existence, as the graft does in the stock, into which it has been inserted.'

as unlearned attention. On the other hand, Ribot could not drop the requirement that a feeling of effort always accompanies voluntary attention, without surrendering his claim that there is a felt basis to the distinction between spontaneous and voluntary attention. Manifestly his twofold distinction is insufficient for his purpose.

[9] Hamilton, like Ribot, denies that all attention is of the voluntary type. Under the heading *Attention possible without an act of free-will*, he says,

'I think Reid and Stewart incorrect in asserting that attention is only a voluntary act, meaning, by the expression *voluntary*, an act of free-will . . .

'*Attention of three degrees or kinds.* – It, therefore, appears to me the more correct doctrine to hold that there is no consciousness without attention, – without concentration, – but that attention is of three degrees or kinds. The first, a mere vital and irresistible act; the second, an act determined by desire, which though involuntary, may be resisted by our will; the third, an act determined by a deliberate volition. An act of attention, – that is, an act of concentration, – seems thus necessary to every exertion of consciousness, as a certain contraction of the pupil is requisite to every exercise of vision. We have formerly noticed, that discrimination is a condition of consciousness; and a discrimination is only possible by a concentrative act, or act of attention. This, however, which corresponds to the lowest degree, – to the mere vital or automatic act of attention, has been refused the name; and *attention*, in contradistinction to this mere automatic contraction, given to the two other degrees, of which, however, Reid only recognises the third.'[1]

This passage is interesting on a number of counts. Hamilton is in agreement with Ribot in maintaining that voluntary attention is not the only type of attention. He recognizes the existence of what I have referred to as rudimentary attention, even though he refuses it the name. He contends that there is no consciousness without attention. And he offers a more flexible classification than the twofold system adopted by Ribot. It is not possible to identify either of Ribot's two types of attention with any of Hamilton's threefold

[1] Bowen, *The Metaphysics of Sir William Hamilton*, pp. 165–6.

schema. Ribot's spontaneous attention is not Hamilton's mere vital attention, because Ribot's is based on desire, and the vital attention mentioned by Hamilton is not. It cannot be identified with Hamilton's second variety, because although this *is* based on desire, it can be suspended by an act of will, whereas Ribot's spontaneous attention cannot. Finally, Ribot's voluntary attention is not identical with Hamilton's attention determined by deliberate volition, because Hamilton contrasts attention based on volition with attention based on desire, and Ribot does not. As far as Ribot is concerned voluntary attention is as much based on desire, or emotional factors, as he calls them, as is spontaneous attention. Even if we prefer Hamilton's classification to Ribot's we do not arrive at a satisfactory position.

Both thinkers endeavour to distinguish types of attention through tracing differences in their origins. They thus reduce the issue to one of motivation, i.e. to the question of the various possible types of cause of an instance of attention. For instance, spontaneous or vital attention is caused by processes in the percipient, a second type of attention is caused by desire, and a third is caused by an act of volition. As opposed to this approach, I wish to argue that the *type* of attention is not determined by the circumstances of its motivation. On the contrary, I hope to show that each type of attention could equally well be motivated by any of the causes identified by Hamilton.

I hold that whether or not the attention demanded an effort, whether or not it was voluntary, and whether or not it was spontaneous, are not factors that are intrinsic to specific types of attention. These considerations are incidental. In short, if there are three types of attention – A, B, and C – it will be true on some occasions that A demanded effort, B was due to an act of will, and C was the result of a desire; and it will be equally true on other occasions that A was effortless, B was the result of desire, and C was due to an act of will. And so on for the other permutations. Where I think it is easy to be misled, and where perhaps Ribot and Hamilton were misled, is in the assumption that if a certain type of attention must originally have had a certain motivation, it must thereafter always retain the same motivation. This assumption commits the *genetic fallacy* according to which the nature of a phenomenon is determined entirely by its origin.

This point can best be illustrated in connection with the form of attention Hamilton describes as 'mere vital attention'. It is evident that he has in mind the 'sense-organ' attention I have been discussing.[1] Now we have seen that this type of attention can be attributed to animals, and this makes it seem entirely reasonable to assume that when it is met with in man it operates in the same way as it does in animals. But this ignores the fact that we also ascribe to man 'higher' forms of attention, which are not found in animals. Voluntary attention is the obvious example. Once this is admitted the whole picture alters radically. There exists at least the possibility that a man may be able to disengage his 'mere vital attention' in virtue of his possession of the abilities intrinsic to his higher forms of attention. But if 'mere vital attention' can be disengaged, it has an altogether different significance from – is a different form of attention from – a 'mere vital attention' that cannot be disengaged by an act of will. Furthermore, in a percipient in which the higher forms of attention are found, it may prove impossible to isolate the lower forms in the purity they possess in those percipients which do not possess the higher forms. Just as in man it is alleged that there are no instances of his behaviour being determined by 'pure' motives (all his motives being mixed), so too it may be the case that in man there are no cases of pure instances of a single type of attention; all attention being a resultant of a number of different types.

These, I suggest, are logical possibilities. It is only necessary to admit that they are possibilities for it to be realized that the assumption that types of attention are determined by their origins is questionable. On these grounds we would be advised to be extremely wary of quasi-evolutionary accounts of the stages of attention, such as Ribot gives us, and such as is implicit in Hamilton's theory.

[10] Let us turn from abstract possibilities to concrete cases, and find out just what does take place. 'Mere vital attention' from its very description must be supposed to take place without the attender willing it. It is compulsive in the sense that the attender has no control over its occurrence. Moreover it must also be effortless, since by calling something an effort it is implied that an easier alternative exists, and in the present case there is, by definition, no alternative. An example of such attention would be the case of a sudden movement catching an eye. When that happens one's eyes are drawn to the spot at which the movement was observed, and they fixate it.

[1] See above, p. 85.

The event has our attention. This is a common experience. When it happens, often the first thing we know about it is that we have *noticed* the movement. That is to say, we may have our attention drawn by a movement without realizing that this has happened. It often happens that it is only after we have been attending for some time that we become aware of attending as opposed to being aware of the object of attention. It may happen that what we notice as a result of attending, itself makes us aware of the fact that our attention has been engaged.

Another possibility is for us not to realize at all that our attention is held. A friend, for instance, may say to me, 'Don't stare', and only then do I realize that I am staring, although I would not have been unaware of the person I was staring at. It is important to recognize that it is quite normal in the situation under discussion for a person to break off his 'mere vital attention', either as soon as he himself realizes that he has been giving it, or as soon as he is told to desist. In either case my act may give rise to feelings of guilt about what I had inadvertently done. The fact that I can be admonished for staring makes even stronger the claim that we are able to disengage 'mere vital attention', since I cannot be required to disengage my attention unless I am able to do so.

Such experiences are not confined to visual attention. One often has the experience of overhearing someone else's conversation and discovering that one has been listening intently in the hope of hearing what is being said. That this may be inadvertent is indicated by the fact that we sometimes stop ourselves from doing it as soon as we realize what we are doing. These very common sorts of cases make it quite clear that on many occasions we do actually disengage our 'mere vital attention'. The fact that such attention begins spontaneously does not mean that it must end spontaneously. And yet if we allowed ourselves to be guided entirely by the *concept* of a 'mere vital attention' we would conclude that the process was from beginning to end incapable of control by an act of will. Of course it is not the case that we have reason to be ashamed of all of our inadvertent attendings, and so it may happen that we may come to realize that our attention is inadvertently being held and yet not on that account feel any obligation to break it off. Thus it is also possible for 'mere vital attention' to be voluntarily prolonged. We learn from these cases that we engage in many attentive activities – staring, overhearing, etc. – without at the time realizing the fact, and that the entire nature of our attention is altered as soon as our attending comes to our notice. What may begin as 'mere vital attention' may thus end up as voluntary attention.

This shows that the relation between spontaneous attention and voluntary attention is not a simple one. It is necessary to distinguish two sides to voluntary attention. On one side attention may be said to be voluntary when it can be engaged at will. On the other side attention may be said to be voluntary when it can be broken off at will. This at once gives us three possibilities for voluntary attention: (a) the case in which attention can be engaged and broken off at will; (b) the case in which it can be begun at will, but not broken off at will; (c) the case in which it is not begun at will, but can be broken off at will. Of (a) we might say that attention was wholly voluntary; of (b) that it was voluntary to begin with, but became *compulsive*; of (c) that spontaneous attention had passed into voluntary attention.

A form of voluntary attention that may easily be confused with non-voluntary attention is *obligatory* attention. Obligatory attention is the attention it is one's duty to pay. When I am ordered to pay attention, and my attention is thereby made obligatory, it is presupposed that the attention in question is voluntary. I could not, for instance, be ordered to be surprised because surprise is not a voluntary form of attention.

A general fault that may be found with the treatment of attention given by Hamilton, Ribot, and James, is that they discuss attention quite by itself as though it described something that could be done on its own even if we were doing nothing else at the time.[1] If it were a *sui generis* act, then it would be interesting to know whether it could be done voluntarily or not. But if attention is not a special mental operation, and if it cannot be meaningfully divorced from the things we do attentively or otherwise, then there is no separate question of whether or not attention *itself* is voluntary. The question of the voluntary nature of attention would then depend on the general question of the voluntary nature of our doings in general.

This survey has shown quite clearly that any attempt to distinguish between different types of attention in terms of the presence or absence of effort, the presence or absence of automatic processes, the presence or absence of desires, and the presence or absence of acts of will, must fail. The framework within which attention is paid is almost always too complicated to admit of such compartmentalization. It remains true, nonetheless, that if we want to

[1] See below, pp. 200–5 for a detailed consideration of the point.

assess the circumstances in which attention is paid to an object on a particular occasion it is essential to go into all the factors I have just been considering.

[11] In this section I propose a different way of making a distinction between types of attention, and I show that this alternative is vaguely foreshadowed in the theories of Ribot and Hamilton. In the chapter as a whole the discussion has concentrated on attention as it is exhibited in its most diffuse forms. I am referring, of course, to pure sensuous consciousness, and the state of reverie. Now these forms of consciousness share the characteristic that in them our intelligence seems to be at its least active. Accordingly, in these states our attention is, in a sense, idle. Since we are not attempting to accomplish anything in such states, no success or failure conditions for attention can be specified. This would be the most reasonable ground on which to base a denial that such states of consciousness are states of attention. Nevertheless, this feature they share with another form of attention that it would be absurd to deny to be a form of attention. Such is sense-organ attention. If I find myself looking at or listening to an object of attention, no question of success or failure arises. Nevertheless, these forms of attention need to be distinguished from those to which success-fail conditions apply. Accordingly, I shall name attention of this type 'unordered' attention. (The point of this choice of term will become apparent as I proceed.) It covers Hamilton's 'mere vital attention', Ribot's 'spontaneous attention' and my 'sense-organ attention'. Unordered attention may be usefully contrasted with two types of attention about which there could be no dispute that they are varieties of attention. The first of these I shall call 'interrogative' attention. This is the attention we pay to an object in order to enlarge our knowledge. Interrogative attention is the attention of a probing intelligence in search of the answer to some question, or the solution to some problem. It comes into operation whenever one is puzzled by something, wondering about it, or determined to find out about it. In this case it is possible to fail in one's quest because one gave insufficient attention to the task. In interrogative attention one's mind is actively engaged; it is attention guided by thought.

The second I shall call 'executive attention'. This is the attention we have to give those of our performances that require a technique for their execution; a technique that cannot be applied unless one has one's mind on what one is doing. The more sophisticated or skilled activities require attention in this sense. Executive attention differs from interrogative attention in that although for its success it is often necessary to bear things in mind, what one has in mind need not be in any way problematic. It may demand that one give oneself self-instruction, or that one warn oneself in connection with tricky parts of the performance, but it does not follow that at the end of the performance one will know something that one did not know at the beginning, or that the performance has failed if one does not end up with some additional knowledge. It is perfectly normal for executive attention and interrogative attention to be found together, since often theoretical problems arise over the perfecting of a technique. But they are distinct none the less. Whereas it is necessarily the case that interrogative attention is propositional, it is not necessary for executive attention to be propositional in form. That is, it is not necessary for one to be bearing in mind some consideration that could be communicated verbally in order for one to be engaged in executive attention. In the case of interrogative attention its success will eventuate in some conclusion being reached, or some facts being noticed. Executive attention need not have a 'noticing' as its result. Its success is not a 'noticing' but a completed performance that has been well done.

Attention may be of the unordered type to begin with and later be transformed into interrogative attention. When this happens our curiosity is said to be aroused. We then view the object of attention in a very different light. By bringing our understanding to bear on the matter, we start noticing aspects of the object that would otherwise have gone unnoticed.

The threefold distinction I have introduced is not meant to be an exhaustive list of the varieties of attention, but is intended as a hopefully more fruitful form of demarcation than those introduced by the writers I have been considering. I shall now indicate how this threefold schema can clear up some of the difficulties we found facing these writers.

I shall begin with a passage of Ribot's which contains a good example of unordered attention (sense-organ attention), and also a good contrast with interrogative attention.

'Thus we may observe how spontaneous attention is natural and devoid of effort. The idler, who loafs around in the street, will stare with gaping mouth at a procession or passing masquerade, and preserve perfect imperturbability as long as the procession lasts. If at any time effort appears, it is a sign that attention changes in character, that it becomes voluntary, artificial.'[1]

As is plain from Ribot's description, the man gawking at the procession exhibits a complete absence of interrogative attention. The description would not lead us to expect the 'idler' to be asking himself where the procession had come from, what it was all about, how it was organized or indeed any set of questions that displayed intellectual curiosity. And yet we can certainly describe the procession as holding his attention. As I mentioned, it is possible for unordered attention to turn into interrogative attention, and this it would do as soon as any of the above questions arose for the spectator. This change, however, need not involve any feeling of effort, and there would be no point in calling it voluntary. Nevertheless, there is reason to believe that Ribot has in mind the very transition to interrogative attention that I have been describing. This is easily explicable in my terms. For interrogative attention is associated with precisely those of our 'doings' that are deliberate and hence voluntary. To try to find out something, or to try to solve a problem are 'doings' which we *do* decide to do, and which we may decide to stop doing. They would qualify as voluntary, and this would explain why the attention associated with such doings should itself be thought of as voluntary. Executive attention would be voluntary for the same reason.

That Hamilton and Ribot really had interrogative attention and executive attention in mind when they referred to voluntary attention is further borne out by their claim that voluntary attention is taxing. For although it is not necessarily true that an activity voluntarily engaged in is *per se* taxing, it is the case that interrogative attention and executive attention are both taxing – they demand concentration. My distinction would also account for the further point Ribot makes that voluntary attention is learned. For while it is implausible to argue that all our voluntary activities are learned, it is unquestionably true that interrogative attention and executive attention have to be learned.

The examination of attention I have undertaken has up to this point concentrated on the object of attention itself. Wherever attention was present, consciousness was seen to divide into a foreground and background. It has been the foreground that I have

[1] Ribot, *The Psychology of Attention*, p. 14.

associated with attention. The background has been left in the background as seemingly irrelevant to the operation of attention. I have deliberately kept it out of the way, so that a number of observations could be made about attention, without the picture being obscured by premature over-complication. The point has now been reached, however, at which a further understanding of attention can only be had by an investigation of the role of the background of consciousness in attention. Moreover the notion of a background of consciousness is to play a crucial role, not only in the analysis of attention, but also in the view of the self developed in chapter five. An understanding of the significance of the background of consciousness, and in particular an appreciation that it plays an *active* role in attention, is, accordingly, vital to my whole enterprise. It is the subject of the next chapter.

CHAPTER FOUR

UNPROJECTED CONSCIOUSNESS

I. THE STRUCTURE OF CONSCIOUSNESS

[1] I give the name 'unprojected consciousness' to those elements of consciousness that together make up the background of consciousness when attention is paid to an object. In this chapter I explore the relationship between those elements of consciousness which may be said to form the object of attention and those which do not (unprojected consciousness). An initial thought is likely to be that there is no connection between the object of attention and unprojected consciousness. The latter would then be looked upon as a residue, which may be ignored as simply redundant. My contention is that this is very nearly the opposite of the truth. I shall argue that unprojected consciousness is as indispensable to attention as is the object of attention itself: the object of attention is to unprojected consciousness as one side of a coin is to the other.

Attention is always attention *to* something or other. It is an absurdity to claim to be paying attention but not paying attention to anything. It is not necessary for me to be able to make a sortal identification of the object of attention in order for me to pay attention to it, but I must at least be able to make a referential identification of it. The question 'What has your attention?' is always a valid question which cannot be answered in the negative once one has conceded that one is paying attention. Moreover, this question itself presupposes that one could be paying attention to any of a number of possible objects of attention – could, because they enter one's awareness at the time. This point is sometimes made by describing attention as 'selective'.[1] While this does convey the idea that there is always more to consciousness than has the subject's present attention, the description is unfortunate in that it wrongly suggests that all attention is deliberate, i.e. the product of *conscious* selection. Even when my attention is compulsive and I cannot disengage it at will, I must – if I am to recognize my state –

[1] For this view, see James, *The Principles of Psychology*, Vol. I, p. 402, and R. G. Collingwood, *The New Leviathan* (Oxford, 1947), p. 22.

at least be aware of the presence of other elements of consciousness to which I could turn my attention if I were able.

If our consciousness were such that we were never aware of anything except the objects of attention, we could not *know* that we were attending: we would have no contrast between attention and nonattention. Let us imagine the possibility of a consciousness the total temporary state of which consisted of but a single element. The question could then be raised whether it would be meaningful to talk of that element of consciousness holding the attention of the person who experienced it. If it could, we should have to be prepared to explain in what respect *attending* to that element of consciousness differed from simply *having* it.

Let us suppose that an excruciating toothache constituted an example of total temporary state containing one element. We should have to imagine the toothache pervading the whole of consciousness, thereby blotting out all other elements. If this were possible, it would be an entirely homogeneous consciousness. What I wish to point out is that in those circumstances it would be impossible on logical grounds to distinguish between attending to the toothache and having it. The sufferer could only distinguish the two possibilities if attending to the toothache were something over and above having it. This might consist in his belief that the toothache now felt worse than it did a minute ago. But as soon as some feature is specified which is the basis of the distinction between having and attending, the attending entails the presence of some element of consciousness in addition to the toothache: viz., in the present instance, the belief that it is getting worse. This example makes it clear that the normal case is one in which our attending to A cannot be fully described without some mention of a concomitant awareness that we are not attending to B, C, or D – where this awareness is evinced by our readiness to regard a shift of attention to B, C, or D, as a distraction. It is in this sense that the existence of elements of consciousness to which we are not paying attention provides a foil to those elements to which we are paying attention.

It is frequently the case that we are first made to realize that our attention has been engrossed by an object, upon being distracted from it by one of the elements of consciousness that erstwhile belonged to unprojected consciousness. That is to say, a shift in attention may make us realize both that we had been paying attention to an object and that we had ceased to do so.

To revert to the example of the homogeneous consciousness, in which there is by definition no unprojected consciousness, nothing could correspond to that element's ceasing to receive attention apart from the disappearance of the state of consciousness itself. But where nothing would count as failing to attend, nothing could count as attending. Such circumstances would render the concept of attention vacuous. It would be like claiming that a landscape painting could have a foreground without a background and that would be an obvious impossibility. For these reasons it would be wrong to think that the existence of a plurality of elements of unprojected consciousness is quite accidental and irrelevant to the operation of attention.

[2] The effect attention has on consciousness is to polarize it into an object of attention and an unprojected consciousness. This polarization I described in the last chapter in terms of foreground and background. That description should now be seen as foreshadowing the present description of consciousness as structured into the object of attention and an unprojected consciousness. The distinction should be understood as a logical one. When one object of attention is replaced by another (because of a change of attention) the elements in consciousness change but the structure is still the same. Frequently, a new object of attention will also be a new element of consciousness, but when an existing element of consciousness becomes the new object of attention it is, as it were, detached from unprojected consciousness and set apart from it. The former object of attention will itself either pass into unprojected consciousness, or else simply cease to be an element of consciousness.

Unprojected consciousness must not be thought of as a solid unchanging mass of elements, for, as we have seen, as attention switches, elements may be detached and later returned to unprojected consciousness. But, in addition, the elements that at the time do not engage attention may nevertheless change, vanish, or be replaced by new ones. If we follow Ribot in taking change to be essential to consciousness, we would expect unprojected consciousness to be continually undergoing such change. This does not mean that the changes can be noticed, because if they were they would have obtruded on attention. At most we may be able to tell in retrospect of their occurrence, but our ability to do this is circumscribed by the fact that at no time are these changes etched on our memories as a result of our having paid attention to them. In this connection I refer the reader to Ryle's sense (*e*) of conscious.[1] He mentions the case of a person being unconscious of the sensations in his blistered heel, because his mind is fully taken up with a heated dispute. Ryle's point is that in this sense 'to be unconscious of' means 'not to heed'. The point I wish to add is that when eventually the pain in the blistered heel is noticed its presence need not come as a complete surprise. The person may recollect that he had after all been dimly aware of it all along. It is this form of awareness to which I am referring when I claim that the elements of unprojected consciousness are elements of awareness. If they were not, there would be no justification in including them in consciousness – unprojected or otherwise. These considerations give us a sufficient basis for rejecting the view that awareness is always linked with noticing and attending.

In fact the very category 'unprojected consciousness' stands as a refutation of the idea that every state of awareness is *ipso facto*, a state receiving attention, and so if my arguments in favour of the recognition of an unprojected consciousness are sound, they are at the same time arguments against the view that an awareness is necessarily an object of attention.

I have up to this point attempted to show that the mere existence of unprojected consciousness is a *sine qua non* of attention. But as far as the *nature* of the unprojected consciousness is concerned, that has been treated as irrelevant. As a foil, unprojected consciousness need be merely other, with its elements having no particular relationship to the object of attention. I shall now try to show that unprojected consciousness is much more than a mere foil to attention.

2. UNPROJECTED CONSCIOUSNESS AND INTERROGATIVE ATTENTION

[3] In the last chapter I distinguished three varieties of attention – interrogative, executive, and unordered, attention. I also accepted the contention that there were degrees of attention. I now wish to argue that the different forms of attention are constituted by the different possible ways in which the elements of unprojected consciousness can be in relation with the object of attention.

Unordered attention defines the lower limit of attention. Hamilton, it will be remembered,[2] even doubted whether it deserved the

---

[1] See above, p. 42.   [2] See above, p. 95.

name. Let us take as an instance of unordered attention the catching of an eye by a sudden movement. It needs no argument to show that in that case the question of what elements make up unprojected consciousness at the time would be quite irrelevant. My attention could be explicated without any reference to the content of unprojected consciousness. In unordered attention, therefore, we have a form of attention in which the relation between the object of attention and unprojected consciousness is one of mere juxtaposition.

We get a very different picture when we come to interrogative attention: the attention we pay when we are on the *qui vive* for something. Let us take the case of a search as an example of interrogative attention. I shall confine what I have to say to the notion of a search in the literal sense, although it will also apply with some modification to the notion of a search in the metaphorical sense; i.e. searching for an answer to a problem. For attention to be interrogative it is not necessary for the attender to have a clear idea of what he is looking for. The idea does not even have to be clear enough for him to recognize what he is looking for when he comes across it. Such attention does not have its success guaranteed. But if the attender can say absolutely nothing about what he is looking for, it can be denied that his attention is interrogative. However, the fact that the attender can give a rough indication of the object of his search is not due to the fact that the object of the search is also the object of attention at the time of the search. The object of the search is 'missing' as it were, and if the attender were to attend to the 'missing' object he would be thinking about finding as opposed to being actively engaged in looking. The actual object of attention during the search must be taken to be either the searching activity itself, or the places that are consecutively searched. In addition to these two aspects of searching, there is a third that is of crucial importance, and that concerns the preparedness of the searcher. No one is likely to deny that the manner in which we go about a search can be affected by our state of preparedness. It is usual, for instance, for the searcher to have beliefs about the place to search, expectations about the probability of success, and so forth. These factors will determine where he looks, how hard he looks, how thoroughly he looks, how long he perseveres with the search, and finally what things he notices during the course of the search. Of these various factors that go to make up the attender's preparedness there is one of particular significance. The attender may have some idea of the state of affairs that would constitute the successful termination of the search. In order words, he may have a mental picture of the scene in which he comes across the thing he is searching for. This picture he may have obtained from memories, or he may have constructed it – it all depends on the circumstances of the search. Such an idea can play an important part in determining the manner in which the search is carried out, and in its absence the searching activity could be expected to take a different form. Moreover, it will partly determine the things we do and the things we do not notice while searching. Because of it we might notice some things we might otherwise have missed, and miss other things we might otherwise have noticed. Since such an idea will predispose us to notice certain sorts of things and overlook others, I shall refer to it as a 'guiding' idea. We may look upon a guiding idea as a partial filter that lets through those 'noticings' that are germane to the search, and that at the same time keeps down the number of extraneous 'noticings'. Equally importantly, if the guiding idea is on the wrong track it will actually make the attender overlook something that is relevant to the search – including in the extreme case the actual object of the search itself.

Now this guiding idea cannot itself be conceived of as the object of attention during the search. Were it to become so, instead of prosecuting the search the attender would at best be engaged in planning a search, and at worst he would be merely distracted by an idea. The question now arises: 'If the guiding idea cannot be the object of attention while the search is under way, in what manner can it be a factor influencing the search?' The suggestion could be made that the guiding idea could only influence the search if at some prior time it had been explicitly an object of attention in the preparatory act of planning the search. Its effectiveness could then be put down to the fact that the idea had not been forgotten. But I do not think this suggestion will do. We can say of someone that he has not forgotten an idea if he is able to recall it when he wants to. But in the sense in which he remembers the idea in the intervening period, we are describing nothing but a disposition. The idea is then in no sense actual until it is expressed in an act of recall. But that is not the sense in which a governing idea influences a search. It cannot be thought of as an idea in the dispositional sense here. It can only have an effect – make its presence felt – by being somehow actual at the time. The idea is 'alive' in the search. Thus a description of it in dispositional terms would miss the point. What we would want to say about such a guiding idea, it seems to me, is adequately represented by the description of it as an element of unprojected consciousness. From this standpoint it would be correct to describe the idea as actual at the time it was influencing the search, and it would also be true to say that it was not itself the object of attention at the time. Furthermore, it would also account for the fact that it is frequently the case that one does not realize that a guiding idea is influencing a search, and it can be a surprise to make the discovery. In this respect the guiding idea behaves like a typical element of unprojected consciousness: its presence is determined in retrospect, either because something makes me realize this myself, or because it is pointed out to me by another.

The sense in which unprojected consciousness may contain ideational elements can be brought out by the following example. People, when they have something on their minds, are sometimes heard to express a thought out aloud when they are speaking to themselves. When this happens there are two things the person might not realize. He might not realize that he expressed his thought out aloud, or he might not realize that he uttered the thought even to himself. Thus, when his utterance is brought to his notice, he might admit that that was what he was thinking, but agree that he had not been aware of making an audible utterance, or he might say that now that it is mentioned he does vaguely recall having had the thought but that if left to himself he would not have numbered it among his thoughts at the time. The latter sort of case is one in which the thought would be an element of unprojected consciousness.

It can happen that in the middle of a search one forgets what one is looking for. What, in terms of the analysis offered here, can be said to have been forgotten? Since the object of the search has been reasoned not to be the object of attention at the time, it cannot be *that* that has passed out of consciousness. Moreover, it has not been argued that the object of the search is represented in unprojected consciousness. Thus the only possibility apparently left open is that the forgetting must be understood dispositionally. The searcher can then be said to have forgotten what he was looking for, either when he stops searching, or when he would fail to recognize the object of his search when he came across it. Now there are obvious objections to analysing the forgetting in this way. All sorts of other reasons could explain why the searcher stops searching, or fails to recognize the object of his search. Some of these reasons would be connected with the searcher's state of preparedness, which I have already discussed. But that is not the point. The point is that the searcher himself would not reach the conclusion that he had forgotten what he was looking for because he observes that he has stopped looking, or has realized that he would not know what would constitute 'finding' in the circumstances. He would realize that he had forgotten because something would have 'gone out of mind'. We can make sense of this happening, I suggest, in terms of the searcher's loss of the idea guiding his search. This we could then explain by saying that the guiding idea had ceased to be an element of his unprojected consciousness. This element having passed out of unprojected consciousness would not itself be noticed, but it could cause one to notice that one had forgotten what one was looking for.

It would be helpful to illustrate some of the points arising out of my analysis with a quotation from Sartre's *Being and Nothingness*. I have in mind the example Sartre gives of himself looking for his friend Pierre in a café. His description of the experience is an acute phenomenological analysis of attention.

'I have an appointment with Pierre at four o'clock. I arrive at the café a quarter of an hour late. Pierre is always punctual. Will he have waited for me? I look at the room, the patrons, and I say, "He is not here." Is there an intuition of Pierre's absence, or does negation indeed enter in only with judgement? At first sight it seems absurd to speak here of intuition since to be exact there could not be an intuition of *nothing* and since the absence of Pierre is this nothing. Popular consciousness, however, bears witness to this intuition. Do we not say, for example, "I suddenly saw that he was not there." Is this just a matter of misplacing the negation? Let us look a little closer.

'It is certain that the café by itself with its patrons, its tables, its booths, its mirrors, its light, its smoky atmosphere, and the sounds of voices, rattling saucers, and footsteps which fill it – the café is a fullness of being. And all the intuitions of detail which I can have are filled by these odours, these sounds, these colors, all phenomena which have a transphenomenal being. Similarly Pierre's actual presence in a place which I do not know is also a plenitude of being. We seem to have found fullness everywhere. But we must observe that in perception there is always the construction of a figure on a ground. No one object, no group of objects is especially designed to be organized as specifically either ground or figure; all depends on the direction of my attention. When I enter this café to search for Pierre, there is formed a synthetic organization of all the objects in the café, on the ground of which Pierre is given as about to appear. This organization of the café as the ground is an original nihilation. Each element of the setting, a person, a table, a chair, attempts to isolate itself, to lift itself upon the ground constituted by the totality of the other objects, only to fall back once more into the undifferentiation of this ground; it melts into the ground. For the ground is that which is seen only in addition, that which is the object of a purely marginal attention. Thus the original nihilation of all the figures which appear and are swallowed up in the total neutrality of a *ground* is the necessary condition for the appearance of the principal figure, which is here the person of Pierre. This nihilation is given to my intuition; I am witness to the successive disappearances of all the objects which I look at – in particular of the faces, which detain me for an instant (Could this be Pierre?) and which as quickly decompose precisely because they "are not" the face of Pierre. Nevertheless if I should finally discover Pierre, my intuition would be filled by a solid element, I should be suddenly arrested by his face and the whole café would organize itself around him as a discrete presence.

'But now Pierre is not here. This does not mean that I discover his absence in some precise spot in the establishment. In fact Pierre is absent from the *whole* café; his absence fixes the café in its evanescence; the café remains *ground*; it persists in offering itself as an undifferentiated totality to my only marginal attention; it slips into the background; it pursues its nihilation. Only it makes itself ground for a determined figure; it carries the figure everywhere in front of it, presents the figure everywhere to me. This figure which slips constantly between my look and the solid, real objects of the café is precisely a perpetual disappearance; it is Pierre raising himself as nothingness on the ground of the nihilation of the café. So that what is offered to intuition is a flickering of nothingness; it is the nothingness of the ground, the nihilation of which summons and demands the appearance of the figure, and it is the figure – the nothingness which slips as a *nothing* to the surface of the ground. It serves as a foundation for the judgement – "Pierre is not here." It is in fact the intuitive apprehension of a double nihilation. To be sure, Pierre's absence supposes an original relation between me and this café; there is an infinity of people who are without any relation with this café for want of a real expectation which establishes their absence. But, to be exact, I myself expected to see Pierre, and my expectation has caused the absence of Pierre *to happen* as a real event concerning this café. It is an objective fact at present that I have *discovered* this absence, and it presents itself as a synthetic relation between Pierre and the setting in which I am looking for him. Pierre absent haunts this café and is the condition of its self-nihilating organization as ground.'[1]

This example brings out very well the point that the manner in which Sartre pays attention to the café is determined by his objective, which is to find Pierre. Everything in the café assumes the character of a background to a non-existent foreground. Nothing in the café is seen in its own right with a being of its own. How completely different this is from the attention the scene in the café would have received, had Sartre not been looking for someone. The preparedness to find Pierre directs Sartre's attention to certain types of 'noticing' and this affects not only what is seen of the café but the way it is seen. It may be that he has in mind a certain image of what Pierre might be looking like and how he might be seated. He would then be looking for that state of affairs, and nothing that did not 'gell' with that image would be the focus of attention. But in those circumstances it would be the search for Pierre and not the image of him that would be the object of attention. The image will guide the search, but it will do so as an element of unprojected consciousness.

It can now be suggested that those philosophers who would as a matter of principle demand a dispositional analysis of the preparedness involved in interrogative attention would do so because they do not have a concept of unprojected consciousness to help them account for those mental factors that quite clearly are not themselves objects of attention. Thus, when Ryle rejects the idea that each of our acts is preceded by a bit of mental rehearsing, he does so because he has no evidence of attending to any such mental rehearsing before acting.[2] He is, we can now see, quite right: there is no such object of attention. However, that does not establish that there are no concomitant mental occurrences playing their part in the overt action. The concept of an unprojected conscious-

[1] Jean-Paul Sartre, *Being and Nothingness*, tr. H. E. Barnes (London, 1957), pp. 9–10.
[2] Ryle, *The Concept of Mind*, pp. 29–32.

ness allows us to admit their existence while at the same time agreeing that at the time of acting nothing but the action holds the attention of the agent. It also nicely explains why Ryle should have claimed that there is no such thing as introspection, but that what seems to be introspection is in reality always retrospection.[1] If there were no unprojected consciousness and every element of experience had to be an object of attention, then it would follow that a seemingly introspected element *had* to be thought of as an earlier object of attention which was simply being recalled. But if we take unprojected consciousness into account we are not forced to say that the 'retrospected' element had to belong to the past. On the contrary, all that will have happened is that its relationship with the other elements will have been altered.

Another point to be noted is that Sartre's account backs up my contention that it is the nature of attention to polarize consciousness into a foreground and a background. When attention is frustrated, as in the above example, an incipient process of division of the field of consciousness into figure and ground irresistibly occurs, but it breaks up before it forms.

[4] I come now to the question of whether it is ever possible to attend to more than one object at a time. We have seen how Hamilton, Ribot, and James agree that the natural tendency of attention is to 'narrow' or 'concentrate' the area of awareness. It is natural, and acceptable, for a person to excuse his failure to pay attention on the ground that he was forced to pay attention to too many different things at once. No one could offer as an excuse for his failure to pay attention the fact that he had only one thing at the time to which to pay attention. If it were not true that the restriction of attention was vital to its successful operation, we would not be able to explain how it was possible to have our attention distracted. For if we could equally well increase the number of things we attend to without our attention to any of the things suffering as a result, we would not be 'distracted' by the new things that had been drawn into attention. The facts of the matter seem plain enough, and I shall follow Hamilton in describing the systematization of these facts as 'the law of limitation'.

'This law is, that the greater the number of objects to which our consciousness is simultaneously extended, the smaller is the intensity

1 *Ibid.*, pp. 163–7.

with which it is able to consider each, and consequently, the less vivid and distinct will be the information it obtains of the several subjects.'[1]

Hamilton's law rests on the assumption that it is possible to pay attention to more than one thing at a time, and this enables a plausible explanation to be given of the existence of degrees of attention: the larger the number of things holding attention which are not connected, the smaller the degree of attention which is given to each. Quite apart from these aspects of the matter, however, Hamilton's law of limitation expresses well the fact that the more restricted, or narrowed, attention is, the more efficient it is. Logically, of course, the limit of such restriction is the case in which attention is paid to but a single object at a time. Those of Hamilton's contemporaries who, like Stewart, have argued against him that it is not possible to attend to more than one object at a time have no doubt been impressed by this fact. It has led to the belief that paying attention to a single thing is the paradigmatic case of paying attention. This belief has persuaded Stewart and others that if, in two instances, attention were narrowed down to a single object, the instances could not be concurrent: i.e. it would be impossible, by definition, to attend to both objects at once.

Many examples seem to bear out this contention. There is the well-known experience of trying to follow two separate conversations at once. What happens is that our attention 'jumps' from one conversation to the other, and we catch a phrase from this discussion and a point from that. We also find a tendency for attention to settle on one of the conversations at the expense of the other, so that we follow and understand more of the one than the other. Here we have an example of conflicting claims upon attention, and there is no doubt that it is a common occurrence to find claims on attention conflicting with one another in this way. But it is one thing for Stewart and others to be right in claiming that there are some cases of conflict of attention, and quite another matter for them to claim that all cases of attending to more than one thing at once are cases of a conflict of attention.

At first sight it looks as though the controversy could be settled by empirical means. It soon becomes obvious, however, that any counter-examples to the hypothesis that we only attend to one thing at a time can be nullified by the claim that even though we

[1] Bowen, *The Metaphysics of Sir William Hamilton*, p. 159.

are not aware of the fact, our attention nevertheless switches (too rapidly to notice) from the one object to the other. The rapidity of the movement from one object to the other would create the illusion that both objects were receiving continuous simultaneous attention; much as a spinning disc of different coloured segments gives the illusion of having one uniform colour. This is a classical case of a conceptual difference being mistaken for an empirical one.

The dispute is, I believe, a conceptual one, but it is also a sterile dispute. It cannot be settled unless and until we know what it means 'to attend to one thing at a time'. We need to know what 'one thing' is, before we know what the disagreement is about. And, I maintain, as soon as we know what constitutes 'one thing' we shall find that there is nothing left to dispute. Let us, therefore, enquire what it means to talk about *an* object of attention. How do we know that we are attending to one object and not several? The artificiality of this question can be brought out most forcibly by considering Sartre's example, in which the object of attention is the interior of a café. We can think of the café as *one* object, but the café in fact comprises a very large number of isolable objects. As Sartre makes quite explicit, the attender is aware of 'its patrons, its tables, its booths, its mirrors, its light, its smoky atmosphere, and the sound of voices, rattling saucers, and footsteps which fill it'. Because the attender is paying attention, all these things are 'taken in'. But in a sense none of them *are objects* of attention. If, afterwards, the attender were asked to say what had been going on in the café, he might have only a hazy idea. He had been paying attention to the café, but not paying attention to everything he saw or heard in the café. He was not, in fact, paying attention to anything in the café at all! As Sartre correctly observes, it was as though the café scene were a 'ground' for a nonexistent figure. That is, it is as though attention were in search of its object of attention. Sartre makes this clear too. He says, 'If I should finally discover Pierre, my intuition would be filled by a solid element, I should be suddenly arrested by his face and the whole café would organize itself around him as a discrete presence.' Were that to happen, we would be in no doubt as to what the object of attention was – Pierre.

Sartre's statement that everything in the café would 'organize around' the object of attention is most important. Whatever it be that our consciousness 'organizes around' is that to which we are said to be attending. But even if Pierre had become the object of attention, what constitutes 'Pierre' would be a number of different things. Pierre is still a complex object. Would that preclude him from being the object of attention? Surely it would be quite unrealistic to claim that Pierre could not be an object of attention on the ground that only the 'ultimate simples' of which he is composed (whatever that might mean) could be so regarded. There might be a variety of things I notice about Pierre as soon as I spot him. Are these features and not Pierre the object of my attention? And if they are, must I have noticed them one after another? We only need raise these questions to see that they presuppose putting a false precision on the whole matter.

A simpler example than Sartre's clinches the argument. Suppose we were asked what our several objects of attention are in relation to the appearance of the printed page before our eyes. Can we attend to several words simultaneously, or are we limited to one word, or perhaps one letter, at a time? If we can take in several words at a glance, would they be our object of attention? If so, would that mean that we had paid attention to only one thing, or several things at once? Or would it mean that we had successively attended to each individual letter? These artificial questions presuppose, I suggest, that there are such things as atomic objects, such that we could make decisions as to what is one object or another, quite irrespective of the purposes of the attender. We need only remind ourselves, however, how different the page must appear to an attender who is a proof-reader looking for misprints from its appearance to the average reader trying to follow the sense of the argument. The proof-reader might treat syllables as the objects of attention, while the ordinary reader might treat meaningful groups of words as objects of attention. Unless we know the purpose behind the attention, we cannot say what should be taken as the object of attention. The object of attention is attender-relative.

[5] Interrogative attention is typically the attention manifested in problem-solving. In a problem-solving context there may be a number of factors that are thought to be relevant to the solution of the problem. When these simultaneously occupy attention there is no question of the investigator being distracted by them. He will only feel distracted by things that have no relation to the object of enquiry. Let us define as a 'relevancy system' the sum of those considerations that are taken by the attender to have a bearing on

his investigative task. A 'divided attention' can then be said to be one in which the objects of attention do not both belong to a reigning relevancy system. When that happens we have a conflict between objects of attention. It should not be overlooked that there is an upper limit to attention which is reached even when one's mind is wholly occupied with a single relevancy system. This occurs when the relevancy system is too complex for all the considerations to be kept before the mind at once. Naturally the limit of attentive tolerance beyond which there is a breakdown of attention will vary from person to person.

The notion of a relevancy system enables us to solve the problem of whether or not it is possible to pay attention to two or more objects of attention simultaneously. When two objects of attention compete for the subject's attention they cannot belong to the same relevancy system. In that case we can only attend to the one at the expense of the other.

To put it differently let us suppose that x is the object of attention of relevancy system S and y that of S'. Now if by paying attention to x consciousness of necessity 'organizes around' x, then y can only become the object of attention by consciousness 'organizing around' y. But it can only do that by destroying its organization around x; i.e. by altering the reigning relevancy system from S to S'. If we find a further object of attention z to which attention may be paid without altering the relevancy system reigning at the time, then z is in no sense a rival object of attention. Whether we would wish to say that in those circumstances attention was being paid to two objects at once, say x and z, or whether we would wish to say that x and z are elements of a compound object of attention seems to me to be a purely terminological question. If a relevancy system were defined as having a single object of attention, we would have opted for the 'compound object' description. However, I see no advantage in that, and to suit myself I shall take the position that we may have more than one object of attention at a time provided they belong to a single relevancy system.

In view of the complexity of the relationship between unprojected consciousness and object of attention in interrogative attention, it is possible to give a more satisfactory interpretation of Hamilton's law of limitation than the one he gives. The degree of intensity of attention must no longer be correlated in simple inverse proportion to the number of objects receiving attention. We must not take it that attention to one object will be n times greater than attention to n objects. The argument of this chapter points to the conclusion that the greater the connectedness between unprojected consciousness and attention, the greater the degree of attention. Interrogative attention is at its maximum when unprojected consciousness and object of attention form a single relevancy system. From this point of view, the complexity of the relevancy system – provided it is not over-complex – is no distraction to attention. On the contrary, the greater the extent to which unprojected consciousness is drawn into the relevancy system the greater will be the concentration of attention. The threat to attention from extraneous elements of unprojected consciousness detaching themselves from unprojected consciousness and obtruding on attention will then be all but nonexistent.

[6] If my reasoning is on the right lines, we are in a position to correct a weakness in Ribot's theory of attention.[1] On his analysis, the effect of attention on consciousness is to suspend the change from one total temporary state to the next, i.e. each total temporary state is succeeded by one identical with itself during the period of attention. That hypothesis, together with the hypothesis that consciousness cannot long survive the suspension of change, entailed the conclusion that attention was a condition inimical to the normal life of consciousness. As against this position I have been arguing that attention has nothing to do with the suspension of change and therefore nothing to do, either, with producing a state of mono-ideism. The unity that comes about when attention is given is the unity of a system, and not the unity of a content. Attention is at its maximum when the elements of consciousness are related in a relevancy system, and not when their number is 'frozen'. Far from demanding the suspension of change, the relevancy system may in fact operate through the occurrence of changes in the elements of consciousness. Thus, if it were possible for change to be suspended, it could well turn out that we would want to say 'X has ceased to pay attention'.

Ribot in fact made a qualification to his theory, which showed his unease about maintaining that attention was a state of mono-ideism, and this qualification is certainly in the direction favouring the position I have suggested. 'Is attention a reduction to a sole and single state of consciousness?' he asks:

[1] See above, p. 84.

'No; for inward observation teaches us that it is only a *relative* monoideism; that is, it supposes the existence of a master-idea, drawing to itself all that relates to it, and nothing else, allowing associations to produce themselves only within very narrow limits, and on condition that they converge toward a common point. It drains for its own use – at least in the proportion possible – the entire cerebral activity.'[1]

This passage exhibits in embryonic form the relation between unprojected consciousness and object of attention that I have called a relevancy system. But the success of attention is not dependent upon eliminating the change from one state of consciousness to another: it is neither monoideism nor relative monoideism.

Possibly Ribot thought that attention did produce a state of monoideism, because he failed to distinguish, as I have done, between a single relevancy system and a single object of attention. I have already shown how easily one can be driven to the conclusion that maximal attention is achieved when only a single object engages attention. I have also argued that we should resist being driven in this direction. Ribot's position nicely illustrates the embarrassments to which it gives rise. There is, indeed, a unity of consciousness when attention is engaged, but the unity is the unity of a system, and not the unity of sheer identity, as Ribot seems to believe. The unity is achieved when, as Sartre puts it, consciousness 'organizes itself around' the object of attention; or as Ribot himself recognizes, when attention is determined by a 'master-idea'. These two ideas are not merely alternative ways of expressing the same thought. The object of attention around which consciousness organizes itself is not itself the 'master-idea'. The position is rather the reverse: the master-idea organizes consciousness around an object of attention. It is evident that the master-idea is none other than that idea in unprojected consciousness which at the time directs the particular instance of interrogative attention, in a way that has already been described.

This is a natural point at which to stop and summarize the conclusions that have been reached so far. I first used a form of transcendental argument to prove that we could not make sense of any form of attention without presupposing the existence of an unprojected consciousness that was not itself engaging attention. I then attempted to show that in the non-intellectual forms of

[1] Ribot, *The Psychology of Attention*, p. 10.

attention, which I have called unordered attention, there is relative separation between unprojected consciousness and object of attention. By contrast the discussion showed that interrogative attention was characterized by a functional inter-relation between unprojected consciousness and object of attention. It has been shown that the concept of 'an object of attention' must not be thought to have the implications of precision and freedom from vagueness which, in the literature, is taken for granted. Finally, I have contended that the connectedness or relatedness between the elements comprising unprojected consciousness and the object of attention must be looked upon as constituting a relevancy system. Attention is concentrated, on this view, when the elements of consciousness are ordered in a single relevancy system. Attention is diffused when its objects cannot be integrated within the reigning relevancy system.

A major implication of the argument is the conclusion that unprojected consciousness contains cognitive elements in addition to sensory ones. This follows from the assertion that unprojected consciousness may contain elements which I have referred to as master-ideas, and that in interrogative attention a number of its elements form a relevancy system together with the elements forming the object of attention. It can thus be appreciated how wrong it would be to look upon unprojected consciousness as a residue of unattended sensory experience.

Some of the ideas advanced in this chapter receive the support of an obscure nineteenth-century writer quoted with approval by James in his *The Principles of Psychology*. The following is the passage in question:

'At every instant of conscious thought there is a certain sum of perceptions, or reflections, or both together, present, and together constituting one whole state of apprehension. Of this some definite portion may be far more distinct than all the rest; and the rest be in consequence proportionably vague, even to the limit of obliteration. But still, within this limit, the most dim shade of perception enters into, and in some infinitesimal degree modifies, the whole existing state. This state, will thus be in some way modified by any sensation or emotion, or act of distinct attention, that may give prominence to any part of it; so that the actual result is capable of the utmost variation, according to the person or the occasion. . . . To any portion of the entire scope here described there may be a special direction of the attention, and this special direction is recognized as strictly what is *recognized* as the idea present to the mind. This idea is evidently not commensurate with the entire state of apprehension, and much perplexity has arisen from not observing this fact. However deeply we may suppose the attention to be engaged by any thought, any considerable alteration of the surrounding phenomena would still be perceived; the most abstruse demonstration in this room would not prevent a listener, however absorbed, from noticing the sudden extinction of the lights. Our mental states have always an *essential unity*, such that each state of apprehension, however variously compounded, is a single whole, of which every component is, therefore, strictly apprehended (so far as it is apprehended) as a part. Such is the elementary basis from which all our intellectual operations commence.'[1]

3. UNPROJECTED CONSCIOUSNESS AND EXECUTIVE ATTENTION

[7] I shall now discuss the relation between unprojected consciousness and object of attention at an entirely different level, and this concerns the connection between the two as found in executive attention. I argue that we are able to exercise control over our attention, in the manner that we do, through the control we exercise over our activities. The next step in the argument is that we exercise control over our activities through the control we have over our 'bodily doings'.[2] I then seek to establish that our kinaesthetic sensations give us our ability to control our 'bodily doings'. Finally, I argue that the kinaesthetic sensations performing this function must belong to unprojected consciousness. In sum, therefore, the argument is that executive attention is dependent upon kinaesthetic sensation, and thereby dependent upon

---

[1] Jas. Wills, 'Accidental Association', *Transactions of the Royal Irish Academy*, Vol. XXI, part 1 (1846), also quoted in: James, *Principles of Psychology*, Vol. I, p. 241.

[2] A word of caution needs to be given about the term 'bodily doing'. Since the investigation is at present concerned with consciousness as such, and not with its relation to the body, the term 'bodily doing' seems question-begging. It should be understood in the sense explained on p. 71 above. The description 'bodily doing' is really a third person description of a doing and as such is strictly ruled out on the *self-approach*. 'Bodily doings' should therefore be understood as those of our 'doings' that another person would describe as bodily. The connection between consciousness and the body will be examined in the final chapter.

unprojected consciousness. The implication of this argument is that the operation of executive attention itself produces some of the elements of unprojected consciousness. In other words, it is shown that even if there were no independently existing unprojected consciousness to act as a foil to attention, the operation of attention in this instance creates its own unprojected consciousness.

I try to establish this thesis first of all in the case of those forms of attention that are necessarily related to 'bodily doings'. I then try to show that the thesis also covers that form of attention that seems to be logically unrelated to bodily doings; namely, reflection.

Ribot is interested in the part played by muscular activity in attention, and it will be useful to begin with a consideration of his view. He sets out his position as follows:

'Are the movements of the face, the body, and the limbs, and the respiratory modifications that accompany attention, simply effects, outward marks, as is usually supposed? Or, are they, on the contrary, *the necessary conditions, the constituent elements, the indispensable factors of attention*? Without hesitation we accept the second thesis. Totally suppress movements, and you totally suppress attention.

'The fundamental role of the movements in attention is, to *maintain* the appropriate state of consciousness and to *reinforce* it.'[1]

In his view the muscles perform their function in attention through the mechanism of *inhibition*: 'Attention, accordingly, means concentration and inhibition of movements. Distraction means diffusion of movements.'[2]

Once again it is possible to turn Ribot's point about physical movement into a conceptual point about a type of activity, namely the activity that I have given the name of 'bodily activity'.[3] We may then understand the thesis as one which maintains that we pay attention by controlling our bodily activities. This is the thesis I propose to examine in the case of executive attention.

We engage in executive attention by bringing parts of our bodies (not excluding the whole) into play, in order to accomplish some task or other. Now, executive attention may be called for either in a situation in which it would be best to keep still (keeping an eye on a

---

[1] Ribot, *The Psychology of Attention*, p. 25.
[2] *Ibid.*, p. 53.
[3] See above, p. 71.

remote object) or in a situation in which it would be best – even essential – to make certain movements (watching a football match). Ribot does seem to be thinking of the first situation to the exclusion of the second, for in the first but not the second it is quite true to say that it is necessary to inhibit movement if we are successfully to attend. Clearly the claim that movement is inhibited in attention is too stringent. However, the claim can be modified by being turned into one specifying that any movement of the body *interfering* with the attentive activity must be inhibited. This would make it possible for us to say that inhibition of movement occurs even in such tasks as threading a needle, without our being committed to the absurdity that one can thread a needle without making any bodily movement.

Ribot's point can best be appreciated by reverting to the case of sense-organ attention.[1] I argued that we engage in sense-organ activity in a spontaneous fashion. That is to say, of such activities as 'looking about', it is not always the case that a reason can be given for one's looking about. On many occasions the proper answer to give to the question, 'Why are you looking about?' is 'I have no reason, I just am.' This is the point I take Alexander Bain to have been making when he asserted: 'Movement precedes sensation, and is at the outset independent of any stimulus from without.'[2] Bain called such movements 'spontaneous', and if we substitute the notion of activity for movement we arrive at the conception of spontaneous bodily activities. It is these activities that have to be disciplined and subordinated when executive attention occurs, and this process of discipline and subordination is covered by what Ribot calls 'inhibition'. This interpretation of Ribot's position would still enable us to understand why he felt that attention was 'unnatural'. When spontaneous bodily activities are interrupted during executive attention the unwanted activities have to be held in check. This inhibition of movement requires muscular effort, and this effort is greater than that required to sustain the activities when they are spontaneous. In short, the exercise of spontaneous bodily activity is 'easier' than is the inhibition associated with executive attention, and this leads to a desire on the part of the attender to break off attention and return to the 'easier' condition at the earliest opportunity. In respect of executive attention Ribot is right to maintain, therefore, that attention is an unnatural condi-

[1] See above, p. 85.
[2] A. Bain, *The Senses and the Intellect* (London, 1855), p. 67.

tion. However, this does not give him an entitlement to make the same claim in respect of unordered attention.

I have been reinterpreting Ribot's theory of physical movement in terms of a theory of action. For 'movement' I have substituted 'bodily activity', for 'inhibition' I have substituted 'keeping in check' these activities. It now remains for me to give a translation of 'muscular movement'. That which from an observer's standpoint is a muscular movement, is from the subject's standpoint a kinaesthetic sensation. Our kinaesthetic sensations are our mode of sensing our own movements. Even more important, they are our means of exercising control over our movements.

Many of the skills that involve the use of instruments can only be practised successfully when executive attention is bestowed upon them. We need only think of the skills of the surgeon, of the maker of precision instruments, of the musician, and of the architect, to name a few. All these skills demand a high degree of coordination of movement, and an extreme sensitivity of movement to perception. Expertise in these matters is denied those who lack the very finest control over their movements. Now the important thing to realize is that it is not attention as such that gives us this fine control over our movements. A person can have great powers of attention, but lack the necessary manipulative skill. This manipulative skill is dependent on kinaesthetic sensation. Our kinaesthetic sensations give us the fine control over our movements that are essential to these sophisticated skills. (Needless to say, the value of kinaesthetic sensation is by no means confined to superior skills.)

It is also clear that when performing a manipulative task that requires great skill we do not consult our kinaesthetic sensations as we might consult a scientific instrument registering an effect, in order to determine the strength and direction of one of our movements. On the contrary we take our kinaesthetic sensations for granted. They give us control over our movements without our having to pay attention to them. All our attention can be given to the actual manipulation that has to be brought off. Were we in the circumstances to turn our attention to our kinaesthetic sensations, that would distract us from the proper object of attention; namely, the bringing about of a certain result. Indeed it would be true to say that one who in the circumstances turned his attention to his kinaesthetic sensations would by so doing be revealing his lack of confidence in his ability; revealing even that he was a novice at the

126   THE SUBJECT OF CONSCIOUSNESS

job. In confirmation of this we need look no further than at the case
of the golfer who gives his attention to his kinaesthetic sensations
during his swing, instead of giving his attention to his shot: his
doing so throws him off his whole performance.

But, another way of saying that the kinaesthetic sensations
accompanying an exercise of skill and guiding it must not themselves be the object of attention at the time is to say that they belong
to unprojected consciousness. Those elements of unprojected consciousness that are the kinaesthetic sensations relevant to the
practice of a skill have a role to play in its successful performance.
They are necessary elements of the relevancy system linking unprojected consciousness and object of attention. Without them there
could be no such thing as executive attention. We reach the
conclusion, therefore, that executive attention is a form of attention
in which it is not possible for unprojected consciousness to be
merely the foil to attention. On the contrary, it is a form of attention
which cannot be actualized without its bringing into existence
certain elements in unprojected consciousness that are necessary to
its actualization. Moreover, the role played by these elements is
involved in the very notion of executive attention. From this standpoint it can no longer be looked upon as a happy accident that an
unprojected consciousness happens to be available as a foil to
attention. We now see that even if there had been no independent
unprojected consciousness, executive attention would still have
brought its own unprojected consciousness along with it. This
means that attention not only produces an unprojected consciousness by the negative method of excluding certain elements from the
forefront of consciousness, but also produces unprojected consciousness in a positive manner through the dynamics of executive
attention itself. If successful, the argument has established the
interdependence of unprojected consciousness and its complement.

[8] Since Ribot has referred to the physical signs of attention –
respiratory modifications, frowning, and so forth – it will avoid
confusion if at this point something is said about the physiological
aspects of attention.

The study of attention from the physiological point of view has
revealed other bodily changes besides the changes in muscular
activity with which I have been dealing. It is claimed, for instance,
that during attention the blood supply to the brain increases. It has
also been suggested that the mysterious alpha-waves in the brain

have a connection with attention.[1] Putative changes of this sort must be distinguished from the changes that take place in muscle activity, because the latter sort of changes are subject to voluntary control, while the former are not (except indirectly). Those bodily changes, the occurrence of which are not directly subject to the control of our will, I shall call *processes*. By contrast the bodily changes that *are* subject to our will, I shall call *activities*. It must be appreciated that bodily changes do not need to be willed in order for them to be activities. They are activities in virtue of the fact that they *can* be willed.

A minor difficulty exists in that it can legitimately be claimed that the ability to contract muscles at will is a sophisticated performance, and that what we normally *will* are movements of our bodies, and not contractions of our muscles. For instance I will that my arm should go up: I do not will the contraction of the muscles which must occur if my arm is to go up. I, in all probability, do not even know what these muscles are. That is to say, I know how to move parts of my body, but I do not necessarily know how to move the relevant muscles. I know how to move my eyes about, but I need know nothing of the existence of the six muscles by means of which the eye movements are effected. This point can be admitted without further ado.[2] We need only remember that when muscle activity is said to be voluntary, what is meant is that certain movements can be performed at will only when the relevant striated muscles are brought into play. Those muscular changes that cannot be innervated by willing are to be excluded from the class of voluntary muscular activities. The muscles for increasing the tension of the tympanum in the ear belong to this latter category. The 'smooth' muscles of the body, and the cardiac muscle are the main types of muscle over which we cannot (normally) exert direct control.

What I call bodily processes are such things as the beat of the heart, digestive action, etc. These processes are governed by the autonomous nervous system, and they go on whether we are conscious of them or not, or indeed whether we are conscious or not.

[1] The EEG record of the electrical activity of the brain reveals a characteristic alpha-rhythm while the subject is not paying attention to anything, but as soon as he attends the alpha-wave disappears. See, W. G. Walter, *The Living Brain* (Pelican, 1963).

[2] For an argument to the effect that we will certain muscular movements primarily and not our limbs, see, C. A. Campbell 'Self-Activity and Its Modes', *Contemporary British Philosophy*, ed. H. D. Lewis (London, 1956).

Although it is possible to exercise some degree of voluntary control over some of these processes, this can only be done indirectly. I can, for instance, make my heart beat faster, but I cannot do it by simply willing my heart to beat faster. I have to use my knowledge that exertion makes the heart beat faster, and first exert myself by making a movement I *can* will. My heart will then beat faster. The difference between the way I raise my arm on willing it, and the way I make my heart beat faster, is the measure of the difference between my control over my bodily activities, and my control over bodily processes. What is of philosophical interest is the connection between bodily activity and attention, and this is of interest only because we seem to have discovered a conceptual link between the two. The connection between attention and bodily process, on the other hand, is contingent. We would not be obliged to alter our concept of attention if it were found that there was no increase of blood to the brain during attention, or that alpha-waves had nothing to do with it either.

4. THE LOGICAL DEPENDENCE OF MENTAL IMAGES AND THOUGHTS ON BODILY ACTIVITY

[9] Ribot's theory that attention is effected by muscular inhibition is not confined to the type of attention we have been considering. He claims that the theory is equally true of another form of attention – inner directed attention – which he calls 'reflection'. Now the dependence of executive attention on muscular activity has been pretty conclusively established. But the idea that muscular activity is the 'indispensable factor' in reflection is much more debatable – not to say paradoxical. How, one might ask, is muscular activity going to help a person to think attentively, or recall a name? It might, admittedly, facilitate attention if we lower our superior orbicular muscles (the muscle of reflection), but we would not deny that a person had thought, or recalled a name, on the ground that he had not lowered his brow at the time. After all, a man may get into the habit of scratching his head before he thinks, and the point could well be reached at which he is incapable of thinking if he is prevented from scratching his head. Nevertheless we would not on that account assert that there is a necessary connection between thinking and head-scratching. Even if it became universally true that head-scratching had to precede thinking, we would not deny that a person had thought simply because he had

not first scratched his head. Quite clearly if the theory of the dependence of reflection on muscular activity is to have any respectability, it must have more to offer than the above would suggest.

Of 'reflection' Ribot says, 'Images and ideas constitute its subject matter.' What he has to do, therefore, is establish a connection between muscular activity and the occurrence of images and ideas. His method of procedure is to use perception as a 'middle term' through which this connection is made. The link between muscular activity and perception has already been established. Ribot's theory hinges, therefore, on the nature of the connection that he tries to establish between perception and ideas and images. An attempt to establish the existence of such a connection was made by Alexander Bain, and Ribot quotes him in support of his position:

'"It does not seem plain, at first," wrote Bain, as early as the year 1855, "that the retention of an idea, an image, in the mind is the work of our voluntary muscles. What are the movements produced, when I conceive to myself a circle, or think of St. Paul's? We can answer this question only by supposing that the mental image occupies in the brain and the other parts of the nervous system the same place as the original sensation. As there is a muscular element in our sensations, particularly in those of the highest order – in touch, sight, and hearing – this element must, in some way or other, find its place in ideal sensation – recollection." Since the time that this passage was written, the question of the nature of images has been closely and profitably studied, and solved exactly as therein indicated. Whereas, to the earlier psychologists, an image or idea was a kind of phantom, without definite seat, existing "within the soul", differing from perception not in degree but in nature, resembling it "at most only as a portrait resembles its original", to physiological psychology, on the contrary, there is between perception and image identity of nature, identity of seat, and only a difference of degree. The image is not a photograph but a revival of the sensorial and motory elements that have built up the perception. In proportion as its intensity increases, it approaches more and more to the condition of its origination, and so tends to become an hallucination.'[1]

Such a passage clearly invites attack. Its assumption that sensations and images are located in the brain might be challenged; as

[1] Ribot, *The Psychology of Attention*, pp. 53–4.

might the assertion that there is only a difference of degree between perception and image. But that is not the point. The point is whether, in virtue of the alleged connections between mental imagery and perception, muscular activity plays the same part in both. Now in perception, muscular activity is concomitant with the perceiving. If the perception consists in my feeling the quality of a rug by rubbing my hand over it, the muscular activity bringing about the hand movement and the tactile sensations are concomitant. The theory that voluntary attention works through control of our muscular activity only makes sense on the assumption that perception and muscular activity are simultaneous. Unfortunately Ribot has not established that the connection, if any, between mental imagery and muscular activity likewise involves simultaneous occurrence. To make matters worse, the examples he gives suggest that on his view the muscular activity is *subsequent* to the existence of the image! He cites the examples of 'people who plunge head foremost into yawning chasms, through fear of falling into them' and of 'people who cut themselves with razors, through the very fear of cutting themselves'. Now these seem to me very bad examples indeed, for it can be debated whether any image need be present at all in the case of such fears, and furthermore if a person does throw himself from a height as a result of having the image of throwing himself from a height, the muscular activity bringing about the fall must occur *after* the image had occurred. Thus even if we grant Ribot his 'motory element' in imagery, this by itself does not establish that image and muscular activity are concurrent, and yet this step is crucial to his argument. Unless that can be demonstrated, it cannot be maintained that attention works through muscular activity in reflection, as it does in perception. It must be said that Ribot's argument simply fails. I shall, therefore, try to rescue his position by offering what I hope are better arguments for it.

[10] I align myself with psychologists such as Ribot and Bain, and philosophers such as Hobbes and Hume,[1] who stress the intimate connection between mental imagery and perception. The position I shall argue for consists of two claims. The first is that no one

[1] Hobbes for maintaining that imagination is but decaying sense, and Hume for maintaining that there is no idea without an antecedent impression. There is a problem for these empiricists as to whether this is an a priori truth or a matter of fact.

lacking the requisite sense modality can enjoy the corresponding form of mental imagery. Thus, no one lacking sight can have visual imagery, no one lacking hearing can have auditory imagery, and so on. The claim must be understood as denying a logical possibility. The second is that it is not possible to pay attention to our mental images without inhibiting spontaneous sense-organ activity. Thus, no one can give his attention to a visual image unless he ceases to engage in activities such as 'looking about', 'looking for' and 'looking at'. His eyes may remain open while he has the visual image, but their being open is not itself a sense-organ activity. Again, this must be understood as a denial of a logical possibility.

Persons, such as Bain, Ribot, and I, who make these two claims (either explicitly or by implication), I shall describe as adopting the 'sentient approach' to mental imagery. With this approach I shall contrast what I shall call the 'phantom approach'. I give it that name because it expresses the view of those who, in Bain's words, hold that the image is 'a kind of phantom without definite seat'. The phantom approach consists of a denial that there is a logical dependency of mental imagery on sense perception. Those espousing the phantom approach might be prepared to concede a contingent connection between the sense modality and the related form of imagery. They could therefore agree that a man without sight from birth might as an empirical fact not have any visual images, but they would insist that there is nothing logically impossible in the idea of such a man having a visual image. The same would be said *mutatis mutandis* of the other sense modalities.

It is worth bearing in mind that on the question of disembodied existence the phantom approach would leave open the logical possibility that a disembodied being could have mental imagery. Such a possibility is ruled out by the sentient approach. Thus the truth of one or the other of these conflicting claims would have a bearing on the intelligibility of the notion of a disembodied existence. The loss of mental imagery would constitute perhaps a decisive impoverishment of the consciousness of a disembodied being granted that sense perception would already have been conceded to be lacking.[1]

I begin by attacking the phantom approach, hoping in the process to clear the way for the sentient approach. The first point to notice is that the very notion of a mental image is dependent upon the notion of the corresponding experience. When a description is

[1] See below, pp. 218–9, where this issue is taken up.

given of an image, it is not ordinarily described *as* image. What is described is the thing which the image is an image of, and even when we wish to describe the image *qua* image we must resort to the language of perceived objects. Thus if we are dealing with a visual image, then the description will draw upon such concepts as 'look', 'perspective', 'colour', and 'shape'. But a person who had lacked the visual experience without which he could not be said to have these visual concepts in the full sense could not apply them to describe imagery, nor could he understand what was meant by imagery described in terms of them.

What I am saying amounts to this. The descriptions we give of our visual images of necessity make use of visual concepts. Now let us suppose that a man sightless from birth claims to have a visual image.[1] How can we ascertain whether his claim is true? Suppose we ask him to describe the image. There are two possibilities: (*a*) he may try but fail to give a description, or (*b*) he may in fact produce a description making use of visual concepts. If he cannot give a description, it seems to me we have every right to be sceptical about his claim that his image is visual. What, we may ask, makes him call it visual? What does he understand the word 'visual' to mean here? If (*b*) is the case, the position is different: sightless people can come to learn the correct use of visual words, such as 'red'; but correct use of the word 'red' does not entail that the user can see red or that he can see *simpliciter*. We have no guarantee, therefore, that when a man uses a visual term to describe his image, it must be a visual image he is describing.

The retort might be made that these are no more than difficulties of verification. We know that sightless people who have their sight restored cannot at first distinguish one geometrical shape from another by sight, in spite of being able to distinguish them by feel. Bearing this in mind, we are not entitled to transfer our doubts about the sightless man's description of his image into doubts about the possibility of his having a visual image. It is theoretically possible, according to this reasoning, for the man without sight to have a visual image without he or anyone else knowing that his image is *visual*. But this point raises many difficulties of the same order as those raised by the question whether a newborn infant sees what we see. If it is allowed that the phenomenal character of our perceptions is altered by our ability to pick out and recognize

---

[1] I shall from now on simply refer to a man as 'sightless', and take the qualification 'from birth' as read.

perceptual objects because of our possession of concepts, then it must be allowed that the phenomenal character of the alleged 'visual' image of the sightless man must be different from our own because no similar abilities and recognitional capacities are exercised in connection with it. Whatever the phenomenal character of his image we could still reasonably doubt that it could be visual. Other considerations, too, tell against this objection and these we shall come to shortly.

Perceptual concepts such as 'seeing' and 'hearing', entail the concepts of 'an organ of sight' and 'an organ of hearing'.[1] Let us continue to confine ourselves to sight. When we look at an object, the object of necessity appears from a certain perspective, determined by the location of our eyes. We see objects in a particular direction, and at a certain distance from our eyes. We see only an aspect of the object, visible from our particular perspective. We do not see, as it were, the object 'in the round' all at once. In other words, we cannot see an object from every perspective at once. That we are limited in this way is part of what we mean by 'seeing'. Now it is true also of a visual image that the description we give of it is logically similar to the description we give when we are seeing rather than imaging. As I have said, we describe the object of which the image is an image, and that means that we describe the object *as though it were being seen*. We would describe the object as though it were being seen from a certain perspective, and this entails the object's presenting a certain aspect, and being at a certain distance.[2] Not even in visual imagery can we entirely escape the limitations of perspectival appearance. The object as imaged presents an appearance from a position, in direction, at a distance, in the same way as does the object as seen.

The question arises: Can a person without sight satisfy these conditions for visual imagery? Or to put it another way: Would he be able to make sense of them? He certainly would have no visual *experience* of these perspectival characteristics, which visual perception and visual imagery have in common. I am not asserting that a sightless person lacks a spatial system, but only that he lacks an experience of perspective. He will have no experience of the real size of an object differing from its apparent size, nor of the characteristic

---

[1] See Shoemaker, *Self-Knowledge and Self-Identity*, ch. 5, where this point is convincingly argued.

[2] The question of the perspectival quality of the visual image must not be confused with the question of the location of the visual image itself. This is a separate question, which is dealt with in the next section.

distortions of shape that result from foreshortening. Further-more, I can have a visual image the phenomenal character of which is due to the fact that it is as if it were of an object I had seen out of the corner of my eye, or due to the fact that it is as if it were of an object the surface of which I was scanning with my eyes. The alleged image of a sightless person could not be an image with such a phenomenal character. In fact the images of a person without sight can have none of the characteristics associated with perspective that I have described. But in that case his alleged image will lack precisely the characteristics that make it *visual*.

The essence of my argument is that the concept of a visual image is logically dependent on the concept of seeing, and the latter, in turn, is logically dependent on the having of 'sight'. Its import is that a sightless person necessarily lacks the conditions necessary to the having of visual imagery. This is one more consideration telling against the phantom approach.

Yet another is that if the phantom approach were true, it would be difficult to understand why there are modes of imaging cor-responding to each of the sense modalities. Why should there not be ten or eleven types of mental image, perhaps including X-ray images, and radio wave images? Furthermore, if the connection between a sense modality and an image is contingent, why should the image be named after the sense modality? Why should the images be described as visual, auditory, tactile, and olfactory, instead of being given some other description, if the description of the one did not logically depend on the description of the other?

[11] There is another respect in which the connection between sense-organ and image cannot be regarded as straightforwardly contingent. In an important sense mental images have their 'seat' in the sense-organ associated with them. Let me begin by drawing attention to an obviously contingent fact that we usually take for granted: those of our sense-organs by means of which we sense remote objects are all clustered together in our heads. It is for this reason, I suggest, that mental images are often said to be situated in our heads. Now let us imagine that it so happened that our 'superior' sense-organs were located in different parts of the body to one another; our eyes in our backs and our ears on our legs, with the remaining sense-organs remaining in their present positions. Had our sense-organs been so placed, there is no doubt that we would take our visual images to 'appear to' the region of our backs

in which our eyes were situated, and our auditory images to 'appear to' the region of our legs in which our ears were situated. We already have some experience of this. If I have a kinaesthetic, or a tactile image of my toe wagging, the image is not 'in' my head, but 'in' my toe. If the phantom approach were true, there would be no reason to think that if the sense-organs were banished to the extremities of bodies, the corresponding images would follow them there. On the contrary, they could be expected to stay stubbornly at home in the head. If, as I maintain, this is not what we would expect to happen, we have further reasons for thinking the sentient approach more coherent than the phantom approach.

I shall try to make clearer what I am claiming in respect of the spatial relation between mental image and position of sense-organ when I say that the mental image 'appears to' where the sense-organ is. Of course I am not wishing to deny that the image 'appears to' the imager, but it is a question of the 'gate' at which it presents itself. Although mental images do not exist in public space, they do have spatial features. These spatial features are not, however, confined to the 'world' of the image; i.e. it is not only the relations of one element of an image to another that can be described in spatial terms. There is, in addition, a seeming spatial relation between the imager himself and his image. This is particularly evident in the case of visual imagery. Psychological subjects have reported on introspective grounds that when their eyes are closed their visual images appear to be about two inches in front of their eyes. The imager, therefore, orients the image in relation to regions of his body. Thus we could say that auditory images are 'in' the eardrums, olfactory images 'in' the nose, gustatory images 'in' the mouth, and so on. If I am right about this, then it follows that when an imager is presented with an image, he will be able to make a spatial distinction between the place he occupies and the place the image appears to occupy. I should like to try to describe how this is done.

The apparent location of an image is, I have argued, fixed in relation to the sense-organ associated with it. This is the natural way to orient the image because of its characteristic of 'appearing to' the particular sense-organ. Now the obverse side of the phenomenon of 'being appeared to', is the locus at which the 'appearing to' is an appearing to. That is, if the appearance gives a certain aspect, we can infer back to the point from which that aspect would be a projection. This point I shall describe as the 'origin' of the mental image (using 'origin' in the sense it has in coordinate geometry). My contention can now be expressed as follows: when we attempt to locate the apparent position of an image, the physical position of the sense-organ is the 'origin' of the image. Another way of looking at the matter is this: just as the sense-organ is the origin of its sense field, so the sense-organ is likewise the origin of its 'image field'. The point can now be made that if the imager's eyes were in his back, the origin of his visual imagery would be that point in his back where his eyes were; and if his ears were on his legs, the origin of his auditory imagery would be those points on his legs where his ears were. Thus, this account gives a sense in which the sense-organ provides the associated imagery with a definite 'seat'.

If we now go back to the phantom approach and consider the possibility of an imager without sense-organs, we can say at once that this notion of the origin of the image with respect to the sense-organ would be without application. The upshot of this would seem to be that the phantom approach rules out the possibility of the imager being able to describe the relation between his image and himself in spatial terms. Moreover, if it were suggested that on the phantom approach the spatial differentiation between imager and image could still be postulated, and the apparent location of the image oriented in relation to regions of the body, it would be quite inexplicable why this should be so. Such a suggestion would be in effect an attempt to get the best of both worlds without making any concessions to either. We are left with the position that an imager without the relevant sense-organ would lack the element of spatiality between himself and his image, which I have tried to describe. I conclude that if I am right about the spatial differentiation between imager and image, and if I am right in maintaining that such a differentiation can only be made in terms of thinking of the sense-organ as the origin of the associated image, then images according to the phantom approach would lack one of the essential characteristics that an image possesses. Consequently, the phantom approach can only be dealing with a form of imagery that lies outside our experience. By lacking 'a definite seat' such alleged imagery becomes unintelligible to us.

[12] The logical dependence of mental imagery on the possession of sense-organs can also be brought out in another, more obvious, way. Once again we return to the question of attention. Some of

the activities we practise we can practise simultaneously: we can whistle while we walk. Others cannot be carried on at the same time: we cannot whistle while we talk. The same is true of our sense-organ activities. I cannot *attentively* listen to something and at the same time listen for something else. The one activity impedes the other. Now the point I wish to make in this connection is that attentive sense-organ activities cannot be engaged in simultaneously with the activity of forming corresponding mental images. Take the case of looking at one's mother attentively. If one is doing that one cannot at the same time form a visual image of her. The 'being appeared to' which is the seeing precludes the 'being appeared to' which is the imaging. The two experiences are incompatible in that they seem to compete for the same logical space, and the success of the one precludes the success of the other. It is rather like the case of the impossibility of an expanse being simultaneously red and green all over. This means that in order, say, to form a visual image I must suspend the sense-organ activity of looking (in any of its modes). I do this by ceasing to focus attentively on what I see, and allow what I see to submerge into a ground for the visual image. (That is if I do not take the short-cut of closing my eyes, in which case there is of course no question but that I cease the activity of looking.)

The importance of this state of affairs for my argument is easy to appreciate. In the first place, this is a result one would expect on the sentient approach, but not one that would have an explanation on the phantom approach – according to which there should be no more difficulty about simultaneously scrutinizing an object visually and having a visual image, than there is in simultaneously whistling and walking. In the second place, it shows that attention is involved in the incompatibility between the perceptual activity and the imaging activity. And lastly, and most significant of all, it shows that the imaging activity is dependent upon the suspension of a bodily activity – viz. sense-organ activity. But the suspension of a bodily activity entails muscular inhibition. Thus the analysis substantiates Ribot's claim that a necessary condition of image formation is the inhibition of interfering muscular movement. But it does more than just show that Ribot is right; it also contains an explanation of why he is right, and this explanation was not one that he was aware of, so it takes the theory beyond Ribot's version of it. It does so by making it clear that we are dealing in both types of case with 'doings' and the 'doings' are ones in which of necessity our bodies come into play. We see, therefore, that even such a non-bodily activity as image formation cannot logically be divorced from bodily activities. The investigation has shown, I believe, that the phantom approach should be rejected in favour of the sentient approach.

[13] By having offered a defence of Ribot's claim that a necessary condition of imaging is the inhibition of appropriate bodily activity, I have supported the thesis that reflection depends on such inhibition in the case of one of its species. It remains to be argued that the thesis is true also of the species of reflection still outstanding – namely, thinking. I mean to refer here to the type of thinking that involves having thoughts.

It would seem difficult to argue – as I did in the case of imaging – that thinking cannot occur simultaneously with certain bodily activities, and in consequence that a necessary condition of thinking is the suspension of competing bodily activity. The connection between bodily activity and thinking will have to be argued for in a more involved manner. The course Ribot chose was to adopt an image theory of thinking. This would neatly solve the problem since if we think 'in' images, no thinking could take place without the muscular inhibition already shown to be necessary to the occurrence of images. This course is no longer open to us because the image theory of thinking has since been shown to be fallacious.[1] In fairness to Ribot, however, it should be pointed out that he was far from being unsophisticated about the image theory of thinking. For many philosophers the image theory of thinking is equated with thinking 'in' *visual* images. This Ribot would have rejected out of hand: he endorsed Galton's work on image thinking, and stressed the fact that many people think exclusively 'in' non-visual images. Some indeed are visual imagists, but some are auditory imagists, and others are kinaesthetic imagists, and so on.

The course I shall take will be somewhat different from Ribot's, but it will lead to the same result: it will show the dependence of our thinking on our bodily activities. I shall not employ an image theory of thinking, but I shall argue that some of our thinking is dependent on imagery, and when it is not it is dependent on perception. Thus in either case it will still be true that thinking depends on bodily activity. I shall argue against any third alternative, and I shall defend my position by arguing against a philo-

[1] See below, p. 140.

sopher who proposes just such a third alternative. In his article entitled 'Thoughts',[1] Ginnane argues that Ryle had, in *The Concept of Mind*, overlooked the existence of thoughts. He means by 'thoughts' such having of thoughts as are described in such standard descriptions as 'it occurred to me', 'it crossed my mind', and 'it dawned on me that . . .' The having of a thought is, he argues, episodic. It is meaningful to ask when and where it occurred. Now with all this I am in agreement. It is the following contention that I dispute:

'How can we reconcile the fact that thoughts are occurrences with the fact that they do not involve the alteration of any stuff at all, not even shadow-stuff such as mental imagery? The answer is vexing but inevitable: we just have to learn to live with the mystery: thoughts are *sui generis*. Thoughts just cannot be "explained" by equating them with something else of a more familiar kind – something we can get our teeth into – and that is all there is to it.'[2]

My objection to this view is based on the argument (*a*) that all the facts mentioned by Ginnane can be adequately explained without its being true that thoughts are *sui generis* in his sense; and (*b*) that the admittance of *sui generis* thoughts into consciousness offends against the Law of Parsimony. It is instructive to compare this passage of Ginnane's with the following one from Price's *Thinking and Experience*.

'In the last two chapters the term "symbol" has been used in a very wide sense, to mean roughly "whatever we think with". It would seem that there is no such thing as pure or naked thinking; or if conceivably there could be, it is beyond the reach of human frailty, even though superhuman intelligences may be capable of it. The human mind, it seems, must always have sensible or quasi-sensible media "in" which we think.'[3]

Now it seems to me that this passage is intended to rule out precisely the sort of view put forward by Ginnane. Thoughts which are *sui generis* are 'naked' thoughts which only a super-

[1] W. J. Ginnane, 'Thoughts', *Mind*, LXIX, 275 (1960).
[2] *Ibid.*, p. 388.
[3] H. H. Price, *Thinking and Experience* (London, 1953), pp. 237–8.

human intelligence might be capable of. Price goes on to identify the media in which we think:

'In free thinking we think "in" all sorts of sensible and quasi-sensible particulars, and indeed in principle there is no limit to their variety. We think in words, in images, in gestures or incipient gestures, in pantomimic actions, with models or sketches or other sensible replicas.'[1]

The symbols 'with' which we think are instantiated either as individual tokens that happen to exist and which we just make use of, or as tokens produced by ourselves. In both cases the awareness of the token may be called an occurrence, and it is this fact, I think, that accounts for the belief that thoughts are occurrences. When Ginnane claims that thoughts are datable as to the time and place of their occurrence, what we really date is the time and place of the awareness of the *token* by means of which the thought is symbolized; whether it be word, image, or gesture.

It must be admitted that after considering this alternative, Ginnane rejects it as 'patently false'. In fact, however, he does the image theory scant justice, and he would I am sure have taken it far more seriously had he taken into account Price's analysis of the Imagist Theory of Thinking. Ginnane's argument amounts to this: since thoughts are not identical with images, the occurrence of thoughts has nothing to do with the occurrence of images. Thus, referring to the image theory of thinking, he says:

'This view, though easily refuted, still has its adherents. It is patently false because there is no self-contradiction involved in someone saying that it occurred to him at a particular time that such-and-such, whilst at the same time steadfastly denying that he had any mental images whatsoever at the time in question. In fact not only could such a claim be made without self-contradiction, it could very often be made quite truly. In any case, no collection of images, however complicated, could ever fully correspond to a thought. No images could, of themselves, amount to, or constitute, the thought that I report when I say, for example, "It occurred to me that Peter might drop in today for a drink". The images are equivocal in a way in which the thought is quite definite. Images can never be anything more than illustrations of my thoughts, just

[1] *Loc. cit.*

as pictures in a book can never be more than illustrations of the text.'[1]

In this argument the premisses are true, but the conclusion is false. It is a *non-sequitur* from beginning to end. Price has shown quite conclusively that a visual image is usually very much more than an 'illustration' of a thought. It is one of the more successful symbols of thoughts. The flaw in Ginnane's argument is his failure to deal with the possibility that on those occasions on which he has a thought without having 'any mental images whatsoever at the time', his thought can only occur because it is expressed in some *other* form of symbol. It cannot be argued that a mental image is never a symbol because it is not always a symbol; but that seems to be the assumption behind Ginnane's conclusion that 'images can never be anything more than illustrations of . . . thoughts'. As I shall show this error vitiates his entire position.

Something first needs to be said about the alternative sorts of token-individuals by means of which thoughts can be symbolized. Undue confusion is caused by an ambiguity in the use of the word 'image'. As Price says,

'The Imagists, we have seen, draw a sharp distinction between image thinking and verbal thinking. But is there not a sense in which some verbal thinking is itself image thinking? Certainly we do often think in or with verbal images – visual, or auditory, or kinaesthetic.

'But these are not the sort of images with which the Imagist is concerned, and this sort of thinking is not what he means by "Image thinking".'[2]

But the Image Theorists are wrong to think that non-verbal visual imagery is the only true source of the symbols 'in' which we think. We can just as well use as symbols the auditory images of the sounds of words, or the kinaesthetic images associated with the articulation of words. In fact we need not use images as symbols at all.

'To placate the Anti-Image philosophers, we now turn to an important point which the Imagists have completely overlooked.

Although mental images are quasi-instantiative particulars, they are not the only ones. Perfectly good perceptible objects, denizens of the public material world in which the Anti-Imagists feel so much at home, may have this quasi-instantiative function, and may cash our words in absence, or approximate to cashing them, in very much the same way as mental images do.'[1]

It can now be appreciated that Ginanne's thesis that thoughts are *sui generis*, is not established by his denial that mental imagery is a vehicle of thought. He should have attempted to refute the view that the vehicle of thought must *either* be a visual image, *or* a non-visual image, *or* a perceptible object, *or* a gesture. This could only be done if it could be shown that a thought could occur that was not instantiated in *any* of these vehicles. In other words, the refutation must consist in a denial of all such disjuncts: a denial of just one is ineffective. It cannot be said that Ginnane even begins to satisfy this condition.

Ginnane's attempt to refute the view opposing his own is so far from being successful that it actually undermines the very premiss on which is based his claim that thoughts are *sui generis*. If we accept Price's account, according to which the symbols 'in' which a thought is carried are drawn either from mental images or from perceptible objects, we have an argument for denying that thoughts are *sui generis*. The occurrence of a thought entails the existence of its symbolic vehicle, and this in turn entails awareness of the token-individual of the symbol. It follows that whenever a thought occurs there is necessarily associated with it a token-individual the awareness of which is itself a datable occurrence. But if we have one such occurrence whenever we have a thought, we have all we need in order to account for the datability of the thought, and we do not need to look for something additional which can be dated when a thought occurs. *A fortiori* there is no need to postulate an ostensibly purely spiritual element of consciousness as the occurrence in question.

If my argument against Ginnane is successful, it supports Ribot's contention that not even in the case of reflection do we find a form of attention that is independent of the condition he has laid down for all attention; namely, the inhibition of movement. The argument has in fact carried us even further. We can now see that the phantom approach can be rejected in the case of the occurrence

1 *Ibid.*, p. 256.

of thoughts. Not even our thoughts are 'without definite seat'. On the contrary their seat (origin) will be determined by the species of the token-individual belonging to the symbolic vehicle of the thought. Thus the sentient approach is vindicated even in the case of that mental phenomenon which would appear to be the chief hope of the phantom approach.

My discussion of the different ways in which unprojected consciousness is involved in two types of attention, interrogative attention and executive attention, also enables us to clear up a difficulty presented by Ribot's theory of attention. Ribot is not as clear as he might be about the connection between the cognitive aspect of attention and its basis in muscular activity. He describes attention as a 'predominant *intellectual state*', but it is by no means obvious how it can be at once an intellectual state and a muscular activity. The answer is suggested by the analysis I have offered of the two ways in which unprojected consciousness may relate to an object of attention. If the relation is effected through a relevancy system in which a master-idea is guiding the attention bestowed on an object, then the attention is an intellectual state. It is to be noted that even here the master-idea can itself only exist because of control over certain bodily activities (as specified by the sentient approach). The attention so described is interrogative attention. If, on the other hand, the relation is effected through a relevancy system in which kinaesthetic sensation is guiding the attention bestowed on an object, then attention is muscular activity. The attention so described corresponds very roughly with executive attention.

The discussion of the last three chapters forms the groundwork for the direct enquiry into the nature of the experiential self which follows. The theory of the self I shall advance is an interpretation of the conclusions already reached, and is based on the distinctions for which I have argued. No substantive propositions of major significance are introduced for the first time in the chapters that follow. From this point of view we have reached a natural turning point in the enquiry, and I now proceed to consider the implications of what has gone before, for our understanding of the self.

THE EXPERIENTIAL SELF

I. THE SELF AS UNPROJECTED CONSCIOUSNESS

[1] The task of examining consciousness in order to determine its structure has now been completed. I argued that this was a necessary preliminary to determining whether Hamilton was justified in affirming the 'Duality of Consciousness', or whether James was right to deny it. The question of the relationship between consciousness and the self was deliberately left in abeyance until this prior question was settled. We are now in a position to see that Hamilton was right in thinking that consciousness displayed a duality, but wrong in thinking that the duality was a duality between one element lying outside consciousness, and another element lying within consciousness. Both elements in the duality, it has been found, lie within consciousness. The results of the analysis of consciousness show, similarly, that James was right in thinking that there was no duality between an element lying outside consciousness and another lying within it, but wrong in thinking that there was no duality within consciousness itself. James denied that consciousness had an 'inner duplicity'. We may concede that while no evidence has been found of its 'duplicity', much evidence has been assembled pointing to its polarization into opposite spheres.

On the basis of this conclusion I now wish to take up the question of the self, and advance a theory that attempts to do justice to the findings of the preceding enquiry. My theory is the startling one that the self is identical with unprojected consciousness. If this theory can be sustained, it will follow that Hamilton was right to interpret the 'Duality of Consciousness' as a duality between self and not-self (subject and object), although wrong to identify the self with an entity external to consciousness. Furthermore, it will follow that James too was right when he maintained that the self must lie within consciousness. To put the position more generally, the theory I am proposing overcomes the difficulties that we saw to lie in the way of both the Pure Ego Theory and the Serial

Theory.[1] Unlike those two theories, mine is based on an analysis of experience itself, and is not inferred from an analysis of entities that are not selves. That is to say, the analysis has abided strictly by the caveat that we look for the solution exclusively from the standpoint of what we experience ourselves as being.

I cannot *prove* the theory I am advocating, just as I cannot *disprove* the theory that the subject of consciousness is a Pure Ego. The identification of self and unprojected consciousness is a deliberate philosophical postulate. My defence of the theory, therefore, must consist in my showing its philosophical superiority over rival theories of the self, and in my showing that the failure to make the identification of the self with unprojected consciousness itself explains the generation of the Pure Ego Theory and the Serial Theory. In short, the theory I put forward has the merit of explaining why the other theories are mistaken. Lastly, my theory accords with our native knowledge of ourselves in that it does not lead to a self which is unknowable and does not lead to a self which is a mere construct. In that sense it is not counter-intuitive as are the two classical theories. A word of caution is necessary here: the theory I am proposing should not be thought to be a theory of the 'empirical' self in the Kantian sense. I am not attempting to identify the self as object (the 'me' as opposed to the 'I' as James puts it). My identification of the self is an identification of the *subject* of consciousness. The position is that the self is experiential, but is not on that account an *object* of experience. It does not follow therefore that the experiential self is the same as the empirical self.

This can be more clearly grasped once it is realized that what we individuate as an experience is always an object of attention: indeed the individuating of an experience by a subject (where there is no question of the subject identifying the experience to another) just *is* to make of it an object of attention. Bearing this in mind it is evident that an experience *of* the self is an experience *qua* object of attention and as such we are dealing with the self as object (the empirical self). But, as will soon become apparent in the course of the exposition, the self *qua* subject – the experiential self – cannot as a matter of logical necessity become the object of attention; cannot therefore become an object. The major implication of the position is that from the fact that the self is not an object of experience it does not follow that it is non-experiential.

[1] See above, pp. 29–30.

I shall now attempt to draw out some of the features that philosophers have maintained are features of the self, and show that these are also features of unprojected consciousness. The conclusion I shall draw from this parallelism is that the philosophers who discerned these features of the self were indeed describing real features: their claims on behalf of the self were true. However, I shall maintain that they misunderstood the nature of their results. They believed not only that they had discovered one of the ultimate facts of experience – namely that each experience had an experiencer – but also that the experiencer must be inaccessible to experience. Instead they had stumbled upon one of the factors essential to the existence of an experience as an object of attention, and because this factor – the existence of unprojected consciousness – could not be 'objectified' in experience they concluded that it was a self that lay beyond experience. My view is that they were right in believing that they had discerned the features of the self (although they could not explain why the self possessed the features they found), but that they were wrong in thinking that only a non-experiential self could possess such features. Conversely, those philosophers who could not accept the idea of a non-experiential self were right to reject the notion, but were wrong in thinking that to do so they had to go so far as to deny the features of the self on which the notion was based. These pronouncements of mine will become intelligible as the theme is developed.

[2] One of the features traditionally claimed to be most characteristic of the self is its essential subjecthood. On this view, the self lies behind its experiences and apart from them, and no attempt to capture the self in experience can succeed because if it did it would make of the self an object and it cannot be an object without ceasing to be a self. On this conception the self is forever hidden from view. Hence it was in vain that Hume looked into himself for some impression of himself, for had he by chance come across anything with the required specifications he would have come across an object and not a subject.

The conception of the self as essentially subject received its noblest and most influential modern expression in Buber's *I and Thou*.[1] But it can be traced back at least as far as Kant's distinction between the transcendental self and the empirical self. 'I have no *knowledge* of myself as I am,' says Kant, 'but merely as I appear to

[1] M. Buber, *I and Thou*, tr. R. G. Smith (Edinburgh, 1937).

myself.'[1] Kant's views on the nature of the transcendental self are obscure, but it is not necessary for us to pursue them in order to appreciate the relevance of his distinction to the approach to the self I am now considering. For in the very next sentence he says, 'The consciousness of self is thus very far from being a knowledge of the self . . .' which suggests that I know *that* I am a self, even though I do not know *what* the self is. The reason Kant gives for our inability to know ourselves as we are is that any intuition I have of myself as object must of necessity be subject to the condition under which all appearances are given: namely, that they are conditioned by *time*. In his view this is a sufficient condition of any experience of the self being merely an *appearance* of the self, and not the real self. But even had Kant not used this particular argument, his view nevertheless lends itself to the idea that the real self can never be met with in experience.[2] In the passage I quoted, Kant describes the empirical self as appearing *to myself*. This cannot be a reference to the empirical self, but must be a reference to the real self: i.e., the subject of the experience of the empirical self. Now if, as Kant does, one makes the assumption that every experience entails an experiencer, it will follow that whatever experience of a self I have, there must still exist a self which has that experience, which is not itself the object of the experience. It follows that we can never experience the self *qua* subject, because as soon as we attempt to grasp the subject-self we find that another subject-self has taken its place. If therefore the subject-self is identified as the real self, the real self forever lies just behind experiences: the experien*cer* cannot be found within experience.

Ryle has referred to this peculiarity of the self in always seeming to be one jump ahead of us in our efforts to experience it, as 'The Systematic Elusiveness of "I"'. He describes the apparent dilemma most evocatively:

'Even if the person is, for special speculative purposes, momentarily concentrating on the Problem of the Self, he has failed and knows

---

[1] Kant, *Critique of Pure Reason*, tr. N. Kemp Smith (London, 1953), B 158. At A 107, Kant says: 'Consciousness of self according to the determinations of our state in inner perception is merely empirical, and always changing. No fixed and abiding self can present itself in this flux of inner appearances.'

[2] I use the expression 'real self' to stand for what Kant calls 'the self as I am', in contrast to 'the self as I appear', in order to avoid embroilment in the doctrine of the Transcendental Ego. It must not be thought, however, that I am thinking of 'the real self' of later British Idealists.

that he has failed to catch more than the flying coat-tails of that which he was pursuing. His quarry was the hunter.'[1]

In Ryle's view it is logically impossible for the 'I' which is the subject of experience to be at the same time its own object. Now, as I suggest, Kant did not himself adopt the position that it was logically impossible for the self to be its own object, although it would not have been difficult for him to have done so. He appears to have thought that another sort of being could conceivably intuit its real self:

'Such an intelligence [as is ours], therefore, can know itself only as it appears to itself in respect of an intuition which is not intellectual and cannot be given by the understanding itself, not as it would know itself if its *intuition* were intellectual.'[2]

But it could be argued that even a being with such an intuitive intelligence might be forced to admit the distinction between the self that has the intellectual intuition, and the self experienced in the intellectual intuition. If he were, the systematic elusiveness of 'I' would recur to plague the intuitive intelligence as well. In any event the mere concept of a non-discursive intelligence knowing itself through an intellectual intuition does not of itself rule out the distinction in question. I am therefore inclined to side with Ryle and against Kant as far as the explanation of the systematic elusiveness of 'I' is concerned. To hope to have an experience of the experiencer, if it makes sense at all, sets going an infinite regress. No matter how many manifestations of the self are experienced, there will always be one left over which has not yet been experienced, and that one is the subject of the last experience. Experience of the self, is, in Ryle's words, 'logically condemned to eternal penultimacy'.

Now the concept of unprojected consciousness, is, as was explained in the last chapter, one of which it makes no sense to say that it could be an object of attention. Elements of unprojected consciousness can be detached and made objects of attention, but they are of necessity replaced by other elements which take their place in unprojected consciousness. It is self-contradictory to say of unprojected consciousness as a whole that it could be an object

[1] Ryle, *The Concept of Mind*, p. 198.
[2] Kant, *Critique of Pure Reason*, B 159.

of attention. In this respect unprojected consciousness refers to experiential elements, but not to experiences which we encounter as objects of attention.

The attempt to experience as object of attention that which can only be experienced as background is frustrated in the same way, and for the same reason, as is the attempt to make of the subject-self its own object. From this point of view unprojected consciousness is systematically elusive. It is systematically elusive to attention. There is a parallel with the 'I' which, as Ryle has argued, is systematically elusive too in the sense that the 'I' cannot be objectified by attention.

If we now identify unprojected consciousness and the self, we explain at once how it happens that they both exhibit the same logical behaviour, and what is more, we provide ourselves with an explanation of the systematic elusiveness of 'I'. If the self *is* unprojected consciousness, then the self can no more become an object of attention and remain subject than an element of unprojected consciousness can become an object of attention and remain an element of unprojected consciousness. If, however, it were possible for the totality of the elements of unprojected consciousness at one instant to become the whole object of attention at the next instant, we would have a situation in which the object of attention was the empirical self as a whole.[1] But, as I have tried to make clear, there would still have to be an unprojected consciousness to back up such an object of attention even though all its elements were new: we would still not have grasped the subject-self. We can therefore envisage, as a theoretical possibility, a succession of attempts to objectify the subject-self. Each time a new subject-self takes the place of the one just objectified, becoming its experiencer. The theory I am advocating explains why this must be so, not on the purely formal ground that an experience requires an experiencer, but on the material ground that a self could not be an object of attention unless unprojected consciousness, with which I have identified the subject-self, existed.

The great attraction of the theory I am proposing can now be explained. In the first place it enables us to resist the logic of the argument according to which the phenomenon of the systematic elusiveness of 'I' drives us back to a Pure Ego: a Pure Ego, moreover, that lies beyond the bounds of experience. According to this

[1] I shall shortly offer reasons for rejecting this as a possibility. See below, pp. 168-9.

logic, if every attempt to grasp the real self in experience fails, this must mean that the self must be something that cannot be experienced. Moreover, it follows that we can gain no knowledge of this self, for such knowledge would imply that we had some experience of it. Therefore, all we know of the self is that it is the subject of every experience – hence its designation as a 'pure' ego. In the second place, and in contrast with this reasoning, I am suggesting that it is indeed true that the subject-self can never itself become an object of experience, and I am maintaining that this has nothing to do with the nature of the self – transcendental or empirical. It is put down to nothing other than the way attention operates. This enables it to be asserted in all consistency both that the self as subject is experiential, and that it is never presented as an object of experience. Furthermore, it obviates the necessity of treating the self as something unknown in itself.

The theory overcomes the paradox that the self, although discoverable in experience, is never an object of experience, and in the process removes the main prop holding up The Pure Ego Theory of the Self. The essence of the matter is, on my view, that the self is experiential (i.e. is composed of elements of consciousness), but is never known as an object of experience. This is one of the factors that accounts for the view that the self lies behind its experiences.[1] It also explains why we have such a lively sense of the *presence* of the self, and why we are so nonplussed by denials of the self's existence.

[3] So much for the general outline of the theory. I have shown why the self cannot be considered as an object, and I have pointed out that unprojected consciousness cannot be considered as an object either. That gives us one reason for suspecting that they are one and the same thing. But account has to be taken of the fact that many philosophers have denied the necessity of the notion of a subject of consciousness. It follows that if they are right and there is no subject of consciousness, then the attempt to argue that it is identical with unprojected consciousness must be abandoned. It is therefore crucial to my enterprise that I offer reason for rejecting the no-subject view of the self.

The philosophers most anxious to deny the existence of the subject have been the Serial Theorists. Their objection has been that if successive states of consciousness have a subject, that

[1] Another is given on pp. 168–9, below.

subject must persist through time in order for it to function as their subject. The self must in that case be considered to be a persisting entity – to wit a Pure Ego.

Now it was precisely this idea of an enduring subject that Serialists such as Russell,[1] Ayer,[2] and Grice[3] wished to avoid. They all suggest that when we refer to a self, what we refer to is revealed on proper analysis to be a relation between total temporary states. As Ayer explains,

'We know that a self, if it is not to be treated as a metaphysical entity, must be held to be a logical construction out of the sense-experiences . . . And, accordingly, if we ask what is the nature of the self, we are asking what is the relationship that must obtain between sense-experiences for them to belong to the sense-history of the same self.'[4]

In contradistinction to this approach, it has been pointed out by J. R. Jones that there is still room for a subject of experiences without such a subject being thought of as a persisting entity.[5] What Jones has in mind are the elements that exist simultaneously in each total temporary state. In other words, he draws attention to that other aspect of consciousness that Serialists have tended to overlook. We are asked to envisage the possibility that each experience has its own subject, and that no two experiences separated in time have the same subject. Such a subject would be transient, since it would not outlast the experience of which it was the owner.

What is of particular interest is the reason Jones gives for wishing to reintroduce this vestigial subject. He points out that it is needlessly paradoxical to deny, as Russell does, that there could be experiences without a subject. Jones recalls the insistence of James Ward that it does not make sense to call something an experience, if there is no one whose experience it is. Similarly, on this argument, there can be no presentation without the presentation presenting itself to a subject. But the main point he makes against Russell's no-subject theory is just that it unnecessarily rules out the possibility of ascribing a single experience to a subject. According to the

[1] B. Russell, *Analysis of Mind* (London, 1933).
[2] A. J. Ayer, *Language, Truth, and Logic*, 2nd ed. (London, 1953).
[3] H. P. Grice, 'Personal Identity', *Mind*, 1 (1941).
[4] *Op. cit.*, p. 125.
[5] J. R. Jones, 'The Self in Sensory Cognition', *Mind*, LVII (1949).

Serialist position a statement such as 'I am seeing this coloured patch' must be analysed in such a way that the statement is really a statement of the relation of the experience of seeing a coloured patch to the experiences which come before and after it. But Jones's objection is that he finds it meaningful to say 'I am seeing this coloured patch' irrespective of whether any other experiences came before or after it. Thus:

'But surely a person never says "I am seeing this coloured patch" or "I am hearing this noise" *merely* as an expression of the fact that this seeing and this hearing are related to other non-contemporaneous mental events in certain characteristic ways. I at any rate am perfectly certain that there is something *contemporaneous* with my seeing the coloured patch or my hearing the noise to which I mean to relate these objects when I say that it is "I" who am seeing the coloured patch or hearing the noise . . . The "I" of which I am thinking seems to be involved in any *one* of the cognitive events which may be combined in the unity of the same total temporary state.'[1]

He proposes therefore that we consider the possibility that the 'I' in sentences describing such experiences refers to something contemporaneous with the experience, which could then be said to 'have' the experience. Some other contemporaneous mental event (element of consciousness) could be assigned this function. This would have the advantage that, provided the mental event selected was always present, there would be a sense in which every experience had a subject, irrespective of its relation to experiences that come before or after it. At the same time it would avoid the myth of a substantival ego, which Russell was anxious to repudiate. It would avoid it without running into Russell's paradoxical position in which it is denied that experiences have subjects. In casting about us for a type of mental event best suited to perform the function of standing as a subject to each experience, there are strong reasons for the choice of bodily sensation for the purpose. This was recognized by C. D. Broad who says:

'I think that the most plausible form of this theory would be to identify the Central Event [i.e. the self] at any moment with a mass of bodily feeling. The longitudinal unity of a self through a period of time would then depend on the fact that there is a mass of bodily feeling which goes on continuously throughout this period and varies in quality not at all or very slowly. At any moment there are many such masses of bodily feeling, which are numerically different however much they may be alike in quality. These form the Centres of a number of different contemporary total states of mind. Each of them is a thin slice of a long and highly uniform strand of bodily feeling; and each of these strands of bodily feeling accounts for the longitudinal unity of one mind.'[1]

Jones follows Gallie in taking up Broad's suggestion.[2] They both equate the subject with what they call 'the somatic field'. I shall not go into the details of this theory because it has been ably expounded and criticised by Shoemaker.[3] The theory rests on the assumption that bodily sensations are not intermittent, for if they were and if an experience occurred during a time at which the somatic field was empty of sensation, the experience in question would be subjectless. But that *ex hypothesi* is impossible. Thus the theory rests entirely on the questionable empirical premiss that some bodily sensation is contemporaneous with every experience.

2. THE PROBLEMS THE THEORY SOLVES

[4] I shall shortly point out some of the advantages which the theory I am advocating has over the somatic field theory, but I first want to pair that theory with another one that has recently been suggested, since much of what I have to say is applicable to both. Ayer, in his book *The Origins of Pragmatism* has produced both a defence and an elaboration of James's theory of the self. At one point he calls it 'our' theory and I shall refer to it as the James-Ayer theory of the self. Ayer's main concern is to produce a theory that will account for the continuity of the self, or in other terms, with the unity of a succession of total temporary states. Now this problem is one that we will come to in the chapter after this one. However, I shall not put off consideration of the James-Ayer theory until then because a number of its aspects are of immediate relevance to the present discussion.

[1] C. D. Broad, *The Mind and Its Place In Nature* (London, 1925), p. 566.
[2] I. Gallie, 'Mental Facts', *Proceedings of the Aristotelian Society*, N.S. XXXVII (1936–37).
[3] Shoemaker, *Self-Knowledge and Self-Identity*, ch. 3, sec. 8.

The significance of James's theory in Ayer's eyes is that he solves the problem left by Hume; namely how to account for the unity of a bundle of perceptions in virtue of which the bundle constitutes a single self. James's solution is that each succeeding member of the series 'appropriates' the preceding member. The appropriation is passed on, or carried over, to each new member in such a way that the current experience appropriates all those that went before it. James recognizes that the experience doing the appropriating has a logically different character to the experiences that are appropriated. He marks this distinction by calling the appropriating experience the Thought. For purposes of exposition Ayer uses the letters T and E to refer to the appropriator and the appropriated respectively, and it will be convenient to follow him in this. The T is defined by James as a subject's 'present mental state'[1] and the E is spoken of as a past mental state. From James's own description, therefore, one would gather that the entire total temporary state which formed a subject's present consciousness was a T for all earlier total temporary states. If that were the case James's theory would in no sense provide us with a subject of the sort Jones had in mind when he said that each experience here and now demanded a subject. James's theory would on that rendering seem geared to account for the continuity of the self alone, and have nothing to offer on the question of the subject that is contemporary with a given mental state. It is significant, therefore, that Ayer does not place this interpretation on James's view. Ayer interprets James's intention as being one of differentiating the T from E's which are contemporary with it, as well as from E's which precede it. That means thinking of consciousness as differentiated at any one time into an appropriating T and appropriated E's. Now this suggestion has much to recommend it. In the first place it is not as counter-intuitive as the interpretation which James' own description suggests: one can conceive of an element of a present total temporary state as a thought which is appropriating experiences, but it is impossible to conceive *all* of one's actual mental state at the time as in some sense a reflective recollection of vanished experience. Further, Ayer points out that James does not think in terms of sharp boundaries between past and present experiences. He describes consciousness as 'sensibly continuous'.[2] With this in mind Ayer makes the following remark:

[1] James, *The Principles of Psychology*, Vol. I, p. 338.
[2] A. J. Ayer, *The Origins of Pragmatism* (San Francisco, 1968), p. 257.

'So the identifying thought appropriates whatever experiences it feels to be continuous with itself, as well as any other experiences, more remote from it in time, which are marked in its recollection with a similar warmth and intimacy.'[1]

Having gone this far the logic of the situation demands that recognition be given to the fact that experiences may be compresent. This category is none other than our total temporary state, and Ayer describes it in terms of the relation of 'sensible compresence'. We may take it, therefore, that T belongs to a set of sensibly compresent experiences.

As I understand it, Ayer's formulation is a detailed emendation of James's theory, and one that increases its plausibility. In the process Ayer has quite inadvertently arrived at a position in which it becomes possible to ascribe to each present experience its own subject. For the T which is sensibly compresent with a number of E's is tailor-made to be the contemporaneous subject of those E's. Now James never reached this conclusion, and the reason is that he had not refined his theory sufficiently to be able to reach it. But Ayer had. Why then did he not reach the conclusion? The answer is obvious. For Ayer the problem of personal identity is exclusively the problem of accounting for the unity of *successive* experiences in a series. The unity of the compresent experiences is independently assured by their relation of sensible compresence. Thus the T as appropriator only needs to be brought in to cover those cases in which experiences are united neither by the relation of sensible compresence nor by that of sensible continuity. I shall in due course link up Ayer's preoccupation with the continuity of the self, with his having failed to keep separate the question of personal identity from that of self-identity.

In the meantime we may simply note that Ayer has missed a golden opportunity to give an interpretation of James's theory which displays its latent power. What I am saying is that Ayer's preoccupation with personal identity causes him to miss the real importance of James's distinction between T and E. Nothing that James says makes it impossible for a T to appropriate an E that is compresent with it. In fact his description of a T as 'the real, present onlooking, remembering, judging thought' actually encourages one to think of it as capable of appropriating compresent experiences. We can even go further and say that for James it *has*

[1] *Ibid.*, p. 257.

to appropriate such compresent experiences, for only if it does so can such experiences be carried forward into future T''s.

It is possible that Ayer was put off the track here because James points out that when a T is itself appropriated it has to be 'dead and gone'. In other words it has to become an E. Now I think it is possible that Ayer assumed that every E that a T appropriates has to be 'dead and gone', and this would entail the consequence that T''s can only appropriate *past* experiences. But no such assumption is warranted. The fact that only a past T can be appropriated by a present T does not mean that present T''s only appropriate past T''s. Their doing so is not incompatible with their also being capable of appropriating *present* E's in addition to past T''s and past E's. This I take to be the case. But then it is a logical feature of T''s that they may function as subjects for compresent experiences. They are a form of mental event which not only could be given the role of subject, but which because their function is that of appropriation *must* be thought of as subjects. From this point of view they are a type of mental event which is much more suited to performing the role of subject than is the somatic field suggested by Gallie and Jones.

It emerges that James's theory contains within it the possibility of satisfying the demand for a subject which Jones laid down. It also has the additional advantage that the subject as so conceived would also account for the continuity of the self from the past, and in this respect it is superior to the somatic field theory which treats the continuity of the self as a delusion produced by the qualitative sameness of background elements in the somatic field.

Certain comparisons and contrasts can now be made between these two theories and the one I offer. All three provide us with a subject of experience such that even an isolated experience can be assigned a subject. In that sense for none of the theories is the self merely a logical construct. Apart from that similarity there is one very great difference between my theory and the other two. On the other two the presence of a mental event with which the self could be identified is something of an accident. As we saw in the case of the somatic field theory it appears to be just a matter of chance that the somatic field is always 'filled'. On James's theory it would also appear to be an arbitrary assumption that within every group of compresent experiences there will be an appropriating Thought. There is no necessity for each and every experience to be appropriated by a Thought. By contrast, no such hiatus plagues my

theory since I have argued that no experience can be individuated
except in so far as it presupposes the existence of unprojected
consciousness. There is nothing merely *de facto* about the presence
of unprojected consciousness when an object of experience has
our attention. Thus on my theory the presence of a mental event
which can assume the role of the subject is a logical necessity. On
the other theories it is not. This seems to me to be a major point
in its favour.

It is interesting to note that James characterizes the appropriating T in just the way I have pointed out that the subject is often
characterized: namely, that a T cannot be an object to itself. We
have seen that James says that a T can only appropriate another T
that is 'dead and gone'. This is reminiscent of the view that we
cannot make of the subject its own object without destroying its
nature *qua* subject, and except in so far as it is an object for a further
subject. It is interesting to see in this connection that James says of
the Thought: 'A thing cannot appropriate itself; it *is* itself; and
still less can it disown itself', and, '. . . the thought never is an
object in its own hands, it never appropriates or disowns itself.'[1]
This is just what we would want to say about the subject. It is
difficult to see how this could be said of Jones's somatic field, or
what reason could be given on that theory for thinking it true. Of
James's theory it seems a bit more intuitively obvious that an
appropriator cannot appropriate itself, but the obviousness may
have more to do with the choice of the word 'appropriate' than
with the clarity of the thought behind it. By contrast, on my theory
if we treat the act of appropriation as the individuation of an
experience as an object of attention, then it is logically necessary
that the subject *qua* unprojected consciousness cannot be appropriated as object of attention. Furthermore, the notion of 'appropriation', which is admittedly obscure, can itself be explicated in
terms of the account I have given of the relation between unprojected consciousness and object of attention.

This can be brought out most easily in contrast to Jones's theory.
Jones, in dealing with the relation between the somatic field as a
whole (the self) and some particular somatic experience, such as a
pain in a part of the body, has this to say about the relation:

'And however many of them I may put forth from myself in a
given inspection, in order again to relate to "myself" as qualities of

[1] James, *The Principles of Psychology*, Vol. I, p. 340.

which I am sensible, there must always be some core of unobjectified somatic content if I am to have a "self" to which I can relate the ones which I notice as being "sensed by me".[1]

It can be seen how close to my theory Jones comes without quite reaching it. It will be noticed that he even goes so far as to talk of 'inspecting' a somatic sensation. His line of argument demands the recognition of attention as the factor responsible for the differentiation of the mass of somatic feeling from those particular ones which are said to be sensed by the self. It is also a striking fact that the somatic sensation to be inspected is described by him as something 'put forth' from the self. Here we have the very idea I have been describing, when I said that attention 'detaches' an element from unprojected consciousness and makes of it an object of attention. Neither Gallie nor Jones realize that the phenomenon they were describing could be put down quite simply to the operation of attention. As a result they were unable to free themselves from the belief that the 'core of unobjectified content' could be anything but somatic. It seems to me that Jones's passage calls for a different interpretation from the one he gives: the pain, or whatever, is the pain of a self, not because it comes from a mass of somatic feeling, but because it has been 'put forth' from the self by attention. This would have been true whatever the composition of the consciousness from which the pain had been 'put forth'. It is not peculiarly due to the fact that it was put forth from a mass of bodily feeling.

Nevertheless, Jones's description of the inspected sensation as 'put forth' from the self is a very important insight. The reverse of the relation is that the self stands 'over against' the object of attention. It expresses the fact to which I alluded in the introduction when I said that the self occupies its own logical space which was separate from the logical space occupied by the experiences it 'owns'. It is now possible to make sense of the other idea to which I appealed in the introduction when I said that experiences 'appear to' their subject. If we separate consciousness into a subject pole and an object pole, and at the subject pole we place unprojected consciousness, and at the object pole an experience 'put forth' by attention, then we have a state of affairs in which both poles of consciousness contain elements. Thus it is possible for an experience to 'appear to' a self in the sense that it comes into a relation to a separate field of consciousness, and the

[1] Jones, 'The Self in Sensory Cognition', pp. 54–5.

relation is one of 'standing-apart-from'. Without this 'standing-apart-fromness' the notion of the experience being an 'appearing to' does not make sense.

[5] I would now like to suggest that it is helpful to interpret James's notion of appropriation in the light of the standpoint I have just described. It is possible for T to appropriate E because E is experienced as 'over against' T. If it were not, there would be nothing independent of T which it could appropriate. I further want to suggest that the so-called appropriation is nothing over and above the relation between unprojected consciousness and object of attention that I have variously described as 'appearing to', 'standing over against' and 'standing-apart-from'. In other words when experiences are individuated as objects of attention, their being individuated is nothing else than their being 'put forth' in such a way that they are describable as 'standing over against' the subject. If we look at appropriation in this light we see that there is no need to look for some special Thought to do the appropriating: the appropriating is done by unprojected consciousness no matter what elements compose it at the time. We are spared having to postulate a special element for the purpose, and an element, moreover, for which introspective evidence could well be lacking.

It seems to me, therefore, that Jame's notion of the Thought as appropriator should be viewed as his attempt to feel his way toward the distinction I have made between unprojected consciousness and object of attention. Since Ayer explored none of the implications of the logical difference between T and E, he missed the most promising side of James's theory. But this is only half the picture. Just as significant for its implications for my theory is James's further view that the experiences appropriated by T are not so much attached to T as to certain kinaesthetic sensations. Speaking of our awareness of T he says:

'It may feel its own immediate existence . . . but nothing can be known *about* it till it be dead and gone. Its appropriations are therefore less to *itself* than to the most intimately felt *part of its present Object, the body, and the central adjustments*, which accompany the act of thinking, in the head. *These are the real nucleus of our personal identity*, and it is their actual existence, realized as a solid present fact, which makes us say "as sure *as I exist*, those past facts were part of myself." They are the kernel to which the *represented* parts of the Self are assimilated, accreted, and knit on; and even were Thought entirely unconscious of itself in the act of thinking, these "warm" parts of its present object would be a firm basis on which the consciousness of personal identity would rest.'[1]

When James says that the E's appropriated by T are appropriated 'less to itself than to the most intimately felt part' of the body, he seems to be suggesting that the appropriation is *by* the Thought but *to* the above mentioned bodily sensations. It is striking how close James comes here to saying that the E's are appropriated by unprojected consciousness, especially when it is remembered that unprojected consciousness necessarily has background kinaesthetic sensations among its elements. We see too that at this point there is not all that difference between James's theory and the somatic field theory, for that theory too depends heavily on those elements of the somatic field that constitute the most intimately felt parts of the body.

It is a striking fact therefore that both James and Jones turn to kinaesthetic sensation, and give it a crucial role to play in their characterization of the self. It is more especially interesting that in the case of James the bodily adjustments he has in mind are clearly due to the subject's paying attention to his experiences. This is made abundantly clear in his chapter on attention, in *The Principles of Psychology*. James could hardly have come closer to my theory without missing it than he does at this point. But once again it must be remarked that no matter how central a role both Jones and James accord to these kinaesthetic elements of unprojected consciousness, they can give no explanation of why they are so central. They are unable to show that these kinaesthetic sensations are a precondition of the appropriation of experiences by their being 'put forth' as objects of attention. Their theories are forced to treat as inexplicable matters of fact factors that on mine have been given a logical explanation.

A final observation about this side of James's theory will dot the i's and cross the t's. Because James lacks the notion of unprojected consciousness, he is forced to classify 'the part of the innermost Self which is most vividly felt' as part of the empirical self or the self as object. He does this in spite of the fact that he describes this innermost Self as 'consisting for the most part of a collection of

---

[1] James, *The Principles of Psychology*, Vol. I, p. 341.

cephalic movements or "adjustments" which, for want of attention and reflection, usually fail to be perceived and classed as what they are.'[1] Had James not missed the implications of his description concerning the logical character of these elements which do not receive attention, he would have had no need to invent a subject to appropriate E's. He would have had no need for his Thought. I have the support of Ayer himself over this point. He says, 'There is, therefore, no necessity for distinguishing between the "I" and the "me". However the concept of the self is to be analysed, there is no reason why the self which acquires the concept should not be identical with the self which satisfies it.'[2]

Commenting on James's view that minute kinaesthetic adjustments in the head are 'the real nucleus of our personal identity' Ayer says that it would seem that it was wrong of him to reproach James with failing to consider that personal identity might be defined in terms of the identity of the body. His answer is that James does not appeal to bodily identity because for him the body is a construct out of experience and as a result the move would be circular. However, Ayer sees it as a weakness in James's theory that he cannot make use of bodily identity in the definition of personal identity, and his supplementation of James's theory essentially consists in his making provision for such bodily identity by showing why 'appropriation' by itself is insufficient, and by showing how the connection with bodily identity is to be effected.

My belief is that James's instinct was right here, and Ayer's is wrong. That is to say, James's theory is superior to Ayer's emendation of it precisely because his does not rely on bodily identity. My grounds for saying this is that James's theory is in this respect true to the *self-approach*, and Ayer's emendation of it is a result of his conflation of the *self-approach* and the *persons-approach*. In short, James offers us a definition of the self as it is to the self, and from that standpoint no question arises of the subject having to identify which subject he is. Ayer, on the other hand, is concerned with the problem of identifying *other* selves, and from that standpoint we might wish to maintain that series of experiences that are not held together by the relation of appropriation, or by any other relation (i.e. membership of a self-contained series), may yet be the experiences of one and the same person. *Qua* subject, experiences

[1] James, *The Principles of Psychology*, Vol. I, p. 305.
[2] Ayer, *The Origins of Pragmatism*, pp. 252–3.

which are not appropriated are nothing to it, and it is meaningless to attach such experiences to it.

[6] Let us, however, for the sake of argument, grant Ayer his claim that the relation of 'appropriation' needs to be supplemented by bodily identity. It is instructive to see how Ayer thinks the attachment of a series of confamiliar experiences to a particular body can be effected. According to him a series made up of experiences that are either sensibly compresent or sensibly continuous with one another are attached to a body if at least one of their number is a kinaesthetic sensation attaching to a body. A kinaesthetic sensation is then defined as attaching to a body in that it must have its 'locus' in a particular body. The theory therefore explains how the attachment is effected, and at the same time provides a means of individuating the body to which the series of experiences are attached – as the body 'in' which the kinaesthetic sensation is located. (In an inexplicable slip Ayer passes from talking about kinaesthetic sensation to talking about bodily sensation as if they were identical; whereas all kinaesthetic sensations are bodily sensations but not all bodily sensations are kinaesthetic sensations.)

Having given an account of the relation of 'attachment' Ayer proceeds to dispose of the difficulties to which his theory gives rise. He faces the same problem that confronted the somatic field theory; namely, how can one be sure that every series of confamiliar experiences will contain at least one bodily sensation as a member? He has no option but to argue in terms of probabilities. He makes such statements as 'Even if it is not true that all our experiences are sensibly compresent with bodily sensations, it can fairly be assumed that the greater number of them are.'[1] Once again we are confronted with a theory which gives a key role to kinaesthetic sensation, and yet because on the theory it is purely contingent that the necessary kinaesthetic sensations should be forthcoming, no theoretical reason can be given for their presence.

In this respect the superiority of the theory I am suggesting is manifest. If the subject is equated with unprojected consciousness, and if there can be no unprojected consciousness without kinaesthetic sensation, then we not only have an explanation of the signal importance of kinaesthetic sensation to self-identity, but have an unshakable logical basis for rejecting any argument for the

[1] *Ibid.*, p. 262.

existence of kinaesthetic sensation in terms of probabilities. We are in a position to see why both James with his encephalic adjustments, and Ayer with his kinaesthetic sensations attached to the body, were both heading in the right direction – but for the wrong reasons—and why on their theory it is inexplicable that such sensations have the importance they accord them. We may further look upon these theories as providing us with a warning of the difficulties one gets oneself into if one does not make the distinctions I have been arguing for. Thus the failures of these theories are an impressive argument in favour of acceptance of mine.

It may have troubled the reader that James should have identified certain kinaesthetic sensations with 'encephalic adjustments' in view of the fact that his theory is not based on bodily identity. From the standpoint of the subject, however, such descriptions should be taken to be no more than appellations of the sensations in question. As such they must not be thought of as presupposing one's ability to identify the heads in which these adjustments occur. But if this is true of James's reference to the body, the same interpretation may be given of Ayer's reference to the body as the 'locus' of bodily sensations. Thus his description of a sensation as 'a sensation of physical pain in a body' could be interpreted as an appellation of a particular type of sensation, and it could be understood without any attachment being made to a physical body. Such is the case when we locate a kinaesthetic sensation in a phantom limb. Ayer would have to show why his account of bodily attachment would not work for a 'phantom body'. This could only be done by forsaking the *self-approach* for the *persons-approach*. As far as the subject himself is concerned all he needs in order to locate his kinaesthetic sensations is a phantom body. The problem to which these issues give rise will be investigated in the last chapter of this book. Enough has been said to show that James is not caught in a contradiction when he describes kinaesthetic sensations in physical terms, and that Ayer needs to do more than he has done to cross the bridge from locatability of bodily sensations to the existence of real bodies.

The judgement Ayer passes on the James-Ayer theory of the self is the following: 'So far as I can see it does not now lead to any counter-intuitive results. Its chief weakness, to my mind, is that the concept of appropriation, on which it relies very heavily, is not sufficiently precise.'[1] I have tried to show that the notion of

[1] Ayer, *The Origins of Pragmatism*, p. 278.

appropriation, as it stands, is *itself* counter-intuitive in that it is implausible to believe that there are any such appropriating Thoughts
unless we consciously call them into being. However, if the interpretation of appropriation I have offered is accepted, then it is
no longer counter-intuitive, for we are all perfectly familiar with
the manner in which our experiences are 'put forth' from us when
we pay attention to them.

Even if the theory is not counter-intuitive at this level, it is
counter-intuitive at a still more fundamental level. When Ayer
claims that 'a self can be defined as any class of experiences which
are confamiliar with each other',[1] he identifies the self with what is,
from the standpoint of common experience, the not-self. A pain I
have is mine; it is not me. Indeed if the pain is 'put forth' from me,
this very result sets it apart from the self. It is because our experiences are 'put forth' from us – because they bear the aspect of
'appearing to' us – that it seems so incredible to say that we just
are our experiences, that we are not in any sense an experienc*er* of
them. It is because we want to get away from this idea that we are
drawn into speaking of ourselves as in some sense behind our
experiences.

Let me digress for a moment to point out why the Serial Theory
seems to be driven into such a counter-intuitive position. The
Serial Theory is unquestionably the classical empiricist theory of
the self: the self is constructed out of 'the given' just as is the
external world itself. Thus the assumptions on which the Serial
Theory rests are themselves determined by the empiricist assumptions about the nature of 'the given'. Now it is incumbent upon
empiricists to explain how 'the given' is arrived at. The logical
method for an empiricist to employ is that of defining 'the given'
by ostensive means. This he does by drawing the attention of the
reader to an item of sense experience, and then giving him directions
on how to recognize an instantiation of 'the given' in the situation
confronting him. It is obvious on reflecting on this procedure that
whatever feature of the perceptual situation is singled out by the
reader will at the time be an object of attention for him. This is
clearly true of the well-known analysis of 'seeing a tomato', which
Price gives in illustration of an ostensive definition of a sense-
datum.[2] If we do not actually put a tomato in front of ourselves to
help us follow the analysis, we no doubt *imagine* seeing one. In

[1] *Ibid.*, p. 259.
[2] H. H. Price, *Perception* (London, 1954), p. 3.

either case the sense-datum is something which is an object of attention at the time of its identification.

This method of arriving at sense-data makes each sense-datum logically independent of every other sense-datum, and since nothing else is given in experience, the self must be viewed as a collection of sense-data. The problem then inevitably arises of how to account for the unity of such a set of discrete units. Some method has to be found of threading them all together. But if I am right the discreteness of the sense-data is necessarily attributable to the fact that they are objects of attention: by singling out for attention *this* rather than *that* in our experience we give the sense-datum its discreteness. If we bear this in mind it is odd then to ask how sense-data are related to one another. They must in the first instance be related as belonging to one consciousness before any particular element can be singled out for attention. Thus, the difficulty only arises if we overlook the reason for the discreteness of sense-data in the first place.

Furthermore, my argument that we should recognize the existence of that part of consciousness which I have called un-projected consciousness no longer compels us to construct the self out of elements which are objects of attention. That is to say, we do not have the difficulty of having to build up the self out of elements which ordinarily would be considered to be elements 'put forth', or 'detached' from the self. The recognition that 'the given' is not exhausted by the object of attention enables a theory of the self to be constructed which is as purely empirical as the Serial Theory, but which does not commit us to its implausible view of the self as a logical construction built up out of elements of the not-self.

Ayer's claim that the theory is not counter-intuitive is, from this point of view, nothing less than paradoxical. But clearly he does not have in mind the sense of counter-intuitive I have been assuming. He means that the definition of the self he has given does not lead us to individuate as a person anything which we would not as a matter of commonsense individuate as a person. In addition, he believes that his theory would allow us to individuate persons in unusual conditions in a way that would produce no paradoxical results. With this claim we may agree. But it is hardly surprising that the theory is not counter-intuitive in this sense, in that Ayer has deliberately chosen as defining characteristics of a person ones which would have as a result that persons thus individuated would coincide with our normal classification of persons. But here again from yet another point of view the results are still counter-intuitive in that the only rationale of the choice of defining characteristics of persons is that they produce the classification Ayer is looking for. Just why the self should be defined in terms of the characteristics he chooses is never explained. Quite obviously this cannot be explained. His theory fails as a theory of self-identity in that he can give no account of the reason for the self's possession of the characteristics in terms of which he defines it.

[7] I turn now to explore some of the implications of the alternative theory I am offering. It is a weakness of the Gallie-Jones theory and the James-Ayer theory that the self is equated with certain somatic sensations. If the self can in any sense be composed of elements of consciousness, it would seem counter-intuitive to confine the elements of consciousness which comprise it to somatic sensations. Far more plausible is a theory which allows it to be a possibility that the self is comprised of ideational elements as well as somatic ones. This possibility is ruled out by the theories we have been considering, but it is more than a possibility on my theory, it is an actuality. I have argued that unprojected consciousness must contain ideational components when attention is interrogative. Then unprojected consciousness will contain as an element a master-idea which is responsible for the direction of attention. Hence my theory does not commit us to thinking of the self in entirely non-cognitive terms – a major drawback of the rival theories. The description 'unprojected consciousness' refers to a logical aspect of the structure of consciousness, and it is on that account not to be confused with the particular content of unprojected consciousness at any one time. There is nothing on my view which rules out the possibility of any particular type of content forming the self at a particular moment – except that elements that are by definition 'attention laden' elements must be excluded. This view of mine coincides with that of Bradley, who says:

'Let us now, passing to the other side of both these relations, ask if the not-self contains anything which belongs to it exclusively. It will not be easy to discover many such elements. In the theoretical relation it is quite clear that not everything can be an object, all together and at once. At any one moment that which is in any sense before me must be limited. What are we to say then becomes of that remainder of the not-self which clearly has not, even for the time, passed wholly from my mind? I do not mean those features of the environment to which I fail to attend specially, but which I still go on perceiving as something before me. I refer to the features which have now sunk below this level. These are not even a setting or a fringe to the object of my mind. They have passed lower into the general background of feeling, from which that distinct object with its indistinct setting is detached. But this means that for the time they have passed into the self.[1]

This means that it is possible for unprojected consciousness to contain as components certain experiential elements which come from our outer senses. That is, it will usually contain elements of perceptual awareness; namely, those elements of perceptual awareness that are not at the time commanding attention. This implication of the theory may seem paradoxical since it could be understood as tantamount to the proposition that the self is partly made up of background 'noise' and peripheral visual awareness and so forth. If that were the case one could well object that one's self was

[1] F. H. Bradley, *Appearance and Reality*, 2nd ed. (London, 1925), pp. 91–2. Bradley's whole discussion of the subject is highly relevant. The above passage clearly contains the view that the polarization of consciousness into self and not-self is the work of attention. This would make it appear that the theory I am putting forward is identical with Bradley's. This is not the case, however much the above passage may make it seem so. For Bradley the distinction between self and not-self is one that emerges from a more primitive condition of consciousness called 'immediate experience'. As I understand it, this is a pre-attentive phase of consciousness, and it is certainly a phase devoid of any reference to a self. Bradley's view that immediate experience does not command even a minimal degree of attention is in sharp conflict with the conclusions I reached in the chapter on attention. For Bradley the existence of a self is dependent upon the operation of thought upon experience. For me the existence of experience cannot be independent of the existence of the self that enjoys the experience. In this matter I side with James Ward in his great debate with Bradley on the question. On the other hand Ward propounded a Pure Ego Theory, and I think Bradley was quite right to attack him on that. My position may be viewed as the reconciliation overcoming Ward's thesis and Bradley's antithesis. I identify the self with something found within experience, and in this way I escape Bradley's stricture against a Pure Ego. At the same time I escape Ward's strictures against Bradley, by making the self basic to all experience. The adoption of my theory entails the abandonment of the most unacceptable aspects of Bradley's and Ward's positions respectively. See R. Wollheim, *F. H. Bradley* (London, 1959), p. 132 ff. Had Bradley made the distinction I have elaborated between interrogative and unordered attention, he might have found it possible to have accepted the idea that immediate experience exhibited the presence of unordered attention. This would have removed many of the obstacles to his accepting the sort of solution I am proposing.

not made up of indistinct noises and indistinguishable visual objects, and so on for the remaining sense modalities. But that would be to misunderstand the position. The perceptual awareness in question is our experience *of* noise, and so forth, it is not the noise itself. This is true too of the other senses. And yet we must be careful not to describe such elements of unprojected consciousness as experiences of noise, because as soon as they are individuated they cease to belong to unprojected consciousness, and even to speak of them as 'noise' presupposes recognition of them; i.e. they have then come to attention. It is only in retrospect, therefore, that we can come to classify such an experiential element as awareness *of noise*. It must be stressed, then, that it is the experienc-*ing* with which the self is being identified, and not the objects experienced.

The question arises 'How much of the content of unprojected consciousness at one time can be turned into an object of attention?' In other words, how much of the content of unprojected consciousness can be objectified as the empirical self? Here again Bradley's thinking is instructive:

'In my opinion it is not only possible, but most probable, that in every man there are elements in the internal felt core which are never made objects, and which practically cannot be. There may well be features in our Coenesthesia which lie so deep that we never succeed in detaching them; and these cannot properly be said to be ever our not-self. Even in the past we cannot distinguish their speciality. But I presume that even here the obstacle may be said to be practical, and to consist in the obscurity, and not otherwise in the essence, of these sensations.'[1]

With this I agree. I would only add that there is a limit to the amount of this content that one can objectify at any one time. If the attempt to detach this inner core is to be made, it will require that attention be directed by a master-idea in order to bring it about. But that master-idea cannot itself be at the same time detached from unprojected consciousness and made part of the empirical self. Moreover, there must also always remain behind those elements of kinaesthetic sensation that make possible the act of attention by which the self is objectified. There will thus always be a residuum which must escape self-objectification. Our

---

[1] Bradley, *Appearance and Reality*, pp. 92–3.

so-called empirical self must forever be no more than partial self-objectification. To my mind this fact goes far to explain the belief that the self is elusive in the sense that there is some aspect of it which experience cannot capture. Even James was prone to this belief, although his theory gave him no justification for it.

If my theory is adopted, the idea can be rejected that self-awareness is awareness of the empirical self. This amounts to a rejection of the view that self-awareness is a special act that describes a special reflective experience which does not occur very often. An attempt at full objectification of the empirical self would indeed be a rare act of the sort in question, but on my theory there is no need to place that interpretation on self-awareness. Instead, in its terms, self-awareness becomes an aspect of all awareness, and as so conceived self-awareness accompanies all our experience. It is this which permits us to view experiences as experiences *to* the self. It is only because there is a self-awareness independent of the particular experience holding attention that the experience is *to* such a self, as distinct from being merely *of* the self. It is in this sense that the subject is present alongside of its experiences.

3. SUPPORT FROM UNEXPECTED QUARTERS

[8] Further support for my contention that unprojected consciousness and the self are identical can be drawn from an altogether different quarter. I shall argue that the theory is corroborated by certain of its deductive consequences. These give rise to expectations which appear to be borne out by experience. Earlier I mentioned the logical possibility of a form of consciousness that I described as a homogeneous consciousness.[1] A homogeneous consciousness was said to be one in which a total temporary state of consciousness consisted of one element and one element only. I spoke of such an element pervading the whole of consciousness, and blotting out all other elements, but I did not commit myself on the question whether such a form of consciousness ever actually occurred; and it is not necessary to my argument that I do so now. My argument is based on the fact that people have *claimed* to experience a homogeneous consciousness. I shall attempt to show that the descriptions that are given of alleged experiences of a homogeneous consciousness are the descriptions we would expect

[1] See above, p. 105.

to receive if my theory were true. In other words, they can be deduced from the theory.

A homogeneous consciousness would, by definition, be a consciousness lacking an unprojected consciousness; i.e. it would not be polarized as a normal consciousness is. It follows from the theory that the single element of a homogeneous consciousness could not be the object of attention. It can further be inferred that if there were such a homogeneous consciousness it would be characterized as a form of consciousness from which the presence of the self had entirely vanished. This inference follows logically from the identification of the self with unprojected consciousness: if no unprojected consciousness, then no self. Were such a homogeneous consciousness to exist, its existence could not be reported first-hand at the time, for to report the occurrence of the state would of necessity mean that a self must be aware concurrently of the state, and this would entail the existence of unprojected consciousness, which, *ex hypothesi*, does not exist. The only first-hand evidence of the existence of a homogeneous consciousness would come from the subject's memory of normal consciousness returning in the wake of some indescribable state of consciousness.

My theory would lead us to expect such a person to say that he had some dim recollection of a form of experience in which awareness of self was completely absent. In other words it would be described as being like having an ownerless experience. Moreover, an inability to characterize the experience more definitely would be connected with the subjectless character of the experience. Now it so happens that Ribot raises the question of the possible existence of a homogeneous consciousness, and concludes that it is realized in some rare types of mystical experience:

'Do there really exist cases of *absolute* monoideism, in which consciousness is reduced to a sole and single state entirely occupying it, and in which the mechanism of association is totally arrested? In our opinion, this we meet in only a few, very rare cases of ecstasy,. . .'[1]

Furthermore, the example Ribot instances, as a case of such ecstasy, is St Theresa's mystical union with God. He traces the seven stations of prayer, or meditation, through which St Theresa says we must pass before we reach the highest stage of ecstasy,

[1] Ribot, *The Psychology of Attention*, p. 10.

which is union with God, and points out that each stage advances to a greater concentration of consciousness than the preceding stage, until ultimately consciousness reaches a single homogeneous state, which he calls 'absolute monoideism'. As he says, 'God has now descended into the substance of the soul, and become one with it.'[1] But it is precisely when the soul has attained this union with God, that mystics claim that all consciousness of self is lost. Indeed some mystics carry their claim to the point of paradox and say that they become God during their mystical encounter.

Ribot points out that such supreme mystical consummations happen extremely rarely. 'The greatest mystics alone,' he says, 'have attained, by a still stronger effort, to absolute monoideism.' There is reason to believe, therefore, that those instances of mystical experience that reach the state of absolute monoideism are also the ones in which the mystic is likely to claim that his self was annihilated in the encounter. I should not neglect to point out that mystical experience is a subject about which authorities disagree. Some contest the preponderant opinion that the self is transcended in the highest types of mystical experience. There is also reason to doubt that all mystical experiences are of one type and that they are all equally describable in terms of an approach to a state of absolute monoideism. The point I am trying to make, however, is that whether or not the claims are accurate, and whether or not they are true, it would be not only intelligible but a logical consequence of my view that a certain type of mystical experience (the highest state of ecstasy) would have to be described in terms of a loss of self-identity. Thus in terms of a theory fitting the facts we have here an unusual set of possible facts which the theory fits. I mention them as an interesting side-light to the theory.

[9] It is a commonplace observation that there is scarcely anything new in philosophy, so if we look for intimations of the theory I am advancing it will be surprising if none are found. It is interesting to discover that something reminiscent of this theory was suggested by Leibniz. In explaining his notion of *petites perceptions*, Leibniz says this:

'Besides there are countless indications which lead us to think that there is at every moment an infinity of *perceptions* within us, but

[1] *Ibid.*, p. 100.

without apperception and without reflexion; that is to say, changes
in the soul itself of which we are not conscious, because the impressions are either too small and too numerous or too closely
combined, so that each is not distinctive enough by itself, but
nevertheless in combination with others each has its effect and
makes itself felt, at least confusedly, in the whole.'[1]

After further elaboration of the idea of *petites perceptions*, Leibniz
adds this:

'These unconscious (insensible) perceptions also indicate and
constitute the identity of the individual, who is characterized by
the traces or expressions of his previous states which these unconscious perceptions preserve, as they connect his previous states
with his present state . . .'[2]

In more recent times essentially the same theory as mine was
sketched by Dawes Hicks in an article he wrote in 1913.[3] His three
basic ideas are these: (*a*) Attention is said to operate in all forms of
consciousness; (*b*) It brings about 'a certain selection or limitation
within the field of what is apprehended of some features and the
relative neglect or disregard of the rest'; (*c*) In its higher, voluntary,
form it is responsible for the distinction between self and not-self.
I shall pass over (*a*) and (*b*) which do no more than endorse the
approach of the earlier chapters. The important consideration is
(*c*), and referring to the distinctions which attention discloses by
operating on its material Dawes Hicks has this to say:

'One such important distinction – it is not too much to say, *the*
most important distinction – which thus comes gradually to
recognition is that indicated by the terms self and not-self. By
degrees in the development of intelligence there is effected a
definitely recognized separation between the trains of thoughts,
sentiments, feelings and sense-presentations which are more or
less constant and habitual, and which thus come to be regarded as
constituting the prevailing centre or background of individual

[1] R. Latta, *Leibniz The Monadology and Other Philosophical Writings* (London,
1951), p. 370.
[2] *Ibid.*, p. 373. I am grateful to Mr J. Schumacher for drawing my attention
to these passages.
[3] G. Dawes Hicks, 'The Nature and Development of Attention', *The British
Journal of Psychology*, VL, 1 (1913).

personality, and the relatively transient presentations and apprehended contents which come and go, and which the subject learns
to contrast with and to distinguish from the totality of the former.
The contents of our knowledge or experience, or rather certain of
them, tend more and more to wear the aspect of an inward possession, and to become the instrument, as it were, by which we
apprehend the world of objective fact. So soon as this distinction
has attained any prominence in consciousness, it must of necessity
influence in a very decided manner the direction, as we may put it
metaphorically, of attention. For it will then become possible for
the subject to differentiate between the cases where attention
comes about through a presented object being connected with the
contents of representations or ideas that are not specially included
in the consciousness of self, and the cases where the activity of
comparing and relating is carried on through means of those ideas
and feelings which are included.'[1]

There are, of course, certain differences between the position
expressed in this passage, and the one I have been developing. In
spite of that my theory clearly has the backing of Dawes Hicks.
Apart from Leibniz and Dawes Hicks, there is some evidence for
the view that the theory I am advocating was also arrived at by
Wittgenstein. If my surmise is right then we will be able to offer an
interpretation of the so-called 'no-ownership' theory of the self
which puts it in a completely different light from that in which it is
at present viewed. However, it suits my purpose better to introduce
Wittgenstein's views in the course of the argument of the next
section.

4. A DEFENCE AGAINST SOME OBJECTIONS

[10] I now come to the difficulties facing the theory which immediately threaten to overwhelm it. In the first place it might be
objected that it is nonsensical to translate 'I have an experience' as
'Unprojected consciousness has an experience'. This at once dis-
qualifies the theory since to be successful a theory of the self must
be able to offer an intelligible analysis of such sentences as 'I have a
pain in my arm' and 'I am swimming'. But if the self is equated
with unprojected consciousness, this would seem to commit us to
the absurdity that one sphere of consciousness could 'have' another

[1] *Ibid.*, p. 22.

sphere of consciousness, and even worse that it could 'have' a swim. Consequently the theory fails, since it does not permit us to say that a self has experiences, or engages in actions. A corollary to this objection would consist in pointing out that although it makes no sense to say 'I have a self', it makes perfectly good sense to say 'I have an unprojected consciousness'. Once again this proves that the self and unprojected consciousness cannot be identical.

In the second place it might be objected that the theory is incoherent in that unprojected consciousness is itself said to be composed of elements, and they too would require a self whose elements they were. But, on the theory, no self exists to which the elements comprising unprojected consciousness could be ascribed. Thus after all the theory is unable to escape postulating experiential elements which are subjectless.

Lastly, it might be objected that the theory fails in that it cannot account for the persistence of the self through time. This it cannot do because it is not only possible but likely that from time to time the entire content of unprojected consciousness will be replaced, and that would mean one self replacing another just as often as that happens. In short, the theory may be allowed to succeed in accounting for the unity of the self at an instant, but it is powerless to account for the continuity of the self through time.

Of these objections I shall leave the last until the next chapter since the issues it raises will be investigated there. Nevertheless it is my contention that in the last analysis *all* the objections originate from a failure to distinguish the *self-approach* from the *persons-approach*.[1] They essentially consist in putting *persons-approach* questions to the *self-approach*, and arguing for the incoherence of a *self-approach* theory on the ground of its inability to handle such questions.

The objections are based upon what it does and what it does not make sense to say in ordinary language. At the level of ordinary language, statements about unprojected consciousness if understood as statements about persons become paradoxical. The reason for this quite clearly has to do with the fact that the conceptual scheme we use presupposes that we are talking about persons, as distinct from subjects of states of consciousness – where it is characteristic of our talk about persons that we are concerned with questions of identification. Now in terms of a subject's

---

[1] See above, pp. 19–26.

enjoying a particular experience, there is no question of his either identifying himself to himself, or of his referentially identifying his experience to himself. Such issues simply do not arise when one is concerned exclusively with one's own case. It is for this reason that Geach is quite right when he points out that when a person is thinking to himself about his own experiences there is no need for him to denote the subject by using the personal pronoun 'I' and no need for him to describe an experience he is having as 'mine'.[1] In other words, in self-address ascriptive language can have no logical point.

But if we *do* use the personal pronoun, then we are doing more than referring to the subject as he experiences himself as being. By using the personal pronoun one draws along with it the entire conceptual scheme for the use of ascriptive language. In short, one presupposes the concept of a person, as Strawson has shown. This means that the identification of the subject with unprojected consciousness is not the same as the identification of the referent of the personal pronoun 'I' with unprojected consciousness. It is for that reason that any such substitution is nonsensical. In sum, we have here the explanation of the fact that the *self-approach* is characterized by a refusal to treat the subject of inner experience as the referent of first person sentences.

This reasoning would still seem to allow, however, that the 'I' as *person* could be said to possess an unprojected consciousness, whereas it would still make no sense to say that 'I' as person possess a subject. The reason the latter statement is nonsensical is that a person *is* a subject and something more. That is to say, the concept of person is logically more complex than the concept of subject, and is logically dependent on the latter concept. It therefore needs to be shown what is odd about the sentence, 'I (as person) have an unprojected consciousness.' If this statement is meant not only to identify the person who makes it, but also is meant to individuate a particular unprojected consciousness then we must understand the unprojected consciousness as 'put forth' by attention. In order to be able to refer to a particular unprojected consciousness it must already have drawn some attention. The ascriber of the unprojected consciousness could not otherwise report its existence. But this is *ex hypothesi* impossible. We can conclude that the statement 'I have an unprojected consciousness' considered as a report of a state of consciousness is meaningless.

[1] See above, p. 23.

If my thinking is on the right lines, we are in a position to understand why so many philosophers have maintained that the personal pronoun 'I' does not refer to an inner subject. We can also understand why they should have been led to conclude that since the 'I' refers to a publicly identifiable person, the search for some other referent for the word 'I' is out of place. In fact all that this proves is that for purposes of communication we require no notion other than the notion of a person as a publicly identifiable particular. It does not prove that there is no subject of experience, and it cannot establish that the awareness of being such a subject is delusive.

Now although on the *self-approach* there is no need to refer to the subject of states of consciousness because it is not concerned with the problem of communication with others, someone who is philosophically minded might wish none the less to describe his experiences to himself in such a way that the description brings out the structure of experience in its exhibition of a subject over against an object. If he simply described his experience as, say, 'this toothache now' his description would fail to do justice to the fact that the toothache is 'put forth' from the self, and stands over against the self. He would have an overpowering reason for wanting to use a personal pronoun, and describe his experience as 'my toothache' or 'the toothache I am having' in order to bring out the subject-object duality of the experience. But he would not want to do this in order to identify the subject: there would be no question of that. What he wants is something with which to symbolize the subject of consciousness in contrast with the toothache that is predicated in the description. Now if the personal pronoun cannot do this because its function is exclusively an identificatory one, some other expression would have to be chosen to symbolize the subject. Now for those philosophers who have not been aware of the need to see the personal pronoun as essentially belonging to ascriptive language about persons, there seemed no reason why the personal pronoun should not be used to perform this symbolizing function as well. They have thus asserted that the 'I' refers to a subject other than the public identifiable person. This has, I believe, been one of the strongest considerations in favour of the Pure Ego Theory.

In order to supply a token which can be used to symbolize the subject of consciousness let us choose the token *I*. This would enable us to bring out the subject-object duality of consciousness in the descriptions we give ourselves of our experiences in the form

'*I* have an experience X'. In such a sentence the *I* has no identificatory use: we are considering its use exclusively in self-address.

This distinction between the ordinary language use of 'I' and the philosophical use of '*I*' to symbolize the self is, I suggest, what Wittgenstein was driving at in his Cambridge Lectures of the early thirties when he was reported by Moore as saying that the word 'I' is used in 'two utterly different ways'.[1] In one of its uses the 'I' denotes a possessor, in its other use it does not. I suggest that we can understand his distinction between the 'I' which denotes a possessor and the 'I' which does not, as being equivalent respectively to the identificatory 'I' of ordinary language, and the symbolizing '*I*' of philosophical description. It is obviously '*I*' in the latter sense which is the origin of the 'no-ownership' theory of the self. If my interpretation of this use of 'I' is correct, then indeed the symbolizing '*I*' does not 'own' its experiences, but the point has no mysterious or counter-intuitive implications. In essence the 'I' which denotes a possessor is the 'I' of the *persons-approach*, and it belongs to ordinary language. The 'I' which does not denote a possessor is the '*I*' of the *self-approach*, and it is not an ordinary language term.

Wittgenstein made a further remark about the meaning of the word 'I' which suggests intriguing parallels to the theory I am developing. As Moore reports:

'In speaking of these two senses of "I" he said, as what he called "a final thing", "In one sense 'I' and 'conscious' are equivalent, but not in another", and he compared this difference to the difference between what can be said of the pictures on a film in a magic lantern and of the pictures on the screen; saying that the pictures in the lantern are all "on the same level" but that the picture which is at any given time on the screen is not "on the same level" with any of them, and that if we were to use "conscious" to say of one of the pictures in the lantern that it was at that time being thrown on the screen, it would be meaningless to say of the picture on the screen that it was "conscious". The pictures on the film, he said, "have neighbours", whereas that on the screen has none.'[2]

This *could* be interpreted as an illustration of the theory I have arrived at. Whether it should be so interpreted is difficult to say.

[1] G. E. Moore, *Philosophical Papers* (London, 1959), p. 310.
[2] *Ibid.*, p. 310.

But I understand Wittgenstein's analogy to mean that the pictures
in the magic lantern represent the 'I' which is identical with
'conscious', in contrast with the picture thrown on the screen
which is not 'conscious' in that sense. The analogy suggests, does
it not, that the pictures in the lantern stand for unprojected consciousness, and the one on the screen stands for the experience
which is detached and 'put forth' as an object of attention. Not
only that, but the suggestion that all the pictures in the lantern are
'neighbours' expresses my thought that unprojected consciousness
contains a plurality of undifferentiated elements in contrast to the
unity of the object of attention. If I am right, then the 'I' which is
identical with 'conscious' is the 'I' which does not denote a possessor: it is the '*I*' of the *self-approach*. It is more than likely that
Wittgenstein has expressed the essential vision that lies behind the
theory I have constructed. If I am interpreting him correctly then
the authorship of the idea for the theory belongs to him, and that I
would be happy to acknowledge. I must confess, however, that I
had to arrive at the theory independently before I was able to
understand Wittgenstein's obscure words.

[11] In *The Bounds of Sense* Strawson makes some remarks which
seem to invite the theory I am advocating, and, in conjunction with
these remarks, he makes others which seem to preclude the
possibility of any theory such as mine succeeding. For this reason
it is worth seeing how my theory stands in the light of what he
says. Strawson maintains in that work that we can ascribe certain
experiences to ourselves (presumably ones which we ascribe to
ourselves not on the basis of observation) without invoking any
criteria of personal identity. As he says,

'When a man (a subject of experience) ascribes a current or
directly remembered state of consciousness to himself, no use
whatever of any criteria of personal identity is required to justify
his use of the pronoun "I" to refer to the subject of that experience.
When "I" is thus used, without any need or any possibility of its
use being justified by empirical criteria of subject-identity, it does
not, however, lose its role of referring to a subject.'[1]

Now in terms of the distinction between the *persons-approach* and
the *self-approach*, Strawson's reference to 'the subject of experience'

[1] Strawson, *The Bounds of Sense*, p. 165.

is equivocal. On the one hand the subject of experience can be understood to be referring to what we take the self to be – i.e. a person for some theorists, and a body for others – or it can be understood to be referring to what we experience ourselves as being. Since Strawson's is exclusively the *persons-approach* we are, of course, not in any doubt about what *he* means by 'the subject of experience'. But the point is that this closes his mind to one of the possibilities suggested by his description. And that is that the 'I' can be used for completely non-ascriptive purposes – criterionless or otherwise. It is only when the speaker intends to communicate to another person that it makes sense to say that he is ascribing an experience to himself (criterionless self-ascription), and it is only when the intention to communicate to another is the reason for an avowal that the *persons-approach* interpretation of the speaker's words is the right one. But we also engage in self-address with the intent of bringing home to ourselves a certain experience we are having. We do this often because attempting to express ourselves by describing the experience is a way of focusing attention on the experience the better to appreciate it. We are then confined to the *self-approach*, and in that case, I maintain, mention of the subject of the experience has nothing to do with ascribing an experience to an owner, and hence nothing to do with criterionless self-ascription. In such cases the 'I' is used symbolically and not referentially. It is used as an '*I*'.

The consequences of a failure to demarcate these two logically different types of situation manifests itself in what Strawson says in the following passage:

'It is easy to become intensely aware of the immediate character, of the purely inner basis, of such self-ascription while both retaining the sense of ascription to a subject and forgetting that immediate reports of experience have this character of ascriptions to a subject only because of the links I have mentioned with ordinary criteria of personal identity. Thus there arises a certain illusion: the illusion of a purely inner and yet subject-referring use for "I". If we try to abstract this use, to shake off the connection with ordinary criteria of personal identity, to arrive at a kind of subject-reference which is wholly and adequately based on nothing but inner experience, what we really do is simply to deprive our use of "I" of any referential force whatever. It will simply express, as Kant would say, "consciousness in general". If we nevertheless continue to think of the "I" as having referential force, as referring to a subject, then, just because we have really nothing left but the bare *form* of reference, it will appear that the object of this reference must be an object of singular purity and simplicity – a pure, individual, immaterial substance.'[1]

It is noteworthy that Strawson acknowledges a 'purely inner' use of 'I', but because of his unquestioned assumption that 'I' can only be used in a referring sense, he concludes that any such use of 'I' must be illusory. We have seen that he is right to deny any such inner directed use of 'I' *as a referring expression*, but this does not rule out the possibility of the use by philosophers of the word '*I*' to symbolize the subject standing over against an experience to which he is attending. Strawson's position rests on his rejection without argument of the Wittgensteinian claim that the word 'I' has two entirely different senses – one of which is a referring sense and the other of which is not. It is this premiss of his that leads him to conclude that any attempt to identify the subject of inner experience must lead to 'a pure, individual, immaterial substance'; i.e. a Pure Ego. In terms of my theory we can say that Strawson was right to reject the idea of a Pure Ego, but wrong in thinking that no alternative could be arrived at on the basis of inner experience. The identification of the self with unprojected consciousness is a clear alternative, and it gives us a self which is experiential and the experiential content of which is rich in diversity and variety. It is the antithesis of Strawson's 'bare *form* of reference'.

We may speculate that Strawson's conviction that awareness of the purely inner basis of self-ascription leads inevitably to the Pure Ego can be traced back to the assumption that a study of consciousness in order to determine its subject can have as its outcome no other result than adoption of a Pure Ego Theory (thesis) or a Serial Theory (antithesis). Until now a third alternative has not been sufficiently explicitly stated to demand consideration. For those who enjoy dialectical language, I am offering a reconciliation between thesis and antithesis in a higher synthesis. We may view Strawson's argument as a challenge to produce a theory of the self based on inner experience which is not a Pure Ego Theory. The theory I offer is my answer to that challenge.

In my introduction I remarked that we have native knowledge of the self and that, therefore, the identity of ourselves as subjects of

[1] *Ibid.*, p. 166.

states of consciousness could only be determined by our looking to our own cases. This is the course I have tried to follow, and the theory I have been putting forward in this chapter is the outcome. I mentioned MacNabb's remark that we have an experience of the self 'more internal than the most personal emotion we feel'. I now suggest that this is the sort of remark we would make were the self indeed identical with unprojected consciousness. Unprojected consciousness has the experiential character and the interiority which MacNabb's description portrays the self as having. The logical features of unprojected consciousness also make it understandable that the Augustinian formula should seem so applicable to the experience we each have of ourselves: if no one asks me what I am, I know; if I am asked, I know not.

CHAPTER SIX

YESTERDAY'S SELF

I. THE PAST OF A SELF AND THE PAST OF A PERSON

[1] Philosophers have been so preoccupied with the question of the persistence of the self through time, that they have overlooked the importance of giving sense to the claim that at any one instant a state of consciousness has a subject. The last chapter attempted to make good this omission. But we in turn must not fall into the opposite error of accounting for the self's contemporaneity with its experiences at the expense of failing to account for its persistence through a succession of experiences. Our theory has explained the manner in which the self gives unity to consciousness in one of its dimensions; namely, its total temporary states. We now have to account for the unity in the other dimension; namely, the unity of a succession of total temporary states. To put it briefly, it remains to be shown that the theory I am advancing also accounts for the continuousness of consciousness and the persistence of the self through time. This I shall now try to do.

It is important to be clear on this question about the implications of following the *self-approach* as opposed to the *persons-approach*. A person suffering loss of memory may ask himself the question 'Who am I?' Such a person does not know who he is in the sense that he lacks certain autobiographical knowledge about himself such as his name, his home address, his relatives, and his occupation. One in such a predicament may be said to lack knowledge of his personal identity. This is pre-eminently the problem that the *persons-approach* is concerned to solve. The question the sufferer from amnesia asks himself is a question about his identification, and he would in the first instance be prepared to accept a statement by a third party telling him who he is, although of course he will only feel completely confident about the third person identification when he gets his memory back and it bears out the identification he has been given. The identity of a person from this standpoint is ascertained in basically the same way as is the identity of a material object. For instance a man's identity can be ascertained by identifying his finger-prints – assuming there is a record of them. Now it is clearly the case that a person asking himself the question 'Who am I?' is not at all concerned with the question of his identity as subject of his present experiences. We could go so far as to say that his being a conscious subject is a necessary condition of his being able to raise the question of his identity of which he is ignorant. Thus a person suffering amnesia about his past is not a person who does not know that he is a self. He wishes to find out certain things that are true of the self he now experiences himself as being. Such a person could wonder philosophically what it is to be a self, and that wonder would not be removed upon his being given certain biographical details about himself.

When a person has forgotten his identity he has lost the connection between his past history and his present situation. Finding out who he is is therefore a matter of finding out who he was. The problem of personal identity is therefore one of establishing that a certain person now existing is one and the same person as one who was known to have existed for a certain time prior to the present. The identity of a person from this standpoint is declared in a statement of the form 'He is the one who . . .' where the clause beginning with 'who' gives a description pertaining to the past. It is quite right, therefore, that philosophers interested in the criteria for the identity of persons in this context should concentrate upon memory and upon bodily identity.

But the *self-approach* is not interested in those questions. It is interested in the question of the persistence of the self *qua* subject of consciousness as it is affected by the passage of time *in the present*. Our native knowledge of ourselves is a knowledge of ourselves as enduring through time. From this standpoint the person suffering amnesia about his past will not necessarily 'lose sight of himself' during the hours that he desperately attempts to recall his identity. He does not need any evidence or criteria for his being the same subject of consciousness now as he was when he first asked who he was. The *self-approach* is concerned to explain in what sense the self has an experience of being a persisting self: a self that is capable of outlasting any individual experience it is having and which preserves its identity despite the changes in the experiences of which it is the subject.

[2] Philosophers concerned with the problem of the existence of the self over a stretch of time have usually for the purpose of argument

phrased the problem in terms of the continued existence of a self from yesterday to today. We find James, for instance, expressing the belief each of us has of his continuing identity in the statement 'I am the same self that I was yesterday'.[1] Now it might seem arbitrary to choose an interval of twenty-four hours for the purpose of discussion, and equally acceptable to choose a different interval in its place. On this line of reasoning all that is needed is to show that it is possible *in principle* for a self to persist through time, and that can be shown in respect of any stretch of time. Why not 'I am the same self that I was this morning, or an hour ago, or a moment ago'? In other words if we think only of the time factor, there is no difference in principle whether we are dealing with a very small lapse of time, or a big one. In theory, therefore, the problem of self-continuity is solved as soon as it is shown that a person is the same self as he was a moment ago.

If this reasoning is accepted it is all the more significant that James looks for the continuity between today's self and *yesterday's* self as opposed to looking for the continuity between experiences closer together in time. Obviously what he has in mind is the possibility that the series of the self's experiences is broken during dreamless sleep. The problem then becomes one of explaining how the series before the interruption is continuous with the one arising after the interruption. (Of course to call it an *interruption* begs the question, because it presupposes that the two series really are subsections of one and the same series. But the question really is: On what ground can two separate series of experiences be said to form sections of a wider series of experiences?) It is clear that the problem arises when there is loss of consciousness due to any cause, and not only when we are in a dreamless sleep.

It would surely be right to argue that before we can handle the question of the continuity of the self in the face of possible gaps in the continuity of a series of experiences, we *should* have an explanation of the continuity of the self in relation to those sections of the series of experiences which have no gaps. Only after solving that problem will we be ready to tackle the problem of the survival of the self across the gaps. From this point of view it would be an

---

[1] James, *The Principles of Psychology*, Vol. I, p. 332. Taken literally the statement 'I am the same self that I was yesterday' is a tautology, since its contradictory 'I am not the same self that I was yesterday' makes no sense. Nevertheless the statement does succeed in conveying the impression we have of our continuing existence through time.

achievement in itself to account for the continuity of the self during a single period of waking consciousness. It would mean that we would have an explanation of what it meant if we said of a subject of a present experience that he was identical with the subject of an experience that occurred earlier in the series. Although self-continuity during waking consciousness is the important issue for the *self-approach*, and the one to which I shall largely address myself, it is necessary to get clear about the effect of breaks in consciousness on our experience of being selves. By saying something about this issue I can explain just how a problem of self-identity can shade off into a problem of personal identity.

The gaps created in consciousness by dreamless sleep, concussion, passing out, and anaesthesia are by no means as damaging to the continuity of consciousness as they may sound. A gap in consciousness can, for instance, never be *experienced* as a gap in consciousness by the person whose consciousness is affected. A person may have the experience of losing consciousness, but that is a conscious experience. No one can be conscious of being unconscious. All we know is that we have the experience of losing consciousness immediately followed by the experience of regaining consciousness. It is only by inference that we know that we have been unconscious, or by being told of this by someone else. In a sense, therefore, consciousness does not record its own interruptions, but gives the impression of being unbroken, although it is not.

This phenomenon can best be understood in terms of a distinction between objective time and subjective time. By objective time I mean clock time. By subjective time I mean our personal experience of the passage of time. In subjective time, if I happen to be waiting for someone, even five minutes can seem a long time. On the other hand, if I am enjoying myself immensely, two hours can seem to pass in a flash. Now what I suggest is that interruptions to consciousness are only interruptions from the point of view of objective time. From the point of view of subjective time, consciousness is uninterrupted. If I had been unconscious for a period, I could only find out about it inferentially, or from the testimony of others. The assertion that a certain period of time had elapsed, during which I was unconscious, must have the status of an hypothesis, as far as I am concerned. By contrast, the statement 'I've had to wait ages for you', belongs to subjective time, and is not in any sense an hypothesis. It is a direct report of a subjective impression.

Thus when from the standpoint of subjective time I say 'I am the same self that I was yesterday' the statement is no more intended to bridge a gap in consciousness than it would be if I had said 'I am the same self that I was this morning'. My recollections of the morning and of the previous night are memory experiences of myself *qua* subject at the time of recall, and the memory is a memory of the subject of recall also being the subject of the experience remembered. But all this would be true even if the so-called 'memories' were delusive. In that case I would indeed be the same self as the one I believed had certain experiences in the past, but whether there was indeed an actually existing person who at the earlier time in question actually had the experiences in question would be another matter. That would be for the *persons-approach* to determine. Thus on the *self-approach* one can claim no more than that one is the same self as the one about whom one claims to make a true memory claim, but from the *self-approach* alone nothing follows about the previous existence of a person and his having had certain experiences in the past.

It follows that the determination of the discontinuities in objective time which must be correlated with the continuities of consciousness in subjective time is strictly a matter for the *persons-approach*. All that one is entitled to say on the subject of the continuity of the self is: 'I am the same self that I "remember" that I was yesterday' – where 'remember' is understood as a memory claim that could be mistaken. I cannot say that I am the same self that I was yesterday if by this I am claiming real existence yesterday. For such a claim can only be made within the framework of the *persons-approach*.

2. AWARENESS AS A STATE AND ATTENTION AS AN ACTIVITY

[3] I have argued that the occurrence of consciousness is dependent upon change and that the change in question comes from bodily activities. I now wish to argue for a further connection between consciousness and bodily activities and that is that the *continuousness* of consciousness is brought about by bodily activities. The point of this approach is that if I can establish that consciousness is continuous in the sense of enduring for a stretch of time, then it will follow that the subject of consciousness too will persist during that stretch of time. Without providing some extraordinary context

it would be very odd to suppose that the subject of a state of consciousness just before the state terminated was not the same subject as the subject just after the state began if, *ex hypothesi*, we were dealing with a single continuous state. Thus by accounting for the continuousness of consciousness we *ipso facto* account for the possibility of the persistence of the subject of consciousness.

The account I shall give of the continuousness of consciousness will be concerned with that aspect of consciousness that I have referred to as the object of attention. To facilitate my account I need to employ a vocabulary which describes the object of attention in a manner better designed to bring out the features of it which are important in this context. When we refer to a perceptual object of attention we usually have in mind an object which is external to ourselves, such as a tree or a train. Now obviously no tree or train can be an element of consciousness, and since an object of attention has been defined as an element of consciousness, some other description has to be given of the object of attention. An object can only become an object of attention at the time we are perceiving it: the object of attention is the tree *as seen* or the train *as heard*. Now I wish to use the word 'awareness' in a special technical sense to refer to objects of attention in so far as they are presented through the subject's sense fields. Thus the tree as presented through sight is an awareness and the train as presented through hearing is an awareness, and so on for the other modalities. If I may borrow Chisholm's vocabulary, when I perceive an object I am 'being appeared to . . . by *x*', where the blank is to be filled in with an adverbial description of the manner in which one is appeared to.[1] Chisholm's concept of 'being appeared to . . .' is identical with the sense I have given 'awareness'. On this definition the object of attention is always an awareness.

It is necessary to stress that 'awareness' is here used in a technical sense because in the ordinary sense of the word if we make our awareness our object of attention we are *not* making the object we are aware *of* the object of attention. To pay attention to the awareness itself in those circumstances means paying attention to the *fact*, say, that one is aware of the old oak, or to the fact that *one* is aware of the old oak, or to the fact that one is *aware of* the old oak, but not to the fact that one is aware of *the old oak*. On my usage, however, it does not follow that if the object of attention is described

[1] R. Chisholm, *Perceiving* (Ithaca, 1957), pp. 120-1.

as an awareness it is the experiencing as opposed to what is experienced that is the object of attention.

It should also be understood that I am using 'awareness' in an occurrence sense and not in a dispositional sense. In a dispositional sense the word 'aware' is often used as a synonym for 'know'. Thus a person can be said to be aware of the circumstances surrounding the assassin's death even though he is not at the time thinking of them, and we could equally well say of the person that he knows the circumstances surrounding the assassin's death. Because I am not using 'aware' in this sense, I have described my usage as a technical usage. Nevertheless the word is often employed in the way I use it, especially by philosophers. In this sense any case of seeing is a case of awareness, any case of hearing is a case of awareness, and so on. In this manner we arrive at the concepts of visual awareness, auditory awareness, tactual awareness, and so on.

One interpretation of such concepts which it is very natural to give is not one that should be given to them in the sense in which I shall employ them. Some philosophers have made use of a concept of sensory awareness such that perception is based upon sensory awareness but is not identical with it.[1] From this point of view sensory awareness is perception minus perceptual recognition. It is important to bear in mind that by perceptual awareness I am not referring to such an inferred sensory basis of perception, but am referring to the full experience involving perceptual recognition. Unless this is clearly appreciated my identification of the object of attention with an awareness becomes unintelligible. First of all, when we pay attention to a perceptual object we are not paying attention to this sensory basis. Secondly, it may be questioned whether it is even possible for a being with recognitional capacities to make of his pre-recognitional sensory experience an object of attention.

In other words my view of awareness amounts to this: if we take up the idea of a 'proper object' of a verb of perception and say that the proper object of hearing is 'sounds', the proper object of seeing is 'sightings', the proper object of smelling is 'smells', etc., then we can take the word 'awareness' to be an umbrella term which allows us to mention any such proper object of a perception verb without having to list the varieties. That is how I am using it. This use parallels the use I have made of the word 'consciousness'

[1] See, D. Locke, *Perception of the External World* (London, 1967), p. 27 ff.

except that the latter word brings in elements to which attention is not being paid in addition to those to which attention is being paid, whereas 'awareness' covers only those elements to which attention is being paid. I shall add just one further stipulation to my use of 'awareness'. Although every perception is an awareness, not every awareness is a perception. Thus a non-veridical perception is still an awareness although not a perception, and an after-image is an awareness although not a perception. This follows from the fact that hallucinations and after-images can just as well be objects of attention as can our perceptions. To take this into account our use of Chisholm's formula must be changed as follows: awareness = being appeared to . . . both in respect of real x's and apparent x's. When the x is real the awareness is correctly called a perception, when the x is apparent we can noncommittally continue to speak of 'awareness'. In spite of this extension of the concept of awareness to cover non-perceptual cases, my main argument centres on the perceptual cases.

[4] Having elaborated the concept of an awareness I am now in a position to advance my main claim. I wish to argue that the continuousness of consciousness is explained by the fact that our awarenesses are kept in being by our bodily activities. For this theory to be intelligible I might give the reminder that I have defined as a bodily activity any activity which cannot be fully described without mention of the sense-organs used in that activity.[1] Thus looking, listening, tasting, feeling tactually, etc., are bodily activities. Now these activities can be practised for a variety of purposes, and so we can make further differentiations according to the purpose for which they are practised. Very often prepositions that go with the verbs designating the activities reveal such differentiations. In the case of the verb 'look' we have 'look for', 'look at', 'look about' and 'look (to see) whether'. In the case of the verb 'listen' we have 'listen for', 'listen to', and 'listen (to hear) whether'. In the case of the other verbs of perception there is a less rich prepositional vocabulary to go with them, and we have to be inventive in finding ways of describing the activities into the description of which they enter. No doubt the reason for this is that our remaining senses are less discriminating.

Of the diverse activities designated by the verbs 'look' and 'listen' in conjunction with prepositions (I shall concentrate on

[1] See above, p. 71.

these two verbs from this point onwards), there are two of particular importance: they are designated by the expressions' looking at' and 'listening to'. Looking at x entails seeing x, and listening to y entails hearing y. Here we have two activities that entail corresponding awarenesses. Furthermore, the point of the activities in question is to *keep in being* a visual awareness and an auditory awareness, respectively.[1] To generalize, there are specific bodily activities whose function it is to sustain perceptual awareness. Obviously whether or not an awareness can be sustained is not dependent upon the sustaining activity alone. If I continue to see an object because I continue to look at it, my seeing it is still conditional upon the object's remaining before my eyes. As Sibley points out, in those cases in which there is a danger of losing sight of the object we describe our activity as one of 'keeping it in sight'.[2] Where there is no such danger, we do not: we simply look at it. None the less both activities are equally retentive.

Philosophers, particularly sense-datum theorists, have been prompted to ask how long an awareness can last. Thus for Russell it was meaningful to entertain the idea that a sense-datum might last a few seconds,[3] and Don Locke suggests that whatever answer we give is arbitrary.[4] However, the connection between the bodily activity and the awareness that goes with it enables us to give an entirely natural and satisfactory answer to this question. The awareness lasts as long as its sustaining activity lasts. Thus if I am looking at a tree, I can correctly claim to see it as long as I continue uninterruptedly to look at it. If, however, I take my eyes off it and then look at it again, I can say that I had seen the tree twice. It is only when we overlook the connection between awareness and bodily activity that we get into difficulties about what constitutes 'one awareness'.

From the criterion of what constitutes one awareness which I have just given it follows that a single awareness may exhibit qualitative change and even will usually do so. For instance, while looking at a tree I can notice various features of it without moving

[1] See F. N. Sibley, 'Seeking, Scrutinizing and Seeing', *Mind*, Vol. 64 (1955). All page references to its printing in *The Philosophy of Perception*, ed. G. J. Warnock (London, 1967), p. 140 ff. Sibley calls the activities I am referring to 'retentions'. I reached the above conclusion before I read Sibley's valuable article, and although my argument goes beyond his, it is reassuring to have such strong support for one's position.

[2] Sibley, 'Seeking, Scrutinizing, and Seeing', p. 145.

[3] B. Russell, *Logic and Knowledge*, ed. R. C. Marsh (London, 1956), p. 203.

[4] Locke, *Perception and Our Knowledge of the External World*, pp. 160 and 179.

my eyes and while remaining motionless. In addition while I am looking at the tree the sun may go in and this will alter the quality of my awareness. Thus sameness of awareness must not be taken to mean sameness of quality of awareness. Probably philosophers have had difficulty in deciding how to distinguish between awarenesses because they have taken it for granted that sameness of awareness was dependent upon sameness of quality of awareness. If that was insisted upon then nothing but an arbitrary answer could be given. However, we may reject the assumption that nothing can retain its identity if it is subject to change, for this assumption engenders Heraclitian-type paradoxes of identity.

The next step in my argument is to make a connection between attention and those bodily activities that sustain awareness. This is quite simply done by pointing out that the activities in question must be attentive activities. In this manner we establish the connection between attention and awareness. I shall try to substantiate this claim in respect of the activities of looking and listening. A minimum condition of looking at an object is that one keep one's eyes on it. If they wander this is not careless 'looking at': it is not 'looking at' at all. The same is true of listening to an object. If one is paying no attention at all to what one claims to be listening to, then it is just not true that one is listening to it. In short, 'looking at' and 'listening to' are paradigm cases of attentive activity. One might wish to deny this in view of the commonness of such remarks as: 'He listened attentively to what I was saying.' But this is not a counter-example when properly understood. If listening is an attentive activity then it would seem to be otiose to say of a person, that he listened *attentively*. The point of such a remark, however, is to stress the fact that he listened with more than usual attention, not that on this occasion he listened with attention as compared with other occasions on which he listened with no attention at all. Because listening is an attentive activity it is not ordinarily necessary to point out that it is done attentively. That is to say, all such concepts as looking, listening, smelling, feeling, and tasting are attention-laden concepts. So also are the higher order concepts such as observing, examining, scrutinizing, and watching. One may practise these activities with greater or lesser attention, but not with no attention.

By no means all awarenesses are sustained by bodily activities. Some instances of awareness are fleeting as when we catch a glimpse of a rabbit, or catch the scent of a flower. If I caught sight of my opponent's cards it would be a serious imputation to say that I was looking at them. Nevertheless the important point is that I cannot give my attention to an awareness without engaging in the attentive activity which keeps it in being. This suggests the view that paying attention to an awareness just *is* attentively engaging in the bodily activity that sustains it. We will find reason to reject that view,[1] but that in no way shakes the conclusion that it is a precondition of paying attention to an awareness that we engage in the requisite attentive bodily activity.

It is now possible to fill in the account for those bodily activities about which I have so far said nothing. I am referring in particular to 'looking for', 'listening for' and 'feeling for'. Do they entail 'seeing', 'hearing' and 'palpating'? The normal situation is one in which we *are* seeing something when we are looking for an object but are not seeing what we are looking for. Similarly with the other senses. In the course of our visual search we look at this and that, and after a brief look to determine that the object is not the one we are looking for we pass it by. Should this account be accepted it would mean that 'looking at' was the basic activity in respect of sight, and 'looking for' an activity dependent on it.

There is obviously something to this, but it will not do as it stands for precisely the reason that it was found misleading to say of the cards that caught the eye that they were being looked at. That is to say, the concept of 'looking at' is conceptually too loaded with the implication of retentiveness to be used to describe a situation in which an awareness is summarily dismissed. Obviously we need a less conceptually enriched concept for the purpose, such as the concept of spotting. Then we could argue that 'looking for' is dependent upon 'spotting'. We would have to imagine an analogous concept for the other sense modalities. 'Picking up' is probably the counterpart to 'spotting' in the case of hearing. If this contention were accepted, it would still remain true that 'looking for' entailed seeing, 'listening for' entailed hearing, and so on for the other senses. But even this can be questioned. In other words, it can be questioned whether 'looking for' logically entails seeing at the time one is looking for. Is it not possible to look for an object at a time when one can't see a thing? I think we must allow this possibility, although the natural thing to say in those circumstances is: 'I am trying to see.' But if the point of trying to see is that one's

<hr/>

[1] See below, p. 207.

inability to see is impeding the activity of 'looking for', then it could be held that failing to see is one of the ways in which one may fail in one's activity of 'looking for'.

The safest conclusion to draw is that 'looking for' is conceptually of a higher order than 'looking at' and is dependent on being able to engage in the activity of 'looking at' and hence seeing. This could be said without it following that no 'looking for' can occur without it being true that on every occasion on which one is 'looking for' one must also be 'looking at' (or rather, 'spotting') at the same time. Essentially the same argument applies to the other senses, and so I shall not go through them one by one.

I do not want to suggest that keeping an awareness in being is the only purpose of perceptual activities. At least two others are important, but they both presuppose the ability to keep an awareness in being. Firstly, one often engages in a perceptual activity in order to give oneself an awareness. Thus I look at the sunset because I want to give myself an awareness of the sunset, and I do this usually because I enjoy sunsets. My enjoying them, however, is premissed upon my ability to retain my awareness of them. Secondly, one often engages in an activity such as 'looking at' in order to see something better, or in order to scrutinize it. If that is one's purpose it is likewise premissed on an ability to retain the awareness.

Up to this point I have tried to establish that perceptual awarenesses are kept in being by certain bodily activities, and I have argued that these activities are exemplifications of the polymorphous concept of attention. I have yet to show how these points establish the fact that consciousness is continuous. Might it not be, for instance, that attention is made up of a series of flashes of attention, or discrete 'quanta' of attention? As we saw James thought of attention in terms of a series of acts of short duration.[1] If this were the case it would be difficult to see how attention could sustain a continuous awareness. What I need to show, therefore, is that attention is an activity, and that activities have precisely the property of continuousness that would account for the continuousness of awareness that we are looking for. I shall then show that awareness is a state sustained by activity and that the continuousness of the activity is transferred to the state which is sustained by it.

To this end I shall first give an analysis of the notion of an

[1] See above, pp. 93–4.

activity and the notion of a state in order to show that activities and states possess precisely the logical feature we are looking for. After this excursus into the logic of 'activity' and 'state', I shall show that what I have been calling 'bodily activities' satisfy the criteria of an activity, and that what I have been calling 'awareness' satisfies the criteria of a state. It may be remarked that in what follows a more sophisticated treatment is being given of Ribot's thesis that consciousness is dependent upon movement (of the body).

[5] The word 'activity' is a very general word used to describe all sorts of goings on. This would lead one to expect that it did not possess a very strict logic of its own. However, philosophers have recently realized that the word is also used to describe a very specific kind of change, which cannot be described as precisely by means of any other concept.¹ It is activity in this generic sense with which I shall be concerned. That is, I shall not be concerned with the use of the word 'activity' as found in such sentences as: 'The activities of the secret society are subversive', and 'Mountaineering is a challenging activity'. In both these sentences a large variety of things people do are brought under the heading of activities. In this wider sense 'activity' is a polymorphous concept which has as its instantiations 'goings-on' and 'doings' which are not themselves activities in the sense in question. In contradistinction to its usage in such sentences as these, I hope to identify a sense of the word 'activity' in which it is not implied that an activity is composed of a number of 'doings' that are not themselves activities.² In the

¹ See Z. Vendler, 'Verbs and Times', *Philosophical Review* Vol. LXVI (1957), A. Kenny, *Action, Emotion and Will* (London, 1963), Ch. 8, T. C. Potts and C. C. W. Taylor, 'States, Activities and Performances', *Proceedings of the Aristotelian Society*, Suppl. Vol., 1965, and C. O. Evans, 'States, Activities and Performances', *Australasian Journal of Philosophy*, Vol. 45, December 1967.

² The sense of 'activity' that I am here ruling out is just the sense that Shwayder believes to be the only sense of the word, and which he summarizes thus: 'The activities of life are distinguished from acts one might do, possibly when engaged in those activities. The background field of activity engaged in often provides the setting against which we may fix units of action. Also, we may begin to analyse a field of activity by specifying kinds of action necessarily or characteristically done when engaged in that activity.' D. S. Shwayder, *The Stratification of Behaviour* (London, 1965), p. 39. Shwayder also claims that whereas 'action is a technical idea', 'activity is a commonsense notion'. My own position is that while I agree that activity is a commonsense notion, its use is not confined to the one described by Shwayder. I should also add that I am not considering the use of 'activity' when it is applied to processes in nature, such as sun-spot activity, or volcanic activity. I have given a more extensive treatment of the ideas I am developing here in the article referred to in note 1.

sense I am after, a definite distinction must be made between an activity and an act such that it is not the case that an activity consists of a succession of acts. I give the name 'generic activity' to any activity of which this is true. (When in future I refer to an activity I wish it to be understood that I am referring to a generic activity, unless I give an explicit indication to the contrary.)

Before I am in a position to give a definition of an activity, certain preliminary distinctions have to be made. In the first place, I wish to make use of a distinction made by von Wright, between the *result* of an act and the *consequence* of an act.[1] The purpose of this distinction is to bring out two totally different ways in which an act may be connected with the changes effected by it. When the connection between the act and the change is intrinsic, or logical, von Wright calls the change the 'result' of the act. When the connection is extrinsic (von Wright regards this extrinsic relation as primarily a causal one), the change is the 'consequence' of the act. For example, if the act is an act of opening the window, it is logically necessary for the window to be opening. The fact of the window's opening is the result of the act. If the window were not opening, the act could not be described as an act of opening the window, but would have to be described in some other way, such as the act of trying to open the window. On the other hand, if the opening of the window caused the door to slam, the slamming of the door would be a consequence of the act of opening the window and not the result of that act. In other words, my act would in this instance be one of opening the window regardless of the slamming of the door (consequence) but not regardless of the fact of the window's opening (result).

Von Wright also notices two possible interpretations that may be given to his use of 'result', and although he believes it to be a matter of indifference which interpretation we adopt, for my purpose the distinction is important. As von Wright explains:

'By the *result* of an act we can understand either the change corresponding to this act or, alternatively, the end-state of this change. Thus, by the result of the act of opening a certain window we can understand either the fact that the window is opening (changes from closed to open) or the fact that it is open.'[2]

[1] G. H. von Wright, *Norm and Action* (London, 1963), p. 39 ff.
[2] *Ibid.*, p. 39.

I shall record this distinction in the following way: when the term is interpreted to mean the change corresponding to the act, I shall identify it as 'result$_c$', and when it is interpreted to mean the end-state of the change, I shall identify it as 'result$_e$'. Now when an agent is said to be doing something, we may describe his doing as the bringing about of a certain result. Two possibilities present themselves: the agent may either bring about result$_c$ or result$_e$. We may at once proceed to identify an activity in terms of these possibilities. An agent is engaged in an activity (in the basic, or generic sense) when he brings about a result$_c$ and he does not stop as soon as result$_c$ comes about. A better appreciation of activity is gained by contrasting it with what in the literature has come to be called a 'performance'. In my terms an agent is engaged in a performance when he brings about a result$_e$ and it takes time for result$_e$ to be produced. To complete the picture, we may identify a third possibility, which is neither an activity nor a performance, but which may be called a 'transitory act'. An agent performs a transitory act when he brings about a result$_c$ or a result$_e$, but in the first case stops as soon as result$_c$ comes about, and in the second case result$_e$ is produced almost instantaneously.

The contrast between an activity and a performance comes to this: in the case of an activity, the result obtains from the very moment the activity commences until the moment it ceases; in the case of a performance the result comes into being cumulatively and is only fully realized at the termination of the performance. Let me illustrate this in the case of an activity and a performance, respectively. If I am whistling, then it will be true that I will have whistled from the moment I started, until the moment I stop: the result$_c$ that I have whistled will obtain right from the beginning, and will not be more fully realized after the activity has been going on for some time, than it was after the first moment. If I am making a bookcase, it will not be true that I have made a bookcase, until the bookcase is produced. The result$_e$ that I have made a bookcase will only be realized upon completion of the 'performance'.

Now it will be noted that from a grammatical point of view I use the perfect tense to describe the results of activities and performances. This is important, because it enables us to distinguish between activities and performances on grammatical grounds. Thus, let the verb describing the activity or performance be represented by 'has øed.'. It is then possible to distinguish between activity and performance as follows: in the case of an activity 'A is øing' entails 'A has øed', in the case of a performance 'A is øing' entails 'A had not øed'. We have already seen that this grammatical distinction operates in the case of the activity of whistling, and the performance of making a bookcase. It will be observed that there is a natural time limit in the case of a performance. The performance continues for as long as it is necessary for the completion of the result. It is possible, therefore, for a performance to be incomplete, or, for instance, half finished. It is for this reason meaningful in the case of a performance to raise the question 'How long does it take?' In the case of activities there is no such natural time limit, and it does not make sense to ask of an activity 'How long does it take?' Performances are completed; activities just stop. The above analysis also supports Kenny's contention that performances *take* time, while activities *go on* for a time.[1]

I have stressed the contrast between activities and performances, not because this is the distinction I most want to utilize, but for the purpose of making the concept of an activity stand out all the clearer. I now come to the contrast between an activity and a state, which for this enquiry is the crucial one. Kenny and others have maintained that the distinction could be made in terms of whether or not the verb describing the putative activity or state possesses a continuous present tense. If the verb has no continuous present tense, it describes a state; if it has a continuous present tense, it describes either an activity or a performance. The characteristic function of the continuous present tense of verbs is to describe what an agent is doing at the time he is doing it. It is perfectly reasonable to expect, therefore, that a verb which does not describe something an agent can do, should lack the tense which implies that it does describe something an agent can do.

The fundamental distinction between an activity and a state is, accordingly, that an activity is a sort of doing of an agent, and a state is not a sort of doing at all. We talk of the state of a person or thing, or conversely, of a person or thing being in a certain state. In so far as we speak of *being* in a state, there is a contrast with *doing*: a person is in a state when he is undergoing something or something is happening to him; and 'undergoings' and 'happenings' are not 'doings'. It must be granted that a person may be able to induce a state, or put himself in a state, but this only means that he is able to bring about the conditions that give rise to the state; it does not mean that he brings about the state itself.

[1] Kenny, *Action, Emotion, and Will*, p. 176.

It is essential to recognize that there are non-dispositional as well as dispositional states. In the case of a dispositional state a person may be said to be in a state under conditions in which he is undergoing nothing in connection with it at the time. Thus Othello may be said to be in a state of jealousy over Desdemona even when he is not feeling any jealousy or behaving jealously, because at the time there happens to be no occasion for jealousy. As opposed to dispositional states there are occurrent states which a person can only be said to be in when he is actually undergoing a certain experience at the time. Among such states are states of shock, pain, drowsiness, excitement, agitation, anger, and depression. Some philosophers have been puzzled about the relation between 'being angry' and 'feeling angry'; 'being depressed' and 'feeling depressed' and so on. The difference between the two types of description, I suggest, is that the former describes a dispositional state and the latter describes an occurrent state. Thus, if a person *is* angry this means that he is liable to do predictable sorts of things under specified circumstances, but if he *feels* angry he is in a certain occurrent state at the time regardless of what he might do next.

Unless otherwise stated, the type of state I shall be discussing and contrasting with activity is the occurrent state. The concept 'state' also implies the idea of its persistence through time. A state which existed for but an instant would less misleadingly be called an event. States, therefore, *last* for a time. The important characteristic that activities and states have in common is that they are both continuous through time, but, as we have seen, activities may be said to *go on* for a time, whereas states *last* for a time. These descriptions of the manner of their temporal endurance reflects the fact that an activity is a certain sort of doing of an agent, and a state is not. This is as far as we need carry the formal analysis for our purpose. I come now to the application of these distinctions to the concepts of attention and awareness.

[6] The preceding section has given us the analytical means to determine the logical categories to which the concepts of attention and awareness belong. I shall argue that attention has the logical features of an activity and that awareness has the logical features of a state. If this can be established it will follow that both attention and awareness have the required temporal continuousness to make it possible in principle for attention conceived of as an activity to

sustain awareness conceived of as a state, since both activities and states have been shown to possess temporal continuousness. The development of the argument will be as follows: I shall first contrast attention and awareness in order to show that awareness is a state and attention is not; I shall then concentrate on attention in order to show that attention is an activity and not a performance or a transitory act.

The first thing to notice is that the verb 'attend' has a continuous present tense (am attending) whereas the verb 'aware' does not: there is no construction with 'am awaring'. This immediately puts attention into the category of a doing of some sort and awareness into the category of a state. More importantly though, it is meaningful to answer the question 'What are you doing?' by saying, 'I am attending (i.e. paying attention) to X'. It would not be meaningful to reply 'I am aware of X'. Even stronger proof of the contention that attention is an activity and awareness a state is forthcoming in that I could give the reply: 'I am trying to attend to x', but not the reply 'I am trying to be aware of x'. To illustrate further that attention is a sort of doing, we need only consider that it is always legitimate to raise the question 'Why are you paying attention to x?' This invites a reply of the form: 'I am attending to x in order to . . .' In the chapter on attention, I pointed out that in certain circumstances attention can be voluntary as well as involuntary. When we choose to pay attention and do so as a result of deliberation we can be expected to produce on request the *reason* for paying attention. Now not all attention is deliberate and it will be especially true of unordered attention that one may have no reason for attending. We can therefore deny that we have any reason for attending: we can say 'There is no reason, I just happen to be attending'. The point remains, however, that it is always legitimate to *ask* for the reason, even when there isn't one. The position is very different in the case of awareness. 'Why are you aware of x?' is not even intelligible unless it be understood as an elliptical way of raising the question 'Why did you put yourself in the position to give yourself the awareness?' It follows that the sentence form 'I am aware of x in order to . . .' does not make sense. *A fortiori* one does not strictly speaking have *reasons* for one's awarenesses. Finally, one may be ordered to pay attention, while one cannot be ordered to be aware: one can be ordered to *do* something, but not to *be* something (except in a very roundabout sort of way).

Awareness will have satisfied all the criteria for being a state if it possesses the feature of lasting through time which as we saw is one of the logical features of a state. Obviously this is the case. The meaningfulness of the question 'For how long were you aware of *x*?' establishes the fact that awareness *lasts* a certain length of time. In spite of the fact that an awareness has all the logical properties of a state, one philosopher in particular has given reasons for declining to call an awareness a state. These reasons will emerge shortly.[1] It is enough for the moment if we agree that to all intents and purposes awareness is a state.

I turn now to attention. It has been argued that when we are attending we are doing something. It remains to be shown that the sort of doing involved is an activity and not a performance or a transitory act. If attention were a performance it would follow that the statement 'A is attending to X' entailed 'A has not attended to X'. But this is false, so attending is not a performance. On the other hand, a person may have been attending for a length of time, so attending is not a transitory act either. It must therefore be an activity. And indeed attention satisfies the grammatical criterion for an activity in that 'A is attending' entails 'A has attended'. That is to say, having attended is the result$_c$ of attending, and this result is brought about concomitantly with its sustaining activity. On this argument we would appear to be justified in calling attention an activity. However, just as in the case of awareness there is a difficulty about identifying awareness as a state, so too in the case of attention there is a difficulty about identifying attention itself as an activity. Unlike the case of awareness, however, there are no expository reasons to hold up an immediate discussion of the difficulty.

The difficulty arises if we accept Ryle's view of the nature of attention. Ryle's view is neatly summed up in this statement by Place:

'There is no special activity called "attending", there is only the attentive performance of an activity.'[2]

This view may be described as the 'adverbial theory of attention', since it finds the paradigmatic examples of attention in our engag-

[1] See below, p. 210.

[2] U. T. Place, 'The Concept of Heed', *The British Journal of Psychology*, XLV, 4 (1954), reprinted in *Essays in Philosophical Psychology*, ed. D. F. Gustafson (New York, 1964), p. 217. (All page references to the latter source.)

ing in activities, carefully, or heedfully. The major implication of Ryle's view is that attention is not itself a separate operation or activity, which occurs concomitantly with the act or activity that is said to be engaging one's attention. As Ryle himself says in this connection,

'Even where it is appropriate to speak of acts of attention, the word "act" carries very little of its ordinary luggage. In ordinary contexts we apply very multifarious criteria in determining what constitutes one act. Perhaps making one move in chess is perform-ing one act; perhaps doing enough to warrant prosecution is performing one act; and perhaps getting from the beginning to the end of a speech without being side-tracked is one act. But a person who has, say, hummed a tune from beginning to end, not absent-mindedly but on purpose and with some application, has not per-formed two acts or accomplished two tasks, one of humming plus one of giving his mind to reproducing the tune; or, at any rate, he has not performed two acts in that sense of "two acts" in which it would make sense to say that he might have done the second but omitted the first. Giving his mind to reproducing the tune is not doing something else, in the way in which a person sawing wood while humming is doing something else besides humming. We should say, rather, that a person who hums a tune with some concentration is humming in a different way from the way in which he hums automatically, for all that the difference might make no audible difference. It makes his humming a different sort of action, not a concomitance of separately performable actions.'[1]

There is at least this indisputable basis to Ryle's argument; namely that it is impossible to pay attention without paying atten-tion to something, but it has been convincingly argued by Penelhum that the dependence of attention on other sorts of episodes does not rule out the possibility of its being an episode itself.[2] There is, besides, another respect in which exception may be taken to the way in which Ryle describes attention. In the passage quoted above, Ryle refers to attention as an 'act', and one of his arguments

[1] G. Ryle, 'Pleasure', *Proc. Arist. Soc.*, suppl. Vol. XXVIII (1954), reprinted in *Essays in Philosophical Psychology*, pp. 200–1. (All page references to the latter source.)
[2] T. Penelhum, 'The Logic of Pleasure', *Philosophy and Phenomenologically Research*, XVII (1956–7), reprinted in *Essays in Philosophical Psychology*. (All page references to the latter source.)

in favour of an adverbial view of attention consists in pointing out the logical embarrassment occasioned by the belief that attention is an act. For instance he says,

'Philosophers and psychologists sometimes speak of "acts" of attention. This idiom too is partially appropriate to certain contexts and quite inappropriate to others. When a person is actually bidden by someone else or by himself to attend, there is something which with some effort or reluctance he *does*. Where his attention had been wandering, it now settles; where he had been half-asleep, he is now wide awake; and this change he may bring about with a wrench. But the spectator at an exciting football match does not have to try to fasten or canalise his attention. To the question "How many acts of attention did you perform?", his proper answer would be "None." For no wrenches had occurred. His attention was fixed on the game but he went through no operations of fixing it.'[1]

Now it seems to me that the proper answer to Ryle here is to deny that attention is an *act*, and to affirm instead that attention is an *activity*. His failure to distinguish an act from an activity leads him to take for granted that if it is inappropriate to call something an act, it follows that it is not a separable episode. But once it is recognized that we are dealing with the different proposition that attention is an activity (and here it is vital to distinguish between activity in the generic sense and activity in the Schwayderian sense in which it is a series of acts), it at once becomes obvious why Ryle's question 'How many acts of attention did you perform?' is inappropriate: while an activity is going on, it is continuous, and that is why we cannot count the number of isolable occurrences of attention, or acts of attention. It cannot be denied that an activity is as much an episode while it is going on, as is an act while it is being performed. I conclude that what Ryle says about 'acts' of attention tends neither to strengthen nor weaken his adverbial view of attention, but is simply beside the point.

All the same, Ryle's adverbial theory makes a negative point, which he is quite right to insist upon. If attention itself is interpreted as an activity, instead of interpreted as a *manner of engaging in activities*, we seem to imply that attention is a purely inner mental operation which we trigger off in conjunction with our

[1] Ryle, 'Pleasure', p. 200.

bodily activities but which is logically distinct from them. Now while I do not reject this view for the reason Ryle does (namely, his rejection in principle of inner mental operations), I find myself on his side in challenging it. I have been maintaining a general thesis to the effect that all activity is bodily, and that thesis will be strengthened if it can be sustained even in the case of such a seeming non-bodily activity as paying attention. Furthermore, those who claim that attention is an inner mental act or operation are themselves involved in great difficulties when it comes to substantiating their claim. This alone is reason for preferring an account which manages without postulating any such inner mental operation. Beyond this point, however, I am in disagreement with Ryle. From what he has written on the subject he gives the impression that paying attention is much simpler than it is. He maintains that paying attention is reducible to doing something with care, or heedfully, or with enjoyment. In each case we are given the picture of an individual act or activity which is practised in a certain 'style' so to speak, and we are led to believe that that is all there is to it.

I do not wish to deny that this simple account might cover some cases of paying attention. What I do want to insist upon is that there are many cases in which we can be sure that this is not the whole story. I think we need to take cognizance of the fact that in these cases it is a precondition of our engaging in an activity attentively that we are simultaneously engaging in another activity. What I have in mind is quite simply this. Often in order to give our attention to what we are doing, we have to think about what we are doing, and often the thinking that is required is not thinking in a dispositional sense, neither is it thinking in the sense of 'being-thought-in-action', but rather thinking in the sense of having *overt thoughts* directing what one is doing. The thinking in this sense may be openly theoretical and propositional in nature. Now it would be a very tough-minded man indeed who would commit himself to the proposition that the entertaining of propositional thoughts is *never* a necessary condition of attention of any kind. If we are not to be unreasonable we must admit the possibility that on some occasions engaging in an activity attentively necessitates engaging in the activity of thinking – in the sense of having thoughts – at the same time. What is *not* implied by this contention, is the idea that such a second activity is itself a *sui generis* activity of attending. And yet this was the idea Ryle was anxious to deny. He could perfectly properly have denied that, without having to deny that the presence of some other sorts of concomitant activity might be detected, which had a role to play in attention.

Provided that this important qualification is made to Ryle's adverbial theory of attention, we may agree with him that attention is not itself an activity. We can then accept his claim that attention is a 'polymorphous' notion,[1] covering a variety of activities whose special characteristic is that they cannot be engaged in at all, unless they are engaged in attentively. Such activities as *perceiving, thinking, watching,* and *enjoying* belong to this class. They are all 'attention-laden' activities. On this interpretation, to say that attention *is* an activity is an elliptical way of saying that there are activities that entail attending. Once it is realized that this is what is meant, there is no harm in referring to attention itself as an activity – as a form of short-hand for this position. This I shall do.

Having sided with Ryle on the question of the nature of attention, I must defend him, if I am to defend myself, against the refutation of the adverbial theory put forward by Place. I must at once confess that I do not really understand Place's argument to the effect that Ryle's case breaks down. According to Place,

'The logical consequence of this theory is that the individual's own activities are the only sorts of things to which attention can be paid.'

His objection to this position is as follows:

'If Ryle's theory were correct it should be nonsensical to talk of someone paying attention to anything other than an activity which he himself is performing. In fact, of course, we can speak with perfect propriety of the paying attention to any kind of object, phenomenon or sensation which is visible, audible, tangible, or otherwise perceptible. In such cases there is no activity which is being performed attentively or heedfully.'[2]

My difficulty with Place's argument stems from the fact that I can only pay attention to a visible object by looking at it, an audible object by listening to it, and a tangible object by feeling it; and as I shall show 'looking', 'listening', and 'feeling' *are* activities. But if this is true, I pay attention to such perceptible objects in virtue of

[1] Ryle, 'Pleasure', p. 202.
[2] Place, 'The Concept of Heed', p. 217.

engaging in attentive activities: it is as much activities which are attentive in these cases as in the cases of actions bringing about changes external to the agent.

Penelhum agrees with Place on this issue. But it is interesting to see that he recognizes the existence of the line of defence I have just offered. I shall quote his remarks about this, but I must just point out that Penelhum is thinking specifically about 'enjoyment' rather than 'attention' as such. Nevertheless this does not affect the argument, since Penelhum is in agreement with Ryle's view that enjoyment is itself a species of attention. We are therefore free to make a mental substitution of the word 'attention' for the word 'enjoyment' in the following passage without violating its intent:

'A possible way out is to insist that what we are enjoying is some activity of our own, *viz.*, that of watching or noticing the actor's performance. But this clearly entails the un-Rylean view that watching and noticing are activities, and therefore occurrences, and although I would not resist this, to hold it in the interest of a dispositional theory of enjoyment would be to construe one heed-concept as episodic and another as dispositional, which is hardly compatible with claiming that both species are of the same genus. What *is* compatible with this is claiming that *all* heed-concepts are episodic, and that some form of attention is part of the meaning of the word "enjoyment".'[1]

In this passage Penelhum mentions the solution I have proposed and then argues that Ryle cannot adopt it. I believe Penelhum is right about this. My response is that if Ryle puts forward a theory of attention that does not square with his general philosophical position, so much the worse for his general philosophical position. All that I am interested in is getting it right about attention, and if I think that Ryle is right on this question, he has my support. I therefore accept Penelhum's way out. It is also evident from my general remarks about consciousness, that, unlike Ryle, I have no wish to avoid 'episodic' accounts of such concepts as 'perceiving', 'thinking' and 'heed-concepts' in general.

[1] Penelhum, 'The Logic of Pleasure', pp. 243–4. The one claim in this passage from which I wish to dissociate myself is Penelhum's claim that noticing is an activity. Noticing is disqualified from being an activity because it lacks the verbal form of the continuous present tense. I can't say 'I am noticing'. Noticing is not something that can go on for a length of time.

3. THE DEPENDENCE OF A PERSISTING SELF
ON SUSTAINING ACTIVITY

[7] I now wish to tie in the analysis of attention just given with what I said about attention in the chapter on unprojected consciousness. Nothing that I said in that chapter suggested that attention itself was one of the species of consciousness and to that extent the claims there made square with the present analysis: namely, the rejection of the view that attention is an inner mental operation. My position was that the forms of attention should be understood as possible structurings of consciousness, with the nature of these structurings being determined by the nature of the relation existing between unprojected consciousness and object of attention. We found this relationship to pass from one of sheer disconnectedness to one of a high degree of involvement, and each stage in this progression was seen to represent different forms of attention and varying degrees of those forms. That is, we passed from unordered attention – the most rudimentary of its forms – through executive attention, to interrogative attention – the most intellectual of its forms.

This theory does not support the claim that attention is itself some conscious process that is *sui generis*. On the other hand, it does support my contention against the position taken by Ryle in those of his works I have been discussing, that attention may sometimes require the co-operation of several activities, and is not always confined to the manner in which a single activity is practised. Interrogative attention is particularly relevant in this connection. As I have argued, in interrogative attention unprojected consciousness and object of attention are united in a single relevancy system. A particular instance of this is the existence of a 'master-idea' in unprojected consciousness, which directs and determines the sort of attention given and the type of object singled out.[1] Such a master-idea itself only comes to be an element in unprojected consciousness, however, in virtue of some additional activity – whether it be thinking, or image formation – that produces it. Interrogative attention, therefore, provides a counter-instance to the simple adverbial theory of attention. A reductive analysis of attention in terms of performing a task in a certain manner, covers only some cases. In others, attention can only occur if two or more activities work in harness.

[1] See above, p. 120.

This supplementation of the Rylean adverbial account of attention allows us to find a place for a feature of attention that would receive no recognition on the unamended account. If one function of an attentive activity is to sustain a state of awareness, then that function is served when the activity in question is practised heedfully. But once the awareness is kept in being it is possible to pay attention to one or more of its features without the sustaining activity undergoing any alteration. For example, I keep a picture in view by keeping my eyes on it and my looking at it is an attentive activity which, if successful, will result in my continued visual awareness of the picture. But now it is perfectly possible for me to pay attention to features of the picture within my field of vision without adjusting the focus of my eyes (it is hard to do this, but possible). That being the case it seems that we have an instance of attention here which comes on top of the attentive activity and is not reducible to it. It looks as though there is a type of attention which has nothing to do with bodily activity at all, although it presupposes it (in order to keep the awareness in being).

However, on my account we can understand this seemingly purely mental type of attention in terms of the concomitant performance of additional activities. In particular we can explain the attention given to one feature within the constant visual field in preference to another in terms of the activity of thinking about the one feature rather than the other, or in terms of the presence of a master-idea directing attention to one feature rather than the other. Our position is then saved due to the fact that the thinking in question has itself been argued to be dependent upon bodily activity. Thus this interesting apparently negative case can be brought under the adverbial theory only on condition it is amended as suggested to include concomitant interrelated activities.[1]

[8] In this section I apply the distinction between an activity and a state to perceptual concepts, in order to make explicit the form of dependence of states of awareness on attentive activities. In other words, the time has arrived for me to show in detail how attentive activities sustain states of awareness, and by so doing to account for the continuousness of awareness. The first thing to establish is that in the case of such pairs of concepts as 'looking and seeing', 'listening and hearing', 'palpating and feeling', the first member of

[1] I am grateful to Mr John Schumacher for drawing my attention to the need to argue for this point.

each of these pairs of concepts designates an activity, and the second, a state. When this is accomplished we will be able to go on to investigate the ways in which these activities and states are connected.

My argument is considerably helped by the fact that Barnes has arrived at conclusions very similar to my own, in a paper 'On Seeing and Hearing'.[1] I shall, therefore, base the discussion on that paper, both for the support it gives to my own position, and for the opportunity it affords me to define my position more precisely by showing the respects in which it diverges from Barnes's position. Moreover, it is Barnes who expresses the reservation about classifying a perceptual awareness as a state, which I mentioned, and it will be convenient to include that matter in the present discussion.

Although Barnes does not attempt, as I have done, to make explicit the logical characteristics that distinguish activities from states, to all intents and purposes he offers the same analysis of looking and seeing, and, by implication, of listening and hearing, that I have given. In the passage that follows he eliminates one possibility by rejecting the idea that seeing and hearing are activities.

'I think there can be little doubt that seeing a tree, hearing a bell, etc., are neither activities nor processes and are only in a partial way states. That they are not activities can be seen from the fact that we do not normally answer questions such as "What are you doing?" or "What did you do?" with "I am seeing the moon rise" and "I saw the moon rise". The normal answers would be "I am watching the moon rise", and "I watched the moon rise". The absence of the continuous present tense seems also to prove that seeing and hearing are not processes.'[2]

In such perceptual contexts as these there seems to be no room for the use of the continuous present tense of the verbs 'see' and 'hear' and that would rule out their classification as performances or transitory acts as well. To this it might be objected that there are after all contexts in which we use the continuous present tense of these verbs: e.g. 'I am seeing stars' and 'I am hearing things'. It should be clear, however, that these uses of 'see' and 'hear' are not

[1] W. H. F. Barnes, 'On Seeing and Hearing', Contemporary British Philosophy, ed. H. D. Lewis (London, 1956).
[2] Barnes, 'On Seeing and Hearing', p. 70.

perceptual ones. The point of such usage seems to be that of making it clear that one is identifying one's condition as hallucinatory as opposed to perceptual.[1] We would, therefore, be put off the track completely if we allowed such usages of 'see' and 'hear' to lead us into thinking of seeing and hearing as types of doing. After all, having an hallucination is not something we do.

A reason for wishing to treat seeing and hearing as performances, which is independent of the one just rejected, is Ryle's analysis of the verbs in question as achievement verbs.[2] But this would be a confusion because an achievement is not itself a performance, rather it is the successful culmination of a performance and that is not another performance in turn. The whole issue has been beautifully cleared up by Sibley in terms of his distinction between the 'spotting' sense of 'see' and the 'retention' sense of 'see'.[3] As he makes clear, Ryle concentrates on the first sense to the exclusion of the second and for this reason he misses the non-achievement sense of 'see'. But it is that sense that I am concerned with and which I take to belong to the category of a state. The most important feature of the 'retentive' sense of 'see' in this connection is that it describes an experience that *lasts* for a stretch of time. I classify seeing and hearing as states because they are not types of doing (as evidenced by the non-existence of the continuous present tense of the respective verbs when they are used in a perceptual context) and because of their characteristic of lasting for a time. This conclusion is supported by what Barnes has to say in the following passage in which he compares looking and seeing to searching and finding:

'While looking for something is like searching for something in referring to an activity, seeing has a dual role, (a) like finding, which refers to the end of an activity and the beginning of a state of affairs, and (b) like possessing, which refers not to an activity but to a state of affairs. In sense (a) I may exclaim "Ah! I see it now." In this case it is plausible to say that seeing is "detecting" or "spotting". But if someone asks "Do you see that tree outside the window?" and I say "Yes, I see it: I've been looking at it for some time," I am using *see* in sense (b) and it does not mean detect here. "I still see it" and "I still have it in my sight" are like "I still have

[1] This point was relayed to me as one made by Mr Malpas.
[2] Ryle, *The Concept of Mind*, p. 149.
[3] Sibley, 'Seeking, Scrutinizing, and Seeing', p. 143.

it" and "I still have it in my possession". Now although we do not use the continuous tenses of a verb such as *possess*, this does not mean that the state of possession cannot have any duration. We say "I had it all the time": and similarly "I saw you all the time" or "I could see you all the time". The state, though it has duration, is complete at each moment of its duration.'[1]

We see therefore, that Barnes agrees with us in finding 'seeing' – and by implication 'hearing', etc. – to have all the logical features which my analysis has shown a *state* to have. In spite of this he is unhappy about calling seeing and hearing 'states' and his reasons are as follows:

'Are seeing and hearing states? They would have to be states in which people and animals could be. Now I can, of course, be in a certain physical state, e.g., filthy, sick, or in a mental state, e.g., depressed, hilarious, or in a state which it is difficult to classify as exclusively physical or mental, e.g., tense, exhausted. And there is also a looser use of "state" in which when I have something wrong with a part of me I can be said to be in a certain state, e.g., when I have a headache or nausea. Seeing something is not very much like being in a state in any of these uses. But there is a class of verbs which refer not so much to a state in which I am as to a state of affairs in which I am central, e.g., *have, possess, own*. The activity or process of buying is followed by the state of having. There seems to be a certain parallel between this sort of verb and verbs such as seeing and hearing. We do not normally use the continuous tense of verbs referring to this kind of state; we do not normally say "I am having the pencil in my hand". And these verbs of ownership further resemble verbs such as seeing and hearing in referring not so much to my state as to my situation *vis-a-vis* something else. But granting these resemblances we should not normally refer to seeing and hearing as states. If they are not activities, processes or states, what are they? The answer, I think, is that they are experiences.'[2]

Now these are no doubt solid reasons for refusing to *call* seeing and hearing 'states'. And yet it cannot be said that Barnes's answer, suggesting that they are experiences, is a happy one. For

[1] Barnes, 'Seeing and Hearing', pp. 74–5.
[2] Ibid., pp. 70–1.

one thing, his answer can be looked upon as a category mistake. It would be logically objectionable to say: 'There are activities, processes, performances, transitory acts, states, events, *and* experiences.' Experiences do not belong in such a categorial list. Rather, experiences are one of the things of which we should like to know to which of the categories in the list they belong. I suggest that we can get around Barnes's objection to classifying seeing and hearing as states, in the following way. We can insist that we are using the word 'state' in a philosophical sense to designate a particular category and not using it in its ordinary language sense. From this standpoint the ordinary language use of the word 'state' could well be more restricted than the use I am giving it such that whatever in ordinary language would be called a state would also be called a state by me, whereas some of the additional things I would classify as a state would not be so described in ordinary language. The reason for the disparity could then be the simple one that from the standpoint of ordinary language we already possess exact concepts for the things in question and have no need to resort to the very general term 'state' to describe them. Thus we have the concepts designed for the purpose, such as 'experience', 'awareness', and more specifically still 'seeing', 'hearing' and 'feeling'. Barnes's mistake, it seems to me, is the one of identifying philosophical distinctions with ordinary usage, and without going any further it can safely be said that the relation between them is not as simple as that. I conclude, therefore, that seeing, hearing, feeling, etc., are *states* from a philosophical point of view, even though it would not be proper in ordinary usage to *call* them states. Having said that, let us proceed to Barnes's analysis of *looking* and *listening*.

In this connection Barnes has this to say:

'Corresponding to the experience verbs *see, hear, taste, smell, feel* are the activity verbs *look, listen, taste, sniff* (or *smell*), and *feel*.'[1]

Barnes does not explicitly make the point, although it is certainly implied in his analysis, that his list of activity verbs identifies activities, because in each case it is true of them that 'A is øing' entails 'A has øed'. That is, if I am looking, I must have already looked, and similarly for the remaining cases of perceiving. In other words, the result of each of these activities comes into being as soon as the activity commences, *lasts* for as long as the activity *goes on*,

[1] Barnes, 'Seeing and Hearing', p. 72.

and perishes the moment the activity ceases. As a matter of fact, Barnes has a concept, which corresponds with my concept of a result$_e$, and this concept he calls an 'upshot'.

He criticizes Ryle for not distinguishing between the concept of an achievement, and the concept of an upshot. Every action has, according to Barnes, an upshot, but not every action results in an achievement. Now Barnes does suggest that every activity also has an upshot. Dealing with the activity of walking, he points out that at each moment the walker reaches a certain point, and adds:

'It would be inappropriate, as we have already seen, to refer to this as an achievement. It is a result or upshot. With any kind of movement there is a continuous upshot, consisting in the fact that at every moment what is moving is at a different point in space.'[1]

However, this analysis gets Barnes into trouble.

If 'looking at' has as its continuous upshot 'seeing' what is the continuous upshot of 'looking for'? The same question arises of course in the case of the other modes of perceiving. The only continuous upshot which is entailed by 'looking for' is 'having looked for', not 'seeing'. Even if we confine ourselves to such activities as 'looking at' and 'listening to' we can still distinguish the two different continuous upshots: namely, 'having looked at' and 'having listened to', and 'seeing' and 'hearing'. Plainly what Barnes has in mind is the latter sort of continuous upshot, but all his argument establishes is the former sort of continuous upshot. This is clear from his remark, 'With any kind of movement there is a continuous upshot'. What Barnes is plainly not entitled to do is to identify result$_c$ in this sense, with the sense in which 'seeing', 'hearing', and 'smelling' are results.

Now it would be conceptually very neat if I were able to claim that Barnes had simply overlooked my distinction between result$_c$ and result$_e$, and that perceptual states were results of the latter sort. But this simple way out would be incorrect. A result$_e$ is an end-state, which only comes into being upon completion of a task, and seeing, hearing, etc., are not states of that sort. We have no option but to recognize that seeing, hearing, etc., are a second type of result$_c$ which is rather the *point* of the activity in question. This gives us grounds for distinguishing between some types of perceptual activity which do not necessarily have such a result (such as

[1] Barnes, 'Seeing and Hearing', p. 73.

'looking for') and those which do (such as 'looking at'). Thus, those activities whose point it is to sustain states of awareness should be understood as ones in which a second type of result$_c$ comes on top of the first type of result$_c$: another type of continuous upshot altogether.

We come now to the crucial question of the relationship between perceptual activity and perceptual state. Barnes has this to say in connection with the particular case of looking and seeing:

'Looking about is a thing that I can do and it has as its continuous upshot seeing first one thing and then another. Looking at some particular thing has as its continuous upshot seeing first one feature of it and then another. Looking for some particular thing, e.g., a gentian, in so far as it involves looking about has as its continuous upshot seeing first one thing and then another: it is crowned by achievement only in so far as it has as an upshot seeing a gentian.'[1]

In this passage Barnes gives us an excellent example of an activity sustaining a state. For it is evident that his description of a 'continuous upshot' is a description of a state that is dependent on a sustaining activity. A continuous upshot must last as long as the activity of which it is the upshot goes on. This means that the continuousness of the activity is reflected in the continuousness of the state kept in being by the activity.

The significance of this example is that it provides evidence of an activity sustaining a state, in one concrete case. This confirms the thesis for which I have been arguing, in as much as a general thesis is confirmed through its instantiations. Moreover, the example in question is not merely a confirming instance of the thesis. It may be regarded as a paradigm case of an attentive activity sustaining a perceptual state. It is thus a demonstration of the thesis that the continuousness of awareness is brought about by the continuousness of a sustaining activity.

We are at last in a position to substantiate the answer I gave to the question about the number of 'sightings' of a tree we make during any given time span.[2] If we think of the seeing of a tree as the 'continuous upshot' – to use Barnes's phrase – of the activity of *looking at*, then we can appreciate that it makes no sense to ask

[1] Barnes, 'Seeing and Hearing', p. 73.
[2] See above, p. 190.

how many 'sightings' of the tree the perceiver registers, after, say, half an hour of solidly looking at the tree. We can only ask the perceiver how many times he has seen the tree if we suppose him to have taken his eyes off it one or more times. He can then reply, for instance, 'I've seen it three times now' – having looked at it thrice. But if the hypothesis is adopted that consciousness is composed of a succession of temporal units, we would have every right to expect an answer to the question 'How many visual experiences have you had of the tree since you started looking at it five minutes ago?' This question is not only manifestly absurd, but, more importantly, we can explain why it is absurd. Given that we are describing a continuous upshot – or a result$_c$ on my analysis – we see that we are dealing with something continuous and not with distinct episodes. We cannot, therefore, break up such a continuous upshot into units, without seriously misrepresenting its character.

We can now, finally, understand the circumstances in which a perceptual activity will be responsible for sustaining a state of awareness. I maintained that attention establishes a logical link between perceptual activity and its corresponding perceptual state. This it does when the awareness holds the attention of the perceiver. It is then a necessary condition of his paying attention to his awareness that it should be the result$_c$ of his perceptual activity. In this circumstance the state of awareness is of necessity sustained by the perceptual activity, and the continuousness of the seeing, hearing, or feeling, is proven.

[9] We can now draw out the wider implications of this investigation for the continuousness of consciousness as a whole, and the persistence of the subject of consciousness. If my argument is sound then we have shown that awareness is a state which lasts for a time. But every awareness is an element of consciousness, so we can draw the conclusion that the consciousness as a whole of which one of its elements is continuous is itself continuousness for just as long as the awareness lasts. But that leaves the possibility that there is a discontinuousness in consciousness from one awareness to the next. Only if the continuousness of consciousness outlasts the continuousness of a particular awareness will we have a state of affairs in which it will make sense to say that the subject of one awareness is the same subject as the subject of another awareness. This condition is fulfilled because the subject can have a number

of contemporaneous awarenesses. One can be seeing an orchestra as well as hearing it with the result that a visual awareness is concomitant with an auditory awareness. It follows also that we must be able to engage in more than one bodily activity at a time: in the present case one must be looking at the orchestra and listening to it at one and same time. However, it is not at all necessary for both activities to end at the same time. I can go on looking at the orchestra long after it has played its last note. This has a twofold consequence. In the first place, because the two awarenesses are concomitant and are both elements of one consciousness they both are awarenesses of a single subject. In the second place, because one awareness may continue after the other has ceased, the subject must persist over the time covering both awarenesses. This was all that we set out to prove. But we can generalize the matter still further by pointing out that the persistence of a subject is assured by the fact that the concurrence of bodily activities ensures the continuousness of consciousness from one awareness to the next provided that these bodily activities are simultaneous for part of their duration.

But what if one bodily activity follows another without either being concomitant with the other or with any other bodily activity? No sooner do we present this possibility to ourselves than we see that we must be describing a situation in which there is a gap in consciousness. That is to say, we are referring to a state of affairs in which we are no longer dealing with a single period of waking consciousness. The gap in consciousness is created, in other words, by the fact that there is for a time no bodily activity whatsoever. But when we are faced with that problem we are no longer in the perspective of the *self-approach* but have immediately switched to the perspective of the *persons-approach*.

It should be noted that the claim that bodily activities can be concurrent – on which my argument for the continuousness of consciousness and hence the self is based – is supported by my theory of a reigning relevancy system. When our consciousness is organized about a relevancy system the bodily activities sustaining the awarenesses that enter that system must be co-operating together and not competing. That is to say, certain forms of attention presuppose the possibility of joint bodily activities, and this consideration closes the door to the objection that it is a gratuitous assumption on my theory that bodily activities must be able to occur concurrently. It can also be pointed out that this analysis would explain why we use the presence or absence of bodily activity as a criterion of the presence or absence of consciousness in the case of another person.

The account of the self's persistence through time was necessitated because we not only have native knowledge of ourselves as subjects of experience, but in addition our experience of being selves is an experience of being selves persisting through time. The account does, however, lend itself to a possible misunderstanding, and I wish to remove the source of this misunderstanding so far as I am able. Once it has been granted that the self persists, we immediately seem to run into the question: Is the self at time $t1$ the same self as a self at time t? We run into this question because to say that the self persists seems to entail that the self at one time is the same as the self at a later time. But this question I claimed to be the concern of the *persons-approach* and here we find it breaking out in respect of the *self-approach*. The answer consists, I think, in seeing that the question cannot break out.

To ask of any particular, Is this the same again? is to ask for a re-identification of it. Such a question implies the existence of an intervening time when the particular was not under observation. If, however, the particular had been kept under continuous observation no question of re-identification could arise. If I have not taken my eyes off the object it is necessarily true that the object at time $t1$ is the same as the object at time t. There could be no question of my finding this out: there could in turn be no question of being mistaken, since the only mistake I could make would be that of believing I had been continuously observing the object when I had not (and then the situation collapses into one of re-identification). Thus just as for the observer the question does not arise whether the object under continuous observation is the same at a later time as it was at an earlier one, so too the question does not arise whether a self at one time is the same as at another time as long as there is the continuous experience of being a self. It should not need pointing out that the parallel in the two cases stops when we reach the notion of continuous observation. In our own cases we do not observe the self – not even continuously. But we do continuously experience being a self. Thus it is only a deity who could say of a self that the self at $t1$ is the same self as the self at t. For oneself the question does not arise.

In this chapter I have tried to show that the view of the self I have been putting forward does not fail on the question of the self's persistence through time. If this attempt has been successful the chapter will also have served to bring together with greater logical coherence many of the concepts that have figured in isolation in earlier chapters. In the final chapter a reconciliation between the *self-approach* and the *persons-approach* will be attempted.

CHAPTER SEVEN

BODILY EXISTENCE

[1] The argument for the temporal continuity of the self has been made to be crucially dependent on bodily activities. At the same time the notion of a bodily activity has been deliberately left up in the air in so far as it was not made dependent on the physical existence of bodies. This standpoint was the consequence of the adoption of the *self-approach* according to which the identification of the experiential self had to be approached through an analysis of consciousness. With the completion of that analysis the time has arrived to give the body its due.

I shall try to show how the connection between the self and a particular body should be viewed, by making a series of transitions from a self conceived as completely independent of a body to one conceived as completely dependent on it. My argument is designed to show that these transitions are ones of progressive concretization such that the final transition in which the self is viewed as necessarily having a body is the one that is consistent with our native knowledge of ourselves and our understanding of our world.

The first conception of the self in inverse order of concretization is that of a disembodied self. Such a conception is based on the premiss that the relation between a self and one or more bodies is logically contingent. That is to say, the self might exist although it no longer has a body and possibly never did have one. One widely believed conception of immortality is based on such a conception of the self. Even philosophers such as Strawson[1] and Quinton[2] who reject the idea of the independence of a person and his body, nevertheless concede that the idea of disembodied survival is at least logically possible. We may note therefore that the theory I have developed does not rule out that possibility when it is taken at one of its levels. We need only reflect that the theory takes consciousness as given and identifies the self with unprojected consciousness, in order to realize that as long as it is logically possible for consciousness to exist apart from a body a self which is identical

[1] Strawson, *Individuals*, p. 115.
[2] A. Quinton, 'The Idea of the Soul', *Philosophical Studies*, Vol. LXIX (1960).

with unprojected consciousness could exist apart from a body. However, we should also be aware of what we must be prepared to sacrifice if we are to countenance this possibility. Such a self would be deprived of sense experience. It would not be able to look at anything, listen to anything, or feel anything; and this would mean that it would neither see nor hear nor have feeling. All there would be left for the self to do would be to think. It would be Descartes' thinking thing. Price has suggested that a disembodied self would have to be thought of as having the equivalent of dream experiences.[1] This is a fascinating suggestion since it helps to give us an idea of what it would be like to be such a self and this is a way of making the idea intelligible to us. Were we totally unable to do that, the conception of the self in question would receive no answering response in terms of our native knowledge of the self, and we would be free to deny that a disembodied self was the sort of self we experience ourselves as being.

However, at a deeper level my theory is not really compatible with this view of the self at all. The argument that images and thoughts are dependent on our capacities to see, to hear, to feel, and so forth would contradict the claim that a self which lacked those capacities would nevertheless be able to have images and thoughts. Thus according to my theory a self which engaged in 'pure' thinking would be unintelligible, as would a self which only had dreams. There is yet another direction in which a disembodied self would be an impoverished self. It would, on my theory, necessarily lack the experience of continuity. I have argued that the continuity of the self is based on the ability of bodily activity to sustain awareness. But a self lacking that ability would be one whose existence would be confined to the single moment of existence during which it was the subject of one momentary experience.

We must conclude that disembodied existence is ruled out by most of the arguments I have used to support my theory of the self. Let us therefore make the transition to the next stage of concretization: the stage at which we allow the self to have perceptual experiences quite apart from its alleged capacity to have Ginnane-like thoughts and dream-like experiences. To make this possible we have to equip the self with bodily activities. But that still does not mean that we have to supply the self with a body in the accepted meaning of the word. We can draw on the Christian tradition for

[1] H. H. Price, 'Survival and the Idea of "Another World"', *Brain and Mind*, ed. J. R. Smythies (London, 1965).

a conception of a self which would be equipped with perceptual abilities and yet not be a self with a body as we know it. I am thinking of the conception of the resurrection of the body in a spiritualized form. The ordinary conception of a ghost of a deceased person would do as well. In both cases the self is equipped with what I shall describe as a *quasi-body*: a body which permits its owner to engage in perceptual activities but which lacks the compensating advantages and disadvantages of the corruptible human body.

It should be evident that although I have introduced the notion of a quasi-body to refer to conceptions of bodies with properties remarkably different from real human bodies, the point of the notion is to tie the notion of body to anything capable of practising the bodily activities involved in perception. Looked at in this way it is necessarily true that anything capable of practising bodily activities has a quasi-body. This means that the concept of a quasi-body enables us to reveal a logical feature shared by all sorts of bodies: namely, the capability they give their owners to practise bodily activities. Considered from this point of view we can legitimately think of real human bodies as one form of actualization of a quasi-body, and ghosts as another possible form of actualization of a quasi-body. If, therefore, we wish to refer to our own bodies in such a way as to disregard all of their properties which are extraneous to their function in the practice of bodily activities (and this includes disregarding the causal conditions for the practice of these activities), we may describe our own bodies as quasi-bodies. A consequence of this extension of the notion of a quasi-body is that it is no longer possible to contrast our bodies with quasi-bodies (of the sort possessed by ghosts). When I wish to contrast the sort of quasi-body possessed by human beings with the sort possessed by ghosts I shall contrast *real* bodies with *phantom* bodies.

It should not be forgotten that kinaesthetic sensation was found to play a crucial role in the successful performance of certain bodily activities. We may add, therefore, that intrinsic to the notion of a quasi-body will be the experience of it as the experience of kinaesthetic sensation. To make this clear I need only mention the phantom limb experience in which a limb is believed to belong to a self, although it no longer does, purely because the kinaesthetic sensations induced by its use can still be induced despite its loss. In other words, the-body-for-consciousness – apart from perception of it as an object – is our experience of kinaesthetic sensation.

It would be logically possible for a quasi-body to be invisible. But even if it were not invisible, there would be no reason for its appearance to remain unchanging – or for it to change only slowly as our appearances do. It would be logically possible for a self with a quasi-body to be undergoing frequent metamorphoses. The successive metamorphoses need not even be restricted to one form: the only restriction that would be entailed by the concept of a quasi-body would be that the positions of its sense-organs relative to one another would have to be relatively constant.

But a quasi-body undergoing metamorphoses would at least belong to a different type of self to the selves we experience ourselves as being in that our appearances do not change like that. Thus, if we conceive of our bodies as quasi-bodies, we would have to conceive of them as quasi-bodies that are not to our knowledge metamorphosing quasi-bodies. Here we find ourselves at the point at which another transition can be made to yet another stage in our series of progressive concretizations. That stage is reached by adding that the quasi-body be subject to the limitation of sameness of appearance. A self with such a quasi-body would obviously come closer in its experience of being a self to the experience *we* have of being selves.

[2] I now want to suggest that we have reached a transition at which the sort of quasi-body we have described is none other than the sort of quasi-body we have: a visible non-metamorphosing quasi-body with a comparatively fixed appearance. But the crucial point to realize is that we have as yet no logical reason for thinking that the quasi-body in question is a real body as opposed to a phantom body. It should be evident on reflection that everything I have said about bodily activity can be understood as applying to a phantom body, and that as far as the *self-approach* is concerned we are not entitled to assume that we have real bodies as opposed to phantom bodies. Obviously the phantom sense-organs of a phantom body would perform the same function as real sense-organs, and they equally make possible the activities on which, as I have argued, the continuousness of consciousness depends. It follows that a self possessing a phantom body would have the same experience of persisting through time that we have.

I am claiming that if we confine ourselves to the *self-approach* we would have no means of knowing that we have real bodies rather than phantom bodies, but two considerations may be suggested which appear to cast doubt on this claim. In the first place, it might be objected that a being with a phantom body would lack many of the types of experience we have because of the type of body we have. But this point can be conceded since it carries no weight. Although we would have no reason to attribute to a being with a phantom body the appetites and attendant bodily sensations which we attribute to the nature of our real bodies, it is not logically impossible for a being with a phantom body to have such appetites and bodily sensations. It would be perfectly possible to locate such bodily sensations in a phantom body. Failure to recognize this was the flaw in Ayer's argument that a (physical) body could be picked out by locating a particular bodily sensation within it.[1] As I pointed out, such location could not ensure the identification of a real body as opposed to a phantom body as far as the subject himself was concerned.

In the second place, it might be thought that a major factor which would differentiate a phantom body from a real body would be the inability of a self possessing a phantom body to act on its surroundings. Thus it might be suggested that a phantom body would lack the capability of physical agency; i.e. it might walk through walls, but be unable to move chairs and comparable objects about. But this objection fails too. It is not logically impossible for such a phantom body to possess the capability of physical agency even though it might contravene the laws of nature. However, at this point we are introducing issues which are strictly beyond the domain of the *self-approach*: we are concerning ourselves with *explanations* of the possible capabilities of various types of quasi-body, and such explanations are not the province of the *self-approach*.

We thus reach the position that as far as the *self-approach* is concerned we could not say that we ourselves have anything but phantom bodies. That is to say, the experience of being a self would be no different whether our quasi-body turned out to be a real body or a phantom body. This conclusion needs no argument, since I have now made it analytically true.

What happens when we try to make the next transition? Obviously the next transition is the last and most concrete of all. It is the one in which the quasi-body gets identified in terms of the

[1] See above, p. 163.

substance of which it is composed. In our case it is the transition to the real body: a body of flesh and blood. We at once see an interesting result: the transition to a real body cannot be made from the standpoint of the *self-approach*, for as has just been noted that approach confines us to thinking in terms of quasi-bodies. We are driven to conclude that the transition to the corporeal body is a move that must be made on the *persons-approach*. We can express this by saying that according to the *persons-approach* we must *take* our bodily activities to be those of a real (corporeal) body. That is to say, we have no incorrigible knowledge of what sort of quasi-bodies we have, although we have incorrigible knowledge that we have quasi-bodies. The move from a quasi-body to a real body must be based on evidence and as such the question whether we have real bodies is a theoretical one. It follows that the transition from a quasi-body to a real body cannot be made on the *self-approach*. To make that transition is the undertaking of the *persons-approach* which is concerned with the question 'What must we *take* the self to be?' In short, what from the standpoint of the *self-approach* is a quasi-body is from the standpoint of the *persons-approach* a real (corporeal) body. The rightness of this conclusion is attested to by the fact that only from the latter standpoint is it important to be concerned about those properties which real bodies possess and which may be lacking in other types of quasi-body. It is only because of the demands of referential identification that it is important that we have real bodies rather than phantom bodies.

I explained in the introductory chapter why it was that the *persons-approach* found it so important to determine whether bodily identity was a necessary – if not a sufficient – condition of personal identity. We can now appreciate why the *persons-approach* is logically compelled to make the transition from the stage in which the self is conceived as having a quasi-body (i.e. the conclusion of the *self-approach*) to the one in which it is conceived as having a real body. The reason is that for the purposes of the *self-approach* the quasi-body need not be visible to other perceivers, or if it is visible to them it need not have the spatio-temporal continuity which is necessary if successful reidentification is to occur.

It is worth remarking just what the *persons-approach* does demand of a body. It must demand that it is real in the sense that it has a continuous spatio-temporal history, that it is visible and of fairly permanent form such that a body can be identified and reidentified as the same again. Obviously any physical body would satisfy these requirements. The body could as well be constructed with the materials of which computers are made as have the soft cellular construction they in fact have. This should make us aware that the question of the composition of bodies – real bodies – is as little the concern of the *persons-approach* as it is that of the *self-approach*. It follows that the developing view of scientists about the nature of bodies are as little threat to our philosophical concept of human bodies as are their theories about the nature of matter to our philosophical concept of a material object. All that the *persons-approach* need insist upon is that the body must have the properties of a basic particular, and the possibility remains that even a phantom body could constitute a basic particular. It is therefore an entirely contingent matter that the only actual bodies we know of (which belong to the type of selves of which we have native knowledge) happen to be corporeal bodies. Thus, if we hope to keep in line with our knowledge of the world, we have little option but to identify what from the standpoint of the *self-approach* is a quasi-body, with what from the standpoint of the *persons-approach* is a corporeal body. If we go through parts of the body one by one, we may then identify the quasi-organs of sight with physical eyes, the quasi-organs of hearing with physical ears, and so on. It is then analytically true that we see with our organs of sight, but a synthetic truth that we see with our physical eyes. This is true also *mutatis mutandis* of the other senses.

This move is essentially the same as the one made on the Identity Thesis in terms of which mental events are claimed to be identical with brain processes.[1] The proponents of the Identity Thesis argue for what they call a 'contingent identity' between mental events and brain processes. The import of the notion of contingent identity is that identity of reference is not the same as identity of meaning. The argument then is that although we do not mean the same by the concepts of mental event and brain process, a particular mental event has as its referent a particular brain process. If we now carry over this idea to the problem of making the transition from a quasi-body to a corporeal body we can say that it consists in taking there to be a contingent identity between a quasi-body (of a certain sort) and a corporeal body. The same move can once again be made of the various parts of quasi-bodies and

[1] See U. T. Place, 'Is Consciousness a Brain Process?' and J. J. C. Smart, 'Sensations and Brain Processes' both of which are printed in *The Philosophy of Mind*, ed. V. C. Chappell (Prentice Hall, 1962).

corporeal bodies, respectively. Thus, we would be claiming the existence of a contingent identity between the organ of sight and the physical eye, the organ of hearing and the physical ear, and so on. The basis for claiming such identity would be the discovery of the coincidence of location of the point of origin of the organ of sight and the physical eye. An additional basis is the fact that the sense-organ (understood conceptually) is impaired or destroyed when the physical organ is impaired or destroyed.

By adopting the theory of the contingent identity between quasi-body and corporeal body we arrive at the point at which the *self-approach* and the *persons-approach* mesh with each other. But even more important, by being able to see the corporeal body as a quasi-body we give ourselves a philosophically far more accurate understanding of the human body. From this standpoint the important thing about the body is not the material of which it is composed, nor yet is it its identificatory role, rather is it the ability it gives us to realize our human potentiality. As the concept of a quasi-body makes clear, the importance of the body is precisely that with it we are able to look, to listen, to feel, among our perceptual abilities, as well as to act, to register emotions, satisfy desires, and communicate with one another.

In other words, this perspective brings it home to us that the *self-approach* forces us to look upon the body as essentially active – as constituted by related and interdependent bodily activities. It enables us to resist those theories of the relation between a self and a body which treat the body in an overly physical way. It gives us a natural corrective to the view once expressed by Ayer when he said:

'I am, however, inclined to think that personal identity depends upon the identity of the body, and that a person's ownership of states of consciousness consists in their standing in a special causal relation to the body by which he is identified.'[1]

We must not forget when reading this remark that for Ayer there is no distinction between the problem of personal identity and the problem of self-identity. If we think of the body as if it were a quasi-body we would appreciate that any causal relation there may be between a self and a body is only one side of the picture. The other side of the picture is to think of the body as instrumental in

[1] A. J. Ayer, *The Concept of a Person* (London, 1963), p. 116.

our bodily activities, and ultimately, therefore, as the 'creator' of a persisting self. It may be remarked that we do not think of our bodies as physical objects except when we lose control over them. Even less do we think of them as physical processes or events. Philosophers come to think of the body in these terms because the *persons-approach* now holds the field as the only legitimate point of view. Thus the only questions that are raised about the body – i.e. is it a necessary or is it even a sufficient condition of personal identity – is one that can be answered quite happily by treating the body purely as a physical object.

This point is well illustrated by the following passage of Strawson's in which the role of bodily activity in perception is completely in abeyance:

'Consider merely some of the ways in which the character of a person's *perceptual experience* is dependent on facts about his own body. Let us take his visual experience. The dependence is more complicated and many-sided than may at first be obvious. First, there is that group of empirical facts of which the most familiar is that if the eyelids of that body are closed, the person sees nothing. To this group belong all the facts known to ophthalmic surgeons. Second, there is the fact that what falls within his field of vision at any moment depends in part on the *orientation* of his eyes, i.e. on the direction his head is turned in, and on the *orientation* of his eyeballs in their sockets. And, third, there is the fact that *where he sees from* – or what his possible field of vision at any moment is – depends on where his body, and in particular his head, is located.'[1]

Strawson goes on to argue, on the basis of these three facts, that although they demand that perceptual experience be dependent on a body, they do not logically demand that it be the *same* body for each of the three facts. But that argument is not my immediate concern. What I wish to draw attention to is Strawson's assumption that it is *facts* about a body that are relevant to the dependence of perceptual experience on bodies. He mentions such things as the eyes being open, the *direction* of the head, the *orientation* of the eyeballs, and the *position* seen from. The picture this conjures up is one of an inert body, 'set up' to face in the appropriate direction. The body is treated as though it were a piece of optical equipment.

[1] Strawson, *Individuals*, p. 90.

Given this assumption it makes sense when he goes on to consider the possibility that a perceiver may be dependent on three different bodies, A, B, and C, such that S (the perceiver) sees when A's eyes are open, but whether B and C's eyes are open is irrelevant; sees from the position of C, but not from that of A and B; sees when B's head and eyes are turned in a certain direction, but not when A's and B's are.

Now my objection to Strawson's argument is that he makes no mention of seeing as a result of *looking*, and in particular he makes no mention of seeing as a result of deliberately actuating one's body in the activity of looking. The facts Strawson mentions, about the eyes being open, the head facing a certain direction, etc., are necessary conditions of deliberately looking, but they are not sufficient conditions of the same. A person can have his eyes open, have his head orientated in a certain direction, and so forth, and yet not be looking at anything, or looking in any sense at all. He could be in a hypnotic trance in which he reports that he sees nothing. It is evident that Strawson leaves out of account the idea of the body as active in a more central sense than causally effective. Once we bring in the idea of 'looking', and the bodily actuation it involves, the artificiality of Strawson's problem becomes apparent.

Let us return to Strawson's example of the perceiver S whose visual perception depends on the co-operation of three bodies. We can at once ask, 'Which of the three bodies belongs to percipient S?' The answer must be that whatever choice we make will be arbitrary. But if we ask, 'Which of the three is looking?' the position is immediately different. We can find out which of the three is willing the looking: i.e., trying to look at this rather than that, taking steps to prevent an object from being lost sight of, and so forth. The one of which this is true, will be S. Therefore one body will still be uniquely the perceiver's body. If, however, S could directly will the movements of all three bodies, so that if S desired to look at an object, he could do so by willing A's eyes to be open and properly focused, willing B's appropriate head movements, and willing C's body to be in the right place, then Strawson would have to admit that the whole idea of a one to one correspondence between perceivers and bodies would have to be abandoned. It is evident that Strawson has failed to establish that the 'facts' of perception cannot themselves guarantee the requirement that each percipient be restricted to one body. His mistake is, I think, that of thinking of the body as a material object, instead of thinking of it as having the active role of a quasi-body.

I think my argument shows that it is wrong to concentrate on the physical facts if one is to establish a non-contingent connection between the concept of sense-experience and the concept of a body. To do so presupposes altogether too mechanical a conception of the relationship between the two. I hope I have succeeded in showing that the line I have adopted, of making the connection between sense-experience and the body depend on the connection between sense awareness and bodily activities, is a sounder one.

[3] My claim that the *self-approach* and the *persons-approach* complement each other receives some support from an interesting passage in *Individuals* in which one can interpret Strawson as feeling his way toward a type of backing to his theory which the one I have constructed attempts to make explicit. He is concerned with the question 'How is the concept of a person possible?' and, in elaboration of the question, part of what he has to say is this:

'For when we have acknowledged the primitiveness of the concept of a person, and, with it, the unique character of P-predicates, we may still want to ask what it is in the natural facts that makes it intelligible that we should have this concept, and to ask this in the hope of a non-trivial answer, i.e., in the hope of an answer which does not *merely* say: "Well, there are people in the world." I do not pretend to be able to satisfy this demand at all fully. But I may mention two very different things which might count as beginnings or fragments of an answer.
First, I think a beginning can be made by moving a certain class of P-predicates to a central position in the picture. They are predicates, roughly, which involve doing something, which clearly imply intention or a state of mind or at least consciousness in general, and which indicate a characteristic pattern, or range of patterns of bodily movement, while not indicating at all precisely any very definite sensation or experience.'[1]

It would not be claiming too much, I submit, to describe the enquiry I have undertaken as one of discovering what there is 'in the natural facts' in virtue of which we are selves, and accordingly, which makes it intelligible that we should have the concept of a

---

[1] Strawson, *Individuals*, p. 111.

person. It is interesting, too, to see what Strawson takes to be a first step in this direction. He suggests moving a certain form of consciousness 'to a central position in the picture': namely the consciousness exhibited in action. There are two points of significance here. (*a*) Strawson is unable to escape according primacy to consciousness, and (*b*) he selects those forms of consciousness that are connected with bodily movement, as being the most likely to make the concept of a person intelligible. It can thus be seen that the direction in which Strawson looks to an answer is remarkably close to the one I have taken. We agree on the position of 'consciousness in general', and we agree on the importance of bodily movement. We disagree only on the type of bodily movement involved. Strawson has in mind the type found in certain kinds of action: he lists 'going for a walk', 'coiling a rope', 'playing ball', 'writing a letter'. By contrast I turn to the bodily activities displayed in sense perception. Once again the contrast between action and activity is in evidence.

[4] The relation I have sought to establish between bodily activity and state of awareness has relevance in a wider philosophical setting than I have yet considered. I shall conclude this study by touching on some of these wider issues.

In the Philosophy of Mind there is a tradition, which goes back to Brentano at least, according to which there exist mental acts or acts of awareness. Brentano himself tells us,

'Every presentation (*Vorstellung*) of sensation or imagination offers an example of the mental phenomenon; and here I understand by presentation not that which is presented, but the act of presentation. Thus, hearing a sound, seeing a coloured object, sensing warm or cold, and the comparable states of imagination as well, are examples of what I mean.'[1]

We find the same view put forward by Moore:

'To begin with, then: I see, I hear, I smell, I taste, etc.; I sometimes feel pains; I sometimes observe my own mental acts; I

---

[1] F. Brentano, 'The Distinction between Mental and Physical Phenomena', *Psychologie vom empirischen Standpunkt*, Vol. I, bk. II, ch. i. Reprinted in *Realism and the Background of Phenomenology*, ed. R. M. Chisholm (Illinois, 1960), p. 41.

sometimes remember entities which I have formerly seen or heard, etc. . . . All these things I do; and there is nothing more certain to me than that I do them all. And because, in a wide sense, they are all of them things which I do, I propose to call them all "mental *acts*". By calling them "acts" I do not wish to imply that I am always particularly active when I do them. No doubt, I must be active in a sense, whenever I do any of them. But certainly, when I do some of them, I am sometimes very passive.'[1]

This view finds adherents right down to the present day. It is a central tenet in the writings of Bergmann;[2] and the proposition that there are mental acts is defended in a recent book by R. Grossmann, a former student of his. As an example of a mental act Grossmann cites 'seeing a tree':

'Consider, for example, the sentence "I see a tree" . . . The . . . sentence seems to mention three things – namely, a person, a tree, and a mental act of seeing.'[3]

Russell was one of the early opponents of the doctrine of mental acts. He stated the objection which many philosophers would now bring against it:

'The first criticism I have to make is that the *act* seems unnecessary and fictitious. The occurrence of the content of a thought constitutes the occurrence of the thought. Empirically, I cannot discover anything corresponding to the supposed act: and theoretically I cannot see that it is indispensable.'[4]

While I am in agreement with Russell about this, I think my own analysis both explains why those philosophers in the Brentano tradition came to believe that there had to be such mental acts, and enables us to replace their analysis with a more satisfactory one. It must be obvious that I would deny that seeing, hearing, etc., are in any sense *acts*. I have classified them as *states* of awareness, and

---

[1] G. E. Moore, 'The Subject-Matter of Psychology', Proc. Arist. Soc., 1909–10. Reprinted in *Body and Mind*, ed. G. N. A. Vesey (London, 1964), p. 237.

[2] Cf. Bergmann, *Meaning and Existence* (Madison, 1960), p. 27 ff., and *Logic and Reality* (Madison, 1964).

[3] R. Grossmann, *The Structure of Mind* (Madison and Milwaukee, 1965), p. 39.

[4] B. Russell, *The Analysis of Mind* (London, 1921), pp. 17–18.

offered my reasons for so classifying them. I maintain quite categorically that Brentano, Moore, and Grossmann are wrong when they assert that seeing, hearing, etc., are acts. But Moore at least is right when he says that we do do something when we see, hear, or taste. Where he is wrong is in jumping to the conclusion that what we do is perform acts of seeing, hearing, or tasting. What we quite incontrovertibly *are* normally doing when retentively seeing, hearing, or tasting, is looking, listening, or tasting. It is only when a philosopher concentrates all his attention on consciousness itself that he is led to believe that what he is doing must be found within consciousness itself. The truth of the matter is that what I *do* when I claim to be doing something when perceiving is engage in the related bodily activity.

Thus it *is* true to say that I am doing something when for instance I see a tree: what I am doing is looking at it. However it is not the case either, that these philosophers have simply made the mistake of believing they had found a mental act when in reality what they had found was a bodily act. As I have argued, looking, and listening – the sorts of bodily doing in question – are not acts but activities. We may well wonder why the obvious *source* of our agency as perceivers should have been missed by these writers. I can only put it down to the fact that it was their chief concern to distinguish the mental from the physical. If the perceiver experienced a sense of agency, therefore, the agency had to be in the category of the mental if the distinction between the mental and the physical was to be upheld.

Of the passages quoted from Brentano, Moore, and Grossmann, Moore's is the most instructive because he finds himself in some embarrassment over the fact that he cannot say that he is particularly active when he performs these putative mental acts. As he remarks, 'When I do some of them, I am sometimes very passive.' This admission is most revealing. If Moore's 'mental acts' are in reality mental *states*, they would of necessity appear to be passive, since being in a state is an undergoing and not a doing.

The view I have been arguing for that seeing is not itself an act or an activity but can be a state sustained by an activity also provides a solution to a problem stated by Sibley. After giving his analysis of verbs of perception Sibley concludes with the observation that 'whether seeing is or is not describable as an activity needs to be reargued with reference to the occurrence uses of verbs.'[1]

[1] Sibley, 'Seeking, Scrutinizing, and Seeing', p. 149.

This remark makes it clear that his own analysis leaves the possibility open that seeing may turn out to be an activity after all. If my argument is correct we can say that this is definitely not the case: seeing is a state and the seeming aspect of the act that goes into it is provided for by the sustaining bodily activity called 'looking at'.

If the philosopher of perception confines his attention to the mental or inner experience of seeing, hearing, etc., he is driven to postulate some sort of mental act to account for the fact that our perceptual experiences are under our control – in the sense of whether we have them or not. Thus our analysis fully bears out and gives us further insight into the judgement passed by Hampshire when he says:

'The deepest mistake in empiricist theories of perception, descending from Berkeley and Hume, has been the representation of human beings as passive observers receiving impressions from "outside" of the mind, where the "outside" includes their own bodies.'[1]

There is, however, a divergence between Hampshire's position and mine when we come to the remedy. For Hampshire it consists essentially in recognizing that the observer is an embodied observer who acts on his physical environment through direct bodily contact. As agents we manipulate physical objects which are external to our bodies by movements of our bodies. Thus:

'I find myself from the beginning able to act upon objects around me. In this context to act is to move at will my own body, that persisting physical thing, and thereby to bring about perceived movements of other physical things. I not only perceive my body, I also control it; I not only perceive external objects, I also manipulate them.'[2]

Obviously nothing I have said about bodily activity conflicts with Hampshire's position. It could, as I have mentioned, be argued that a self with a quasi-body could not use it to manipulate physical objects even though he could use it in his perceiving. If this were so we have the best argument of all for the identification of our own bodies considered as quasi-bodies with corporeal bodies, since our

[1] S. Hampshire, *Thought and Action* (London, 1959), p. 47.
[2] *Ibid.*, p. 47.

ability to act on the things around us is an integral part of our experience of being selves. The difference between Hampshire's position and mine does not require of me that I deny anything he says about the involvement of the body in perception, it rather requires of him the recognition that there is a logical stage prior to the one he describes; namely, the stage in which we engage in those bodily activities involved in perception prior to our ability to act on our environment. That is to say, my view gives recognition to the fact that the precondition of the existence of a self is not the bodily contact we make with other objects, but the spontaneous bodily activities themselves which involve our moving parts of our own bodies independently of effecting any changes in the positions of other objects. If we think of the matter in terms of a child's development, it is clear that the child learns to stare, or to gape, and then it learns to follow the movements of objects, long before it learns to manipulate objects. In other words its earliest activities include the activity of unordered attention. Thus the child has the experience of being a self before it manages to push objects around. It is true that the child will as yet have no conception of himself, and Hampshire might be correct in thinking that he is describing some of the necessary conditions of developing such a conception of self, but I have nowhere claimed that the *self-approach* gives us a conception of ourselves: it only gives us the self in respect of which such a conception can be formed.

The differences between the position of the empiricists, Hampshire's position, and my own, can be loosely categorized in terms of the three varieties of attention with which I have been working. The empiricists may be looked upon as taking interrogative attention as their starting point, since in interrogative attention the involvement of bodily activity is at its least conspicuous and is consequently easily overlooked – as it is by them. Hampshire's position operates at the level at which executive attention comes into play; namely, when we are dealing with manipulative skills. As far as his account is concerned this level exhausts the role of the body in perception. My position goes back to the most rudimentary stage of all at which unordered attention operates. There we reach a stage of bodily involvement which is a precondition of any other type of bodily involvement, and there too we find a form of control over bodily activity which is a precondition of developing any other type of bodily control. Until we can control those of our movements which adjust the 'focus' of our sense-organs we cannot be capable of either executive attention or interrogative attention. We have, therefore, every reason to see such activities as the basic bodily activities such that the selves we experience ourselves as being are necessarily quasi-embodied. When we add stage two to this last stage we are compelled to take selves to be not merely quasi-embodied but really embodied.

I claimed in the introduction to be able to show that a view of the self could be constructed which was a *via media* between the Pure Ego Theory and the Serial Theory. The identification of the self with unprojected consciousness is just such a view. It gives us a self which is the subject of every experience and it gives us a self which in no way takes us beyond experience. The theory put forward in these pages is offered as an account of the experiential self. I also claimed that a theory of this sort was no threat to theories developed on the *persons-approach*. I have tried to show that the self of which we have native knowledge can be *taken* to be a self with a real body, and indeed that we have overpowering reasons for so taking it. In essence the enterprise I have just concluded should be viewed as an attempt to explain what the self is which has the experience of being a self and which takes itself to be a person.

INDEX

INDEX